SIGN LANGUAGE INTERPRETING

SIGN LANGUAGE INTERPRETING

Theory and practice in Australia and New Zealand

2nd edition

Jemina Napier

Rachel McKee

Della Goswell

THE FEDERATION PRESS
2010

Published in Sydney by:
    The Federation Press
    PO Box 45, Annandale, NSW, 2038
    71 John St, Leichhardt, NSW, 2040
    Ph (02) 9552 2200 Fax (02) 9552 1681
    E-mail: info@federationpress.com.au
    Website: www.federationpress.com.au

National Library of Australia
Cataloguing-in-Publication entry

    Sign language interpreting: theory and practice in Australia and New Zealand.
        Jemina Napier, Della Goswell, Rachel McKee

    Includes index.
    Bibliography.

    ISBN 978 186287 780 1. (pbk)

    Australian Sign Language – Translating.
    New Zealand Sign Language – Translating.
    Translating and interpreting – Australia.
    Translating and interpreting – New Zealand.
    Interpreters for the deaf – Australia.
    Interpreters for the deaf – New Zealand.

419.94

Typeset by The Federation Press, Sydney, NSW.
        Printed by McPhersons Printing Group Pty Ltd, Maryborough, VIC.

PEFC

PEFC/21-31-16

Foreword

This book is water to a parched earth. The need for multicultural, evidence-based texts on interpretation is significant. This volume not only addresses the general field of interpretation, it explicates the local context, and it also includes recent research and trends in practice as reflected in international professional literature.

The authors of this book bring together a rich set of resources, knowledge, skills and experience. Further, they are each actively, respectfully and meaningfully involved in the communities Australasian interpreters are likely to be working with. The practical and the theoretical are nicely married in this text by authors who are wise teachers, fine researchers, excellent practitioners and women of integrity.

Students, working interpreters and teachers of interpretation will find this book a valuable resource. We are so fortunate to have such a fine tool at our disposal, filled with useful and sophisticated information, yet accessible even to those who are just beginning their studies. From recent entrant into training to advanced interpreter with a great deal of experience in the field, this book will offer many benefits and is sure to become a necessary volume in every interpreter's library.

Sharon Neumann Solow
ASL & International Sign interpreter,
interpreter educator & consultant

Contents

Preface

Why the need for a 'local' text book?

Is sign language interpreting in Australia and New Zealand different in principle or practice to anywhere else in the world? Yes ... and no.

'No', because the interpreting profession in this region shares in the theoretical and professional knowledge developed by our pioneering peers overseas. That established body of knowledge and experience offers a common basis for our professional identity and practice in Australasia. As authors and teachers, we gratefully acknowledge that legacy and hope our efforts will enrich it.

But our practical experience as interpreters in this part of the world also tells us, 'Yes', there are some recognisable differences in context and approach that are not reflected in overseas texts. Time, place, and culture-specific experience are vital ingredients in initiating new practitioners into the field. The Australian and New Zealand interpreting landscapes differ from Northern hemisphere environments (and from each other) in several ways: the particular educational and political history of our Deaf communities, the characteristics of Auslan and NZSL (not forgetting spoken English and Māori), the development of interpreting services, systems for training and accreditation, the influence of government policies, the relationship with spoken language interpreting fields, and of course the cultural backgrounds of interpreters and their consumers. All these factors uniquely shape our professional position in our own countries.

As interpreter educators we have often wished for a relevant resource for Australian and New Zealand interpreters which integrates the best of current international knowledge with an understanding of our own languages and communities, and work environments. By articulating this knowledge in a locally-focused book, we hope that interpreters will more readily identify with the content, and be able to make international and historical comparisons as advance local practice.

Who is this book aimed at?

Our main target audience are entry-level interpreters who are in training or recently qualified: reader feedback on the first edition of this text confirmed a need for an accessible yet comprehensive text on theoretical and practical aspects of interpreting. We assume that readers will have fluency in Auslan/NZSL, and be familiar with their local Deaf community.

By presenting an overview of current theory and research perspectives from the international literature, and local work contexts and conditions, we also hope that qualified interpreters, interpreter trainers and potential researchers will find the book useful as a reference text or a stimulus for further study and investigation. We encourage teachers and other readers to use the extensive bibliography for further reading on specific topics.

A word about theoretical approaches and terminology

Interpreting is a complex activity, and theories about interpreting have borrowed insights from numerous disciplines, including communication, linguistics, psychology, anthropology, and sociology. This book reflects that eclectic tradition, but emphasises a sociolinguistic approach to explaining the interaction between social, linguistic and cultural factors in interpreted situations. This framework acknowledges that interpreters are active, decision-making participants in their role of facilitating communication, always having to consider human and situational demands. We suggest that the more interpreters explore insights from sociolinguistic research about how and why people communicate in particular ways, the better they will understand and manage their task.

In doing the research for this book, we informally interviewed a number of colleagues to get a range of perspectives and genuine anecdotes about the work of interpreters. We have included quotes from these discussions, with permission, throughout the book, but have chosen to keep the contributors anonymous.

There is a range of conventions and views on whether and when to refer to deaf people as uppercase 'Deaf' or lowercase 'deaf'. In this book we use uppercase 'Deaf' only in reference to the collective entities of Deaf community or Deaf culture. Lowercase 'deaf' is used as a generic term when referring to deaf people, especially as clients or consumers of interpreting services, due to the variety of ways in which deaf individuals may prefer to describe and identify themselves in print form.

We have not generally used the terms 'hearing-impaired', 'hard of hearing', nor the compound 'Deaf and hearing impaired', because this book is about interpreting for deaf NZSL or Auslan users, and we have found it rare for people in those signing communities to call themselves hearing-impaired.

Finally, there were also choices to be made in how to refer to interpreters themselves. Even though interpreters work between specific languages, and should therefore technically be referred to as 'Auslan/English' or 'NZSL/ English/Māori' interpreters, this is rather cumbersome to keep repeating, especially when we want to talk about them all together! We have therefore chosen to use the following shortcuts: 'Auslan' interpreter, 'NZSL' interpreter, 'Auslan/NZSL' interpreters, or just plain 'sign language' interpreters. We trust that no-one will feel shortchanged.

Jemina Napier, Rachel McKee, Della Goswell
January 2010

About the authors

Jemina Napier is a Senior Lecturer in the Linguistics Department at Macquarie University, where she established the Auslan/English interpreting program, and is now Head of the Translation and Interpreting section. She has over 20 years experience as a sign language interpreter in the UK, Australia and internationally, working in either BSL, Auslan or International Sign. She has published over 40 book chapters and articles on sign language interpreting, and is immediate past President of the Australian Sign Language Interpreters' Association.

Rachel Locker McKee is Program Director of Deaf Studies in the School of Linguistics and Applied Language Studies at Victoria University of Wellington. She has worked extensively as a sign language interpreter in both New Zealand and the USA since 1985, and established university training programs for interpreters and for Deaf teachers of NZ Sign Language (NZSL). She was the founding president of SLIANZ. Her publications have focused on analysis of sign language interpreting, linguistic description of NZSL, and the New Zealand Deaf community.

Della Goswell is co-ordinator of the Diploma in Interpreting (Auslan) Course at Petersham TAFE, and the PG Diploma of Auslan/English Interpreting at Macquarie University. She has been accredited as a NAATI Auslan/English interpreter since 1987, has interpreted at national and international level, and is past President of the NSW branch of the Australian Sign Language Interpreters Association. She has taught courses in Auslan, Auslan/English interpreting, and teacher training. Her publications are predominantly teaching/learning resources.

Acknowledgments

We are indebted to several interpreters, interpreter educators, researchers, Auslan/NZSL teachers, and linguists for their contribution to this book. Many people have assisted in different ways – providing case studies of experiences, discussion of interpreting practices, consultation on linguistic aspects of signed languages, and reviews of earlier drafts of the book. We would like to acknowledge all of these people, as we feel that the book would not be as robust or representative without their input.

Particular thanks to: Nadine Ardati, Stephanie Awheto, Meredith Bartlett, Peter Bonser, Karen Bontempo, Andy Carmichael, Breda Carty, Julie Coxhead, Louise de Beuzeville, Mandy Dolejsi, Sabine Fenton, Darrel Firth, Danielle Fried, Rosie Henley, Shannon Knox, Marcel Leneham, Patty Levitzke-Gray, Megan Mansfield, Maree Madden, David McKee, Sharon Neumann Solow, Evelyn Pateman, Thornton Peck, Petersham TAFE Auslan Interpreting Diploma class of 2005, Lynette Pivac, Adam Schembri, Liz Scott Gibson, Kirsten Smiler, Merie Spring, Micky Vale, Wenda Walton, Alan Wendt, Sue Williams, and Shiz Sameshima.

CHAPTER 1

INTRODUCTION

Interpreting between people who use different languages is not a simple or mechanical process of substituting words from one language into another. It involves being in the messy midst of human beings trying to communicate and relate to each other. Accurately conveying one person's ideas, feelings, experiences and intentions, in a way that is meaningful to someone of a different cultural and linguistic background, is a delicate and often difficult task. It is still beyond the capability of the most advanced information technology.

Interpreting is often described as a process of mediation between languages, cultures and communities. No matter which languages are being used, interpreters need to call on their intellect, social instinct, physical and emotional stamina, and professional judgment; all these need to be cultivated through training and experience. The challenges and variety that interpreters encounter make for a job that can at times be exhilarating, uncomfortable or even onerous, but ultimately richly rewarding.

This book

This book is an introductory text for sign language interpreting students, professionals, and educators in Australia and New Zealand. It is written by practising interpreters and interpreter educators drawing together insights from experience, research findings and a body of professional knowledge. It offers a theoretical foundation and a practical guide for interpreting.

This chapter sets the scene by introducing some key concepts about sign language interpreting, giving an overview of how the profession has developed in Australia and New Zealand, and considering the relationship of interpreters to the Deaf[1] community.

Chapter 2 explores the nature of communication and the actual process of interpreting. This chapter introduces theoretical models which explain important components of the process, and also discusses criteria for evaluating whether interpreting is effective.

---

1   We will use capital 'D' to refer to the Deaf community as a collective who identify themselves as having a cultural and linguistic identity which is expressed by the use of a natural sign language – in this case Auslan or NZSL. However, we will use lowercase 'd' to refer generally to deaf persons as potential consumers of interpreting services, since not all of these individuals identify as culturally 'Deaf', even if they use sign language in some form.

Chapter 3 outlines the kind of linguistic knowledge and skills needed by interpreters, including knowledge of Auslan/NZSL and English/Māori, and bilingual skills.

Chapter 4 describes the further knowledge, skills and attributes that assist interpreters to manage the rapid transfer of messages between people. This includes cultural knowledge and particular cognitive and emotional skills.

Chapter 5 introduces key aspects of professional practice, including the role and ethics of the professional interpreter and preparing for interpreting assignments. It also covers the interpreter's responsibility for managing physical and environmental impacts on the interpreting situation, including personal presentation and the positioning of participants.

Chapter 6 identifies the dynamics and demands of interpreting communication in one-way (monologic), two-way (dialogic) and group interactions. This chapter also identifies common challenges faced in interpreting assignments.

Chapter 7 introduces contextual knowledge relevant to each of the settings in which sign language interpreters commonly work. These include education, employment, social services, legal, medical, mental health, conference, religious, and performance interpreting.

Chapter 8 describes specialised techniques that may be needed in particular settings, or with particular clients. These include team interpreting, telephone interpreting, video remote interpreting, relay interpreting, working with deaf people who have minimal language competence, working with deafblind clients, diplomatic interpreting, oral interpreting, and international sign interpreting.

Chapter 9 highlights issues for sign language interpreters working in Māori-specific settings in New Zealand and with Indigenous Australians.

Chapter 10 provides a snapshot of the employment environment for interpreters in Australia and New Zealand, including training and accreditation, salaried versus freelance employment, and occupational health and safety considerations.

The appendices contain useful reference materials including recommended readings, the Codes of Ethics of interpreter associations in each country and other documents relevant to professional practice.

What is an interpreter?

The word 'interpreter' is derived from Latin, and refers to someone who explains the meaning, and makes sense of, what others have difficulty understanding. When people need to communicate with each other but are separated by a language barrier, they often feel frustrated at being unable to use familiar communication strategies to get the message across. In these situations, interpreters are a necessary intrusion into other people's lives.

Although interpreting is a relatively newly recognised profession, interpreters have been around for as long as groups of people speaking different languages have needed to communicate – for the purposes of trade, politics, war, religion and colonisation. References to interpreters appear in the early texts of many cultures and empires, for example, in 2600 BC in Mesopotamia, and 165 BC in China. The importance of the role of the interpreter is highlighted in the Bible: St Paul urges the Corinthians to use an interpreter wherever 'any man speak in an unknown tongue … but if there be no interpreter, let him keep silence'.[2]

Who are sign language interpreters?

Pathways into a sign language interpreting career are diverse; these comments reflect some typical journeys:

Deaf family member / CODA (child of deaf adult)

> I was interpreting before I knew what the word meant. With deaf parents who sign, I think you just start being the interface between them and the hearing world – it didn't feel strange or different at the time, it was just how things were. I didn't think of interpreting as a career choice, until much later on.

> My oldest brother is deaf and went to a deaf school so he really taught the rest of us how to sign – we weren't really fluent though. I thought everyone signed like we did, but later on I found out that we used lots of home signs, and there were so many more 'new signs' to pick up once I started formal training.

Language interest

> I'd always wanted to learn sign language – ever since I was at school and we learned the manual alphabet. Later on, I saw a sign language course advertised in a community college brochure – that was it, nothing could have stopped me. I went to every course I could find!

> I landed in interpreting by accident really. I was learning sign language out of interest, no particular plans, and someone at the local college who knew I was studying, called me and asked if I could help out because they needed an interpreter desperately. I really thought I was just an emergency stopgap, but here I am, still working there. To be honest I've learned most of my skills on the job.

---

2   II Corinthians, Chapter 14, verses 27 and 28, King James Version.

Contact with deaf people

We had neighbours who were deaf, and I used to be fascinated by how they communicated when I was a child. I didn't do anything about learning to sign until I was thinking about a career change – at that stage Signed English classes were being offered locally and I didn't know that there was any difference. It's taken some time to break those habits.

The Australian Theatre of the Deaf came to my high school and it was love at first sight. So, I actually studied to be a teacher of the deaf, but got waylaid and ended up working as an interpreter!

My church has a small group of deaf members, and the services are interpreted, so I've been watching signing and seeing how interpreters work for quite a few years – it always seemed so expressive, especially the songs. I slowly but surely gravitated towards interpreting; I think it was inevitable.

At work, there was a deaf woman in my department and I started asking her how to sign different things. Over time I picked up more and more signs and started doing really basic interpreting. She encouraged me to take it further, so I started sign language classes, and then enrolled in an interpreter training program.

Signed[3] language versus spoken language interpreting

Sign language interpreting involves the same basic process as spoken language interpreting, however, one key difference is modality: how the languages are produced and received. Spoken languages are auditory-verbal languages, relying on speech and hearing to produce and receive words. Spoken language interpreters therefore work in the auditory-verbal modality. Sign language interpreters, however, usually work between a spoken (auditory-verbal) language and a signed language, which is visual-gestural. Sign language interpreting is therefore bi-modal, which creates some unique cognitive and physical demands. In Australia, sign language interpreters generally work between the languages of Auslan (Australian Sign Language) and English; in New Zealand, interpreters work between NZSL (New Zealand Sign Language) and English or Māori.

Interpreting settings

Another difference between signed and spoken language interpreting work is the range of settings in which the services are required. Spoken language

---

3   We will generally use 'sign language' interpreter and interpreting as this reflects common usage amongst practitioners. However, we note that the term 'signed language' is used in the linguistics literature to distinguish between signed and spoken languages. We will also use this term for clarity and grammatical accuracy wherever we are comparing the two language modalities.

interpreters usually work with speakers of minority languages, who need to access mainstream services (for example, medical, legal, government departments). However, most people from non-English speaking backgrounds are able to acquire spoken English as a second language over time, and so reduce their reliance on interpreters. As a result, spoken language interpreting is not generally provided in education or employment settings. Minority language communities also tend to have bilingual spokespeople who represent them at a political level, using English.

In contrast, a deaf person, because they are deaf, can never develop complete access to a spoken language. This means they have a potentially life-long relationship with sign language interpreters across a much broader range of settings. For example, as well as working in most of the spoken language interpreted settings, Auslan and NZSL interpreters also work extensively in education (primary, secondary and tertiary), in professional workplaces, government consultations, important family occasions (for example, births, weddings, funerals), and at community events in which hearing 'outsiders' also participate.

Diversity of deaf consumers

The work settings and particular challenges faced by sign language interpreters vary according to the communication choices, educational opportunities, and the overall demographic profile of their local Deaf communities.

As most deaf people have not had early access to signing at home, their exposure to, and therefore fluency in, sign language depends very much on how, when and where they first met and socialised with other deaf people. For example, residential schools were a very fertile environment for sign language development, whereas currently, many deaf students in non-signing mainstream schools do not acquire sign language until after they leave school and start mixing with the Deaf community.

This relatively haphazard language acquisition process, and natural variation within signing communities (such as regional and age differences) means that deaf consumers are extremely varied in terms of sign language fluency, style, vocabulary choices, and English influence. Interpreting work is therefore interesting but challenging, and requires the development of a broad repertoire of signs and grammatical approaches.

As diversity in the language use of the Deaf community is strongly shaped by historical changes in deaf education, the next section gives a brief overview of that history in Australia and New Zealand respectively.

Australian deaf education

Language use in the Australian deaf population has been influenced by a variety of educational policies in different places over time. In the late 19th century most States established residential deaf schools, where signing (or at least fingerspelling, that is, the Rochester method) was used and deaf teachers were employed. These schools continued through the first half of the 20th century, but from the 1950s onwards their teaching methods came under the influence of oralist approaches, which forbade manual instruction. This meant that signing was relegated to the playground and dormitories.

During the 1970s and 1980s, residential schools started closing and deaf units within mainstream schools became more common. Oralist instruction methods did not produce the results they had promised, and Total Communication programs, using Australasian Signed English (ASE) as the manual component of instruction, became the predominant teaching methodology for deaf children across Department of Education facilities.

In the 1980s and 1990s, mainstreaming deaf children in public schools became government policy, and the majority of remaining deaf schools were phased out. ASE remains the official method of instruction in a number of state Department of Education deaf programs, however some deaf students are accessing Auslan via a few small bilingual education (Auslan/English) programs, and/or the use of Auslan interpreters in mainstream classrooms.

New Zealand deaf education

The use of sign language in the New Zealand deaf community has been even more influenced by a history of strictly oralist educational policies than Australia; signing was officially prohibited in all New Zealand schools for the deaf from their beginning in 1880 until 1979 and no deaf teachers were employed. Sign language has always been used by deaf children and adults in New Zealand, but until relatively recently it was not used openly outside the Deaf community.

In 1979 Australasian Signed English was introduced into schools as part of Total Communication; this system incorporated mainly Auslan signs, a few NZSL signs, and some contrived signs. NZSL was recognised in deaf education in 1993 with the opening of the first bilingual NZSL/English class in a deaf school. As in Australia, the majority of deaf students are now mainstreamed, with minimal access to NZSL language role models. Few deaf school students have communication support from a trained NZSL interpreter. Students in deaf resource classes (units) and the small number who attend deaf schools have more opportunity to use NZSL with teachers and peers.

Although the Australasian Signed English system was perceived as foreign to the Deaf community when it was introduced in 1979, its use in education for more than a decade paved the way to the acknowledgement of NZSL. Modern NZSL includes a significant amount of ASE vocabulary, although Auslan and NZSL remain distinct 'dialects' with a strong relationship to British Sign Language.

Sign language interpreting in Australia and New Zealand

The pre-professional/ BYO era

In both Australia and New Zealand, the profession of sign language inter-preting was established and recognised in the 1980s. However, prior to this time, interpreting in each country had a slightly different profile.

In Australia, interpreting services originated in the religious welfare provisions of the Deaf Societies in each State. From the late 1800s to the early 1900s, missionaries, responsible for moral and spiritual guidance to the Deaf community, provided interpreted church services. This later developed into a welfare officer role, and services expanded to include employment, legal, housing, aged care and other social support. Deaf people often brought their own interpreters; family members (for example, parent or CODA), friends who could sign and teachers of the deaf provided assistance to the Deaf community on a voluntary basis.

In New Zealand, the role of welfare workers, family and friends was also important, but the negative perception of signing and strong emphasis on oral skills meant that deaf parents often discouraged signing in the home, and were uncomfortable signing openly in public. This created a legacy of CODAs who were not always bilingual and were less likely to provide the same levels of 'public' interpreting support as their Australian counterparts. Although interpreting certainly happened informally through family, tea-chers and welfare workers, the stigmatisation of signing discouraged demand for interpreting as a formalised service.

Professionalisation

The professionalisation of sign language interpreting in Australia and New Zealand has followed closely in the footsteps of the US and UK, with the US leading the way.

In the US, American Sign Language (ASL)/English interpreters began to be recognised as professionals from the late 1960s following the acknow-ledgement of ASL as a language and funding linked to rehabilitation legislation. The Registry of Interpreters for the Deaf (RID) was established in 1964. Historically, there have been two certification systems in the US: one through RID, the other through the National Association of the Deaf (NAD). However, in 2002 the National Council on Interpreting (including represen-tatives from RID and NAD) announced a formal collaboration. Training programs in the US are offered at community college and universities, offering qualifications up to post-graduate level. The Conference of Inter-preter Trainers (CIT) was established in 1979 and is an organisation that provides professional development opportunities for interpreter educators and standards for interpreter training.

In the UK, British Sign Language (BSL)/English interpreters work in England, Wales, Northern Ireland and Scotland. In 1980, research into BSL as a distinct sign language was being led by Mary Brennan, and the Council for the Advancement of Communication with Deaf People (CACDP) was established. CACDP began offering short interpreter training courses, and established a BSL interpreter register for England, Wales and Northern Ireland. CACDP initially offered an interpreting exam as a route to qualification, but this was later replaced by a National Vocational Qualification (NVQ). There are now several training programs linked to the NVQ. In Scotland, interpreter assessment and qualifications are administered by the Scottish Association of Sign Language Interpreters (SASLI).

In Australia, interpreting services were originally provided by the State Deaf Societies via combined interpreter/welfare officer positions. This welfare model provided 'cradle to the grave' assistance for deaf clients, but little autonomy. Members of the Australian Deaf community became aware of the emerging interpreting roles and services available in the US during the 1970s and 1980s. Individuals attended conferences, studied at Gallaudet (a university for the deaf in Washington DC), and brought back news of a more empowering and professional interpreting model.

During the 1980s a number of factors combined to change the face of interpreting in Australia:

- Anti-discrimination legislation was established in individual States and later federally, requiring that people with disabilities be 'reasonably accommodated' in areas of public life, including education, employment, and provision of goods and services. This meant that for the first time, deaf people could claim the right to interpreting services for some settings.

- Multicultural politics in Australia provided a platform for recognition of cultural diversity generally, and interpreting services and accreditation were expanded via the establishment of the National Accreditation Authority of Translators and Interpreters (NAATI) and Telephone Interpreter Service (TIS). NAATI introduced 'Deaf Sign Interpreting' into its testing regime, largely due to the efforts of John W Flynn in Victoria.

- Deaf people started attending tertiary educational institutions in greater numbers, increasing the demand for access, and gaining employment in more prominent positions.

- Trevor Johnston named the language in the early 1980s and created the first Auslan dictionary in 1989. Auslan was included in the National Languages Policy in 1987 (although it is still not recognised in law).

- Deaf Societies moved to split previously combined welfare/interpreter roles, so the concept and position of interpreters began to change. Interpreters were paid for their language services, and were required to be NAATI accredited.

- Individual State sign language interpreter associations were established and informal training of interpreters began. Western Australia established the first formal interpreter training course in 1986, whereas other States did not commence formal training until the 1990s.

In New Zealand, the push for professional interpreting services came from the New Zealand Association of the Deaf (NZAD), established in the mid-1970s. As in Australia, Gallaudet College (now University) had a significant influence on the perception of interpreting as a recognised service in New Zealand. In the early 1980s a group of deaf academics from the College visited New Zealand and described the interpreting services, educational access and sign language research happening in the US at that time. The Gallaudet professors' recommendation that the New Zealand deaf community aim for a similar path of development inspired NZAD to work with parents of deaf children and the Department of Social Welfare to establish New Zealand's first sign language interpreter training course in 1985. This training was led by Dan Levitt, an interpreter trainer from California, who also started documenting the signs he saw, as an authentic, independent sign language. At the same time, linguistic research was being done by Marianne Collins-Ahlgren, which was vital in legitimising NZSL as a real language.

There was no further sign language interpreter training in New Zealand for a number of years, and shortfalls in interpreting supply were met by recruiting interpreters from Australia and the UK. However, in response to increased demand and lobbying for local interpreter training, the Diploma in Sign Language Interpreting was established at the Auckland University of Technology in 1992. In 1996 the Sign Language Interpreters Association of New Zealand (SLIANZ) was formed.

Sign language interpreters and the Deaf community

The relationship between interpreters and members of the Deaf community has more facets than just a 'service provision' transaction, for several reasons:

- Hearing people rarely encounter a sign language interpreter, whereas interpreters may be a common presence in a deaf person's everyday life and in the wider social networks of their community. Deaf people therefore usually know more about interpreters, and how to communicate via an interpreter, than the hearing consumers we work with.

- Interpreters have a symbiotic relationship with the Deaf community, since each depends on the other for certain benefits. Deaf people need interpreters to communicate with hearing people who cannot sign, in a wide range of public and private situations. Interpreters need the Deaf community, first, to acquire the linguistic and cultural knowledge which underpins their professional skills, and ultimately for opportunities to earn a living and maintain professional status in society.

- Each side of this partnership also gives up something in exchange for benefits gained. The presence of interpreters in deaf people's everyday lives impinges on their privacy and autonomy, while the role interpreters take on, means they forego various forms of personal expression (such as dress style and personal opinions) while on the job. The role can also oblige interpreters to be available for work at times and places that conflict with the priorities of their own lives (for example, being called on after hours to a police station, or interpreting in situations that are outside their personal comfort zone).

- Interpreters choose their occupation, and can manage the impact of their work, whereas deaf people have not chosen to need interpreting services throughout their lives. This creates a potential power imbalance; deaf people are acutely aware that interpreters can determine the quality and quantity of their access to information and opportunities in mainstream society.

- Interpreters' hearing status also affects the amount of power they hold in any situation that involves deaf and hearing people in contact with each other. Interpreters are automatically members of the majority group, while deaf people are usually perceived as 'different'.

- And finally, the legacy of poor educational standards for many deaf people (particularly, limited English literacy) means that they are often socially and economically disadvantaged, and dependent on interpreters for access to information.

Interpreters need to be sensitive to this predicament and to minimise the impact of this imbalance by striving for the highest ethical and technical standards in our work.

Beyond the personal level, interpreters have an indirect political significance in the Deaf world, as a necessary tool for Deaf leaders to advocate for the goals of their community. These include access to information, improved education, sign language recognition, and consideration in government policy. As a Deaf leader, Hilary McCormack, former president of the Deaf Association of New Zealand explains:

> The advent of interpreters marked a radical change for New Zealand Deaf. The Deaf could speak for themselves, the hearing could understand, and they in turn could make themselves understood to the Deaf. It was the beginning of learning about each other. (McCormack 2001: 22)

This introduction has signalled some of the many dimensions to the study of interpreting: interpersonal, political, ethical, cultural, linguistic, and technical. The next chapter explores what is involved in the actual process of interpreting, looking at the nature of communication in general, and what happens both within the interpreter's head and within the broader context, when meaning is transferred between languages and people.

Thought questions

1. If you are a working or training interpreter, reflect on your own entry to the interpreting profession:

(a) What originally motivated you to become an interpreter? Has your motivation for being in the field changed at all?

(b) What personal skills or background experience do you bring to your work as an interpreter?

2. If you are familiar with the Deaf community in your locality, consider:

(a) What kind of educational experiences have most deaf people had?

(b) What variation in language and communication styles have you noticed?

(c) In what situations do they most often use interpreting services?

(d) What kind of awareness and attitudes do the wider hearing community have towards deaf people, sign language and interpreting?

CHAPTER 2

THE INTERPRETING PROCESS

What is interpreting?

People observing sign language interpreters sometimes have a slightly romanticised impression of their work, evident in comments such as 'I really enjoyed watching you sign, it's so beautiful and expressive'. What may appear as seamless output in an effective interpretation belies the underlying skills and effort involved.

Certainly interpreters have always drawn on innate language and communication talents in their work. However, learning about current research on interpreting and translating enables professional interpreters to acquire a deeper level of technical knowledge of interpretation, as a basis for better performance.

This chapter introduces theoretical and technical concepts about communication and the interpreting process, and explains different models of interpreting. These models relate to the internal operations within the interpreter's brain, as well as the external cultural, social and physical contexts which affect the interpretation of meaning between people.

We explain different techniques (consecutive and simultaneous) and approaches (free and literal), and discuss criteria for judging quality in interpretation. And finally, we identify areas of research that are refining our understanding of how interpreters do what they do.

Translating and interpreting

The terms 'translating' and 'interpreting' are used interchangeably by the wider community. 'Translation' is often used as a generic term to refer to the transfer of a message between two languages – regardless of the mode of the languages (spoken, signed or written). Television news reports often superimpose 'voice of translator' as a description of the person providing the English voice-over of a foreign language speaker. However, in the professional interpreting and translating fields each term has a more specific and discrete use.

Translation is the process of transferring meaning between languages in written or recorded texts (for example, translating a book from German into English, or creating a recorded Auslan/NZSL translation of an English text). Translators can make extensive use of reference materials in their preparation and are able to edit and correct their work until they are satisfied with the outcome (Nord 1997). This creates a fixed text, which can be revisited. Translators usually work alone in an office environment and cannot predict exactly who will read their translation or what background knowledge the reader might bring to it. Recent studies have described-techniques and considerations for translating written English into a signed language, in order to maintain the integrity of the original text and to achieve the purpose of the translation (Tate, Collins and Tymms 2003; Montoya et al 2004; Conlon and Napier 2004).

Interpreting is also a process of transferring meaning between languages but is done in real time between people. Interpreters work 'through the airwaves' (signed and/or spoken), in the presence of people who need to communicate immediately. Interpreting occurs in a variety of physical and social environments, involving the interpreter and at least two other participants, which means they must continuously attend to the social dynamics. While interpreters don't have the luxury of presenting a 'polished' translation, having contact with a live audience means that interpreters do have scope to adjust the delivery of their message throughout the process, to respond to, and enhance, their clients' comprehension.

Despite these differences, the overall goals of the translation and interpreting processes are similar, so translation theories and principles are often relevant to sign language interpreting. Translation theories focus on the idea of equivalence – what it means, and how to achieve it (Baker 1992). Translators seek to achieve equivalence at different content levels: word (lexical), grammatical (syntactic), meaning (semantic), and overall function (purpose of the text). Like interpreters, translators also think about the broader context of their work, that is, why something is being translated, what overall message the speaker is trying to convey, and the desired impact on the people reading the translation (Nord 1997). Interpreters and translators refer to the language they are working from (receiving) as the *source language* (SL); the language they are work into (producing) is called the *target language* (TL).

The interactive nature of communication

Communication is not as simple as just sending and receiving 'packages' of information; it is an interactive process that happens within a particular time, place, and relationship between people. A speaker and listener both take an active part in constructing meaning from the language that passes between them and both are participants in the discourse. *Discourse* means the language used in a particular context or in a particular interaction. Even amongst native speakers of the same language, miscommunication is common; sometimes what a speaker says and what a listener hears are two different things, and sometimes several participants listening to the same speaker will construe the message in various ways. In other words, meaning is filtered through our own experience, knowledge, attitudes, expectations, and other personal and cultural factors. Differences in cultural background, gender and age of participants in a situation compounds the potential for different understandings of a 'message'.

Sociolinguists (for example, Hymes 1972; Brown and Fraser 1979)) have identified features of communication situations that influence how people use language. For the purposes of thinking about interpreting, these can be grouped into contextual and message factors.

Contextual factors

Setting – The physical space (for example, GP's office, university classroom, church, sports ground) and time of interaction (for example, beginning or end of an encounter, time of day) can influence people's choice of language style or register. Specific references to time and space (for example, 'last time', 'the main door', 'over there', 'upstairs', 'go back') may only be understood with shared knowledge of the setting.

Purpose – The reason people are together (for example, wedding reception, lecture, mortgage application, job interview) influences the topic of communication, the underlying aims, mood and feelings of individual participants, and how turn-taking and other conversation strategies occur. Within these broader events, individual speakers also have specific communication purposes such as sharing or withholding information, threatening, explaining, belittling, praising, placating, joking, boasting, encouraging, arguing, comforting, teasing etc. These individual purposes are known as language or discourse functions.

Participants – The way people talk reflects who they are: their ethnicity, gender, social class, education level, age, region and personality. The participants' role and status in the event (for example, host or visitor, minister or congregation member, staff or customer, insider or outsider) also have an effect on the communication. This includes the level of language formality, who opens, leads and closes discussion, who controls topics, and whether technical or fixed expressions (formulaic language) are used (for example, in court or at a job interview).

Language code – This refers to which particular language or dialect is being used, and the modality of that language (spoken or signed). Interpreted situations involve communication across two languages, with a bilingual intermediary. This gives the communication a different texture than the usual monolingual format; people tend to feel less sure about how the communication will proceed – what to say, when, and how to say it.

Audience adjustment – People don't always talk the same way in every situation; they adjust their speech style to match who they are speaking to, or to project a particular impression of themselves to an audience (Bell 1984). A teenage boy, for instance, talks to his mates differently than to his grandmother or his girlfriend or his teacher; a Māori person may switch between an in-group form of Māori-English to a Pakeha (non-Māori) style of English, depending on who they are communicating with and where; deaf people adjust their signing style to match the language use of the people they are with, and the situation (Lucas and Valli 1990). This is called *code-switching* (that is, switching between languages, or varieties of the same language), and is used to express affinity with, or difference from, the other participants (Stubbe and Holmes 2000).

Culture – This is like a mental map that sets out how people behave, think and relate to each other and their environment. A person's cultural background establishes their expectation of 'normal' communication behaviour in any given situation – the purpose and protocols of particular settings and the likely topics of talk. Language encodes shared cultural knowledge that is not fully explained in words, so our cultural framework also helps to make sense of references to people, places, concepts and things. For example, in English-based cultures the word 'cousin' means the child of our parents' sibling (aunt or uncle); but in Māori and Aboriginal cultures, these close relatives may be called brothers or sisters, and the word 'cousin' is applied to a much wider circle of relatives or even friends. So, the same word can mask different underlying cultural experiences and meanings.

For interpreters, important contextual factors which influence communication situations can be remembered as *the four 'Ps'* (Eighinger and Karlin 2003):

- Participants – who is there?

- Place – where are they?

- Purpose – why are they there?

- Point – what do they want to achieve?

In any given interpreting assignment, the answers to these questions can guide an interpreter's decisions about how they understand and convey meaning. The purpose and point of what people want to achieve in a situation can influence how interpreters manage the process – for example, determining how much effort to devote to: conveying the participants' emotion or tone, capturing every detail that is stated, or focusing on the speaker's overall idea or underlying meaning.

Message factors

We have all heard a teacher or parent say: 'Now say "sorry" as if you mean it!' The *way* something is said is a crucial part of the meaning of *what* is said. Because interpreters aim to communicate meaning and not just words, they must attend to two layers of any spoken or signed message: content and packaging (Gile 1995).

Content

The content of a message is the information or ideas that a speaker intends to convey. This is also known as *denotative* or *propositional* meaning. It is often easy to identify the denotative information content of a message, but also very important for interpreters to recognise meaning carried in the smaller details – how things are phrased or expressed. Consider the difference in meaning between:

- 'Give it to me', and, 'Just give it to me' – 'just' alters the strength, urgency or politeness of the request;

- 'I'm sure she's coming back tomorrow' and 'I'm fairly sure she's coming back tomorrow' – 'fairly' is qualifying the certainty of the statement;

- '*He's* not my boyfriend', and 'He's not my *boyfriend*' – vocal emphasis or stress can focus on the identity of the person, or the nature of the relationship.

Paying attention to words that hedge or qualify the strength of a statement, and vocal intonation and pauses, can help interpreters better understand the speaker's meaning and intent beyond denotative content.

Implied meaning

Message content can be expressed explicitly (stating information and intent directly), or implicitly (relying on the listener to pick up the underlying meanings of the words in the context). For example, a teacher giving a student feedback on an unsatisfactory assignment could say bluntly: 'This essay is not up to scratch – it's superficial, disorganised and isn't written in academic style'. This choice of words may be informative, but will probably have a more negative than useful impact on the student. A more sensitive teacher would take into account social and psychological factors: their position of power, and the need to maintain a student's motivation. They might choose an indirect way of delivering the same points: 'You've got the beginnings of some good ideas here that need developing and organising further, and you need to check your formatting'. The real message here (that the essay is not up to expectations in various respects) is implied rather than explicit.

People often express meaning indirectly, leaving a listener to work out the real meaning from what is left unsaid, or the tone of voice and other non-verbal clues. For example, a customer in a cake shop reaching for a second chunk of the free gateau samples on the counter may feel repri-manded by the shopkeeper's comment, 'It's very *rich*, Madam'. Clearly, the intended message is something like, 'One piece per customer, you greedy woman'. This 'between the lines' level of meaning is known as *connotative* meaning (related to the word, 'connotation'). An important reason for expressing a message indirectly is to minimise confrontation and potential embarrassment (saving face) for the speaker and receiver.

Interpreters need to be alert to both explicit and implicit content in a message, so that they can decide how to express it. Sometimes it is necessary and appropriate to make implicit information more explicit in the interpretation, and sometimes vice versa.

Innuendo is a particular type of connotative meaning that is expressed indirectly, often through humour (for example, sexual innuendo). Innuendo means 'a hint or sly, usually derogatory, remark or insinuation' (Tray 2005: 96) and does not always transfer well between languages. It often involves a play on words, or knowledge of cultural meaning. Picking up and expressing innuendo is a sophisticated skill to acquire in a second language and can be difficult to convey in interpretation.

Packaging

Listeners pay attention not only to a speaker's words (linguistic information) but also to the additional (paralinguistic) information, or how the words are said. People intuitively recognise verbal and visual clues about a speaker's social background, and get emotional cues from the speaker's tone of voice, facial expression and body language (affect). A listener's understanding of message content is also affected by the comprehensibility of the speaker's language, including their fluency, pace, and volume.

Information that listeners derive from the 'packaging' is known as *metanotative* meaning (Cokely 1983). It is not unusual for metanotative meaning to conflict with the denotative meaning of what is said; people don't always mean what they say, or say what they mean. Consider a speaker who reads from her notes in a dreary monotone: 'I am delighted to welcome you to this exciting event'. The way she is delivering the words, means that the message the audience responds to is more likely to be the metanotative meaning (that is, a sense of flatness), even if that wasn't her intention. Sarcasm is an example of where the metanotative meaning in the delivery is deliberately intended to contradict the words, for example, 'I *really* like the way you keep interrupting me'.

Register

Register refers to differences in speaking or signing style which change according to the level of formality, the familiarity between participants, and the use of specialist jargon. Speakers often vary their register according to the context, through features such as word choice, grammatical complexity, pronunciation, volume, and pace. For example, a manager who addresses a staff meeting at a measured pace, in complete sentences, using technical words, with a commanding voice, is signalling that this is a formal situation. But during the coffee break, the same manager can shift to a more informal (colloquial) register, by using slang, less careful pronunciation, and less complete sentences spoken at a more spontaneous pace; this register shift signals that the context has changed to an informal 'off-duty' situation.

Joos (1967) identified five commonly used spoken language registers:

- *Frozen* – Where the text always stays the same and is usually part of a ritual, for example, the Lord's Prayer in a church service or the National Anthem at a graduation ceremony.

- *Formal* – Where the text is often a monologue (one-way), with one person in a more authoritative position than the audience, doing most of the talking, and using technical terms and complex language, for example, a university lecture or conference presentation. Formal register language is often 'planned' in advance.

- *Consultative* – Where one person is seeking advice or service from another person who is an expert (for example, doctor-patient interaction), or two people who are not intimate, discussing or exchanging information.

- *Informal* – Typical of conversations between friends or work colleagues, using colloquial phrasing and shorter sentences, with a lot of overlap in turn-taking. Informal register speech is usually more spontaneous or unplanned.

- *Intimate* – Interactions between people who know each other very well (such as family members or best friends) who have a shared social life and a lot of assumed knowledge, and can therefore make inferences from what is said. Conversations in intimate register are often difficult for eavesdroppers to understand, as speakers may not finish sentences, rely on the listener's background knowledge, and use code words that are meaningful only to them.

Technical registers that include specific jargon and ways of relating information are characteristic of professional and technical contexts (eg as used between medical personnel or mechanics). As yet, there is little research on register within Auslan or NZSL. However, research into BSL (Sutton-Spence and Woll 1998) and ASL (Zimmer 1989) has suggested the following differences between informal and formal registers in these sign languages.

Informal (spontaneous) register includes:
- more use of colloquial signs;
- more non-manual expression of adverbials and topicalisation;
- reduction of two handed signs to one hand;
- less distinct marking of spatial locations and role-shifts;

Formal (planned) discourse uses:
- an expanded signing space;
- more precise articulation of handshapes and spatial locations;

- more explicit discourse markers (for example 'now', and rhetorical questions) to move between topics and sub-topics;
- more English influence such as use of lexical conjunctions (for example, 'and' and 'then') and fingerspelling.

In Auslan, it has been noted that increased English mouthing and finger-spelling are features of an academic register, reflecting the importance of English in this context (Napier 2006). Signed languages in general tend not to have the range of technical registers found in English.

Interpreters working between Auslan/NZSL and English need to develop their repertoire of speaking and signing styles through experience in both language communities. Appropriately 'matching' the register of the source text in the interpretation is an important part of getting the whole meaning across. For example, a study of an ASL lecture interpreted into English found that the interpreter made the deaf presenter sound child-like because they did not use the appropriate formal register and discourse features (Roy 1987). In this case, listeners would have formed judgements about the lecturer's credibility based on the interpretation.

The first step in interpretation is to work out what the speaker means, so that the interpreter can construct an equivalent version of this meaning in the other language. The more aware interpreters are about the various layers of communication – context, message content and packaging – the more accurate and complete the transfer of meaning.

Interpreting as a process

Sign language interpreters experience interpreting as a physical, mental and emotional effort, and often emerge from a job in a whirl of thoughts and feelings about the experience, with a gut sense of whether it went well or badly. Often they dwell on a linguistic mistake, or a problem with the interaction that looms out of proportion, as they mentally replay their performance.

To develop a greater sense of control over our work and to refine our skills, it is important to move beyond just reacting to experience, towards a more analytical and critically reflective approach. A theoretical under-standing of the task enables an interpreter to evaluate the outcomes of their work in more detail than just 'good' or 'bad'. This is a valuable tool for trouble-shooting problems and identifying areas for skill development (independently or with a mentor). Being able to identify the *reasons* for errors, or good choices in interpreting outcomes, is known as a 'process-oriented approach' (Gile 1995).

A process-oriented approach is based on 'models' of interpreting that practitioners can use to understand and discuss what they do and to justify the decisions they make. A model represents a complex idea or process which is not directly visible (such as the universe, or family dynamics, or interpreting). Models identify key components and/or stages, and show the relationships between them.

Although the physical act of sign language interpreting can be observed externally, and can be superficially described as 'signing what is said/saying what is signed', there are many more subtle factors and unconscious operations in the process. By using models to name the factors involved and suggest how they impact on the interpreted situation, interpreters can describe more precisely what may have helped or hindered their interpreting outcomes. Several models have been developed to assist teaching, assessment and critical reflection.

Models of the interpreting process

Changing theories about the nature of communication and interpreter's roles have influenced the development of different interpreting models in our field. All these models have contributed to more precise and complex ways of thinking and talking about the interpreting task.

Information processing models

The first interpreting models emerged in the late 1970s and early 1980s, based on the work of conference interpreters, and drawing on the theories of information processing and psycholinguistics, for example, Moser (1978), Gerver and Sinaiko (1978), Ingram (1974, 1985), Ford (1981) and Lörscher (1996). These models focus on the cognitive activities within the interpreting task, analysing them into stages of:

- Receiving (the source message);

- Decoding/analysing (the meaning from source language);

- Converting/encoding (the meaning into target language);

- Delivering (the target message).

These early models were valuable in representing the sequence of mental and physical sub-tasks involved in interpreting. They generally assumed the interpreter's function to be like a physical and mental conduit (channel), through which messages are processed and passed. The interpreter is seen as a 'machine' not affecting the process, other than to switch the SL of the original speaker into the TL of the audience. The 'message' is treated as something rather static or independent. Social, environmental, and cultural factors in interpreted situations do not feature strongly in these models.

Interactive models

More recent interpreting models have drawn on sociolinguistic theories, which explain the ways in which language and communication is related to social identity, culture, and processes of interaction. Interpreting models inspired by a sociolinguistic framework highlight cultural and interpersonal aspects of interpreted communication, and view the interpreter as a participant in constructing the interaction, rather than as a neutral or mechanical conduit who just 'processes' it.

Writers, researchers and interpreter educators such as Seleskovitch (1978), Cokely (1992), Colonomos (1992), McIntire and Sanderson (1995), Stewart, Schein and Cartwright (1998), Wadensjö (1998), Roy (2000) and Wilcox and Shaffer (2005), have taken a wider and more active view of the interpreting process. Their analysis places more emphasis on understanding the interaction between the interpreter, the message, and the other participants. These writers acknowledge that decisions about meaning and interpretation are filtered through the lens of the interpreter's own cultural, linguistic, and personal experience.

Figure 2.1: An interactive model of interpreting

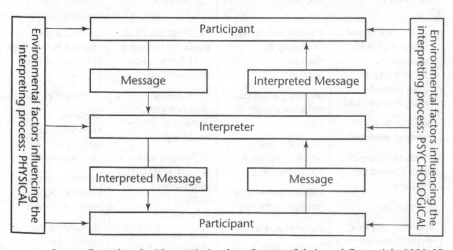

Source: Reproduced with permission from Stewart, Schein and Cartwright 1998: 35

Interactive models focus on 'the way utterances are used in communicative situations and the way we interpret them in context' (Baker 1992: 217). This is a more pragmatic or holistic approach, where less attention is paid to the internal operation of decoding and re-encoding information, and more emphasis is placed on the message that is delivered, and the meaning it conveys in the context. These models encourage interpreters to be aware of:

- The background knowledge and expectations that all participants bring to the interpreted situation including, of course, the interpreter;

- Interpreter strategies for managing the communication;

- Environmental and psychological distractions;

- The effect of participants' differing roles and status;

- How language and culture are intertwined in the expression of ideas.

These models show interpreting as a highly interactive and context-dependent process.

Stages in the interpreting process

Interactive interpreting models incorporate the stages proposed by cognitive models in processing the SL into the TL, and also identify environmental, physical, psychological, and cultural factors. Various terms have been used to represent stages of the process, but the key ideas can be summarised into three basic stages, with four cognitive tasks, as follows:

Figure 2.2: Interpreting process stages

SL INPUT	PROCESSING		TL OUTPUT
Reception	Analysis	Conversion	Delivery and Evaluation
Concentrating and perceiving the SL message (in auditory and/or visual channel) taking into account: Speaker gestures, pointing, posture Audio-visual input, other contextual referents Affected by: External/ physical distractions, for example, dim lighting, noise, audience activity, speaker's accent, body odour, etc Internal/ psychological distractions – for example, interpreter's thoughts, emotions, or physical discomfort	Understanding and analysing SL meaning, taking into account: Meaning of words, phrases, sentences, text Context – place, situation, actions, participant roles Cultural knowledge implicit in message Speaker goals Paralinguistic cues- style of delivery, affect, emphasis, body language SL communication norms Using short-term memory to link incoming message with previous parts of SL text Using long-term memory and personal experience of SL language and culture, to derive meaning	Re-constructing the message meaning in TL form, taking into account: TL linguistic structures to express equivalent meaning TL cultural frame – transferring shared or unfamiliar cultural information TL discourse norms (organisation of ideas and interaction) Using short-term memory to retain SL message elements and their relationship Using long-term memory of TL language and culture, to construct meaning	Delivering an equivalent message in TL, taking into account: TL modality Audience knowledge and language preferences Context – place, situation, actions, participant roles TL communication norms – for example, expected style of delivery, or interaction Monitoring and repairing errors, in response to self-evaluation and/or audience or team interpreter feedback on TL output

In reality, these tasks do not occur in a neat linear sequence; a skilled interpreter receives, processes and outputs chunks of the incoming message in a continuous overlapping cycle. Some of these tasks are executed automatically by a competent interpreter, with a number of tasks being executed at the same time, including revising earlier decisions and output. Fundamentally, though, accurate perception and comprehension of the SL message must be the first step in the interpreting process; without these, accurate interpretation is impossible.

Memory

In order to understand and process the information exchanged in any communication, people rely on two main types of memory: short-term (working) memory (STM) and long-term memory (LTM). Information received from all the senses (hearing, sight etc) is filtered, so that a limited amount of selected information is held in the short-term memory. This information can be verified against, or draw from, existing 'records' in the long-term memory:

Figure 2.3: Basic model of memory

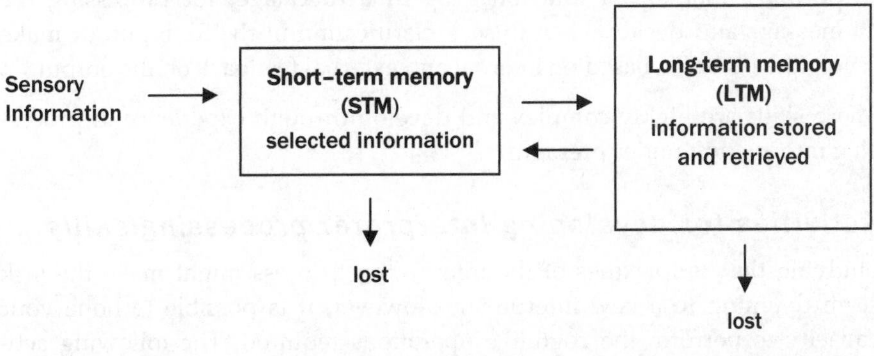

Interpreters rely on extensive knowledge of the languages and cultures they work between, as a basis for understanding the information they are processing. This needs to be consolidated in long-term memory so that it is available for retrieval. They also need to develop their short-term memory so that they can hold enough chunks of information for long enough to determine the meaning, and convert it into the TL form, without losing the threads of the ongoing SL input and their TL interpretation. Memory skills are therefore imperative to using time lag effectively. Information held in STM is usually lost unless it is consciously committed to LTM, for example, by rehearsing or repeating it, or by connecting the new information to existing LTM information. Information can also be lost from LTM over time.

Processing skills

The specific skills needed to cope with the cognitive processing demands of interpreting have been identified by Colonomos (1992) as follows:

- *Analysis* skills include the ability to concentrate on the input and filter distractions, quickly analyse and derive meaning from words in context, access background knowledge in long-term memory for comprehension, and store and retrieve SL message form and meaning in STM.

- *Composition* skills include the ability to retrieve message meaning from STM, access TL cultural and linguistic knowledge in long-term memory, and rapidly plan and construct an equivalent message using appropriate TL lexicon, grammar, and cultural references.

- *Monitoring* skills include the ability to notice and assess one's delivery, and adjust TL output accordingly to reduce errors and improve compre-hensibility, taking into account audience feedback and new information in the incoming SL message.

- *Process management* skills include the ability to manage the information flow by chunking the incoming message into meaningful and manageable portions, maintain a functional lag time (décalage) for processing the message and decide when to seek clarification in the SL input, or make repairs in the TL based on internal and external feedback on the output.

These skills are highly complex and develop through experience in proces-sing information under pressure.

Activities for developing interpreter processing skills

Studying the complexities of the interpreting process might make the task seem daunting to a new interpreter. However, it is possible to hone your capacity to perform the cognitive operations required. The following acti-vities may assist in building your processing sub-skills:

- *Listening* and *analysing* a spoken/signed text: Concentrate on understanding meaning. As you listen, make a written or graphic map of key ideas and their relationships. You can also practice identifying different kinds of meaning while listening to a spoken/signed text by noting these in separate columns, colours or boxes on a page – for example, explicit and implicit meaning, cultural references, and paralinguistic aspects of speaker's delivery. Start by listening to the text several times and focusing on just one of these aspects at a time.

- *Paraphrasing:* Listen and re-phrase short messages within the same language. You can start by working from English to English, then from Auslan/NZSL to Auslan/NZSL, and then between the spoken and signed languages. Be aware that the ability to paraphrase within the same language is essential to successful interpretation.

- *Summarising*: Similar to paraphrasing, but with the goal of identifying and describing only key points. Use passages at least a paragraph long.

- *Shadowing*: Repeat a spoken or signed message exactly, almost immediately after the speaker/signer. Gradually increase the gap between the speaker's output and yours by counting progressively more seconds before you are allowed to begin.

- *Recalling*: Strengthen your short-term memory. Listen to short passages of connected ideas (spoken or signed) and recount as much detail as you can immediately afterwards in the same language. Challenge yourself to listen and immediately recall increasingly long strings of items in a list or facts embedded in a story – numbers, dates, names, words in a category (for example, sports). The average STM span for separate items or a series of items is seven plus or minus two, (that is, between five and nine). Try to extend your STM span.

- *Dual tasking and filtering distraction*: Combine a language task with another sensory task, such as concentrating on understanding an audio message while watching a silent but moving TV screen, or concentrating on a sign language message with background music or conversation going on. Tell a short narrative while you stack an untidy pile of numbered pages in order. Try and maintain a phone conversation while a signer distracts you with simple questions or comments.

- *Predicting*: Given the title of a talk, or the background context of an interaction, brainstorm a list of topics, terms, related ideas, and communication issues likely to arise.

- *Making closure*: Practise completing sentences with deleted items, or completing unfinished short passages (verbally or in writing), based on your knowledge of language structures and the surrounding content.

- *LTM store:* Increase your mental archive of general knowledge by being alert to current events, ideas, and history in both the communities you work in; become an eavesdropper and listen to people around you talking; read widely, including media and Deaf community publications; when you come across new information or ideas, make a conscious effort to mentally relate these to things you already know or examples within your personal experience – this strengthens learning and memory. Build your memory bank of linguistic and cultural knowledge by taking opportunities to absorb new information and experiences in both of your languages.

Levels of processing during interpretation

When interpreters analyse SL input, they may process the message at various structural levels (Colonomos 1992):

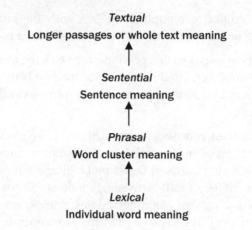

Textual
Longer passages or whole text meaning

↑

Sentential
Sentence meaning

↑

Phrasal
Word cluster meaning

↑

Lexical
Individual word meaning

Lexical level

People usually gain meaning from stretches of language longer than single words. Sometimes interpreters get stuck processing at a lexical level (ie, word for word) if they don't understand the source message, or their sign language production skills are limited; it is rarely an adequate level of processing for interpreting complete ideas. However, 'one word/sign at a time' processing is a necessary strategy when the SL message contains names, numbers, or technical terms that need to be remembered exactly and transferred literally into the TL. Or interpreters might choose to use a more word-level processing approach to manage short passages in the SL which they don't understand, but which their client does, for example:

> A deaf person at a weekly staff meeting expected some technical dis-
> cussion about chemicals in a swimming pool. She briefed the interpreter –
> 'Don't worry when you don't understand what they're talking about, just
> tell me exactly what they're saying'. The deaf employee was able to make
> sense of certain information passed on at a lexical level, because she
> recognised the meaning of the technical terminology and phrases, even
> though the interpreter didn't.

Phrasal and sentential level

Interpretation tends to be processed mainly at the level of phrases and sentences. One reason for this is that these chunks of meaning can be comfortably retained and processed. Psycholinguistic research shows that one of the natural efficiencies in human language processing is that we comprehend and store thousands of frequently used groupings of words as 'frozen' chunks or units. This means that interpreters can predict the content of many phrases and even complete sentences, without expending effort on processing the individual words. Interpreters often process at this level because phrases and sentences provide the minimum amount of meaning needed to form an interpretation – although it is also essential to consider how these units of meaning relate to the overall text and purpose of the communication.

Textual level

Processing at textual level means the interpreter has a solid understanding of the overall purpose, content and structure of the message, and aims to create an equivalent version which makes sense to the TL audience. Interpreting information at this level requires skills in prediction, closure, and memory, as well as awareness of how ideas are connected and how communication events are structured. Preparation and prior knowledge make it more possible to interpret at this level, so that the interpreter is familiar with the speaker's overall aim, key concepts and linkage of ideas. For example, reading a conference paper before a presentation, or a lesson plan before a classroom teaching session, or being familiar with medical dialogues, or set courtroom procedures. (See discussion of discourse mapping as a preparation tool in Chapter 5).

Interpreting techniques or modes

There are two main interpreting techniques (also known as interpreting modes): *consecutive* and *simultaneous*.

Consecutive interpreting

Consecutive interpreting is where a speaker/signer delivers their message in discrete chunks, pausing for the interpreter to pass on each piece of the message. These segments can be as short as a phrase or as long as the entire speech, but are commonly around 300 to 600 words. Consecutive interpreting is a technique typically used by spoken language interpreters working in dialogue settings, to avoid overlapping voices and ensure accuracy. Sometimes the consecutive mode is used at more formal levels of spoken language interpreting, when it is impractical or inappropriate for the interpreter's voice to overlap with the speaker's voice, such as a diplomatic speech, or a business negotiation.

Spoken language interpreters working consecutively often rely on note-taking to aid retention of information within each chunk. Note-taking for interpreting purposes is a skill in itself, using abbreviations, symbols and layout to represent key ideas and relationships in the text. When interpreters are required to consecutively interpret long passages, their notes act as a map or prompt for reconstructing the message in the TL. To our knowledge, note-taking is seldom used by sign language interpreters, due to the need for directed eye gaze while either receiving signed input or producing signed output.

Simultaneous interpreting

Simultaneous interpreting is where the speaker/signer talks continuously, while the interpreter passes their message on as soon as they hear/see enough to understand. Simultaneous interpreting requires different skills from consecutive interpreting as it requires the interpreter to:

- Listen to/ watch the SL message and analyse its meaning;
- Identify a meaningful chunk (or concept) to be interpreted;
- Restructure and deliver the concept into the TL.

At the same time as:

- Continuing to listen to/ watch the SL;
- Identifying the next segment to be interpreted;
- Monitoring one's interpretation in the TL.

For this reason, working simultaneously creates more cognitive demand than using the consecutive technique, where the interpreter is processing only one chunk of information at a time and has less interference between input and output languages.

Time lag

When interpreters are working in simultaneous mode, they generally do not know what the speaker will say, or mean, until they have said it. So rather than starting their interpreting at exactly the same time as the speaker, there is always some time lag (also called décalage). This brief delay allows the interpreter to listen to and analyse a chunk of the SL message before passing it on. This processing time varies depending on the familiarity and complexity of the incoming chunks of information. Interpreters may need to use a long time lag to fully understand an unfamiliar concept, or to find the point in a meandering introduction. However, when passing on statistics or telephone numbers, for example, minimal time lag is required – in fact a longer time lag would jeopardise remembering all of the details, given short-term memory typically holds only five to nine items. Also, when a topic is very familiar to the interpreter, or the speaker/signer is using common phrases or expressions that are well known, time lag can reduce considerably and even disappear altogether (become negative). You may have seen segments of interpreting that are ahead of the speaker, because the interpreter knows where the talk is heading. Of course this can backfire, and require repairing, if the prediction is incorrect.

Many interpreters aspire to a long time lag, seeing this as the mark of a competent practitioner. Certainly the development of short-term memory capacity and the ability to use a long time lag where appropriate are valuable skills, however time lag needs to be understood as an average of different degrees of delay throughout a text. No interpreter maintains a continuous, fixed time lag – they move along a continuum. Cokely (1986) analysed how interpreters working from English into ASL used time lag to process the incoming message, and looked at the effects of shorter and longer lag times on the accuracy of the interpretation. Overall, he found that either a very short average time lag (producing output before properly analysing meaning), or an excessively long average lag, resulted in loss of information and accuracy in the TL output. Cokely's study identified that interpreters with an average time lag of two seconds made more miscues (that is, inappropriate omissions, additions, and alterations) than inter-preters with a longer average lag of four seconds. In addition, effective processing was not just dependent on the length of time between input and output, but on how the interpreter used pauses to chunk SL input into meaningful TL output chunks.

Which technique is appropriate for sign language interpreting?

Because sign language interpreters work between a 'silent' language and a spoken language, the interpreting process can, and usually does, happen simultaneously. There is no auditory conflict between the languages being vocalised, one over the top of another, so there is less obvious need to break the process into segments. Sign language interpreting consumers generally expect interpreters to work in simultaneous mode, regardless of the setting.

Another reason behind the use of simultaneous mode by sign lang-uage interpreters is that taking notes in order to interpret consecutive chunks of information presents two problems. First, they cannot afford to take their eyes off a deaf client's signing or they will miss vital content, so note-taking becomes scrappy at best. And, because they need their hands and eyes to interpret into sign language, they cannot hold or read their notes while interpreting from them.

However, some research indicates that using the consecutive tech-nique can be more effective (Russell 2002), especially in legal or medical contexts, where interpreting accuracy and clarity is critical. Working with segments of one language at a time allows the interpreter time, and proces-sing space, to get a clearer idea of the specific details and the overall aims. Experienced sign language interpreters sometimes argue for the use of con-secutive interpreting in these sensitive situations, so that they can digest complex, technical or confused information, and express it as clearly as possible in the TL, with proper attention to finding cultural and linguistic equivalence.

Less experienced sign language interpreters often find the prospect of consecutive interpreting more daunting – they are nervous that they will forget information if they wait too long, and feel that simultaneous interpreting is easier because they can process information immediately, in smaller chunks. This usually means they are not used to the process of interpreting consecutively, and lack confidence in their own short-term memory skills.

In fact, the consecutive technique can be more effective for less experienced interpreters, because it allows more time to produce an intact message in a more natural TL style with less interference from the SL. Research has shown that shorter time lag is associated with higher rates of error and incomprehensibility in the TL output (Cokely 1992). For example, interpreters working simultaneously who do not use enough lag time, can end up processing only one or two words at a time rather than whole concepts, or making incorrect predictions about the direction of the speaker's message. Processing at a lexical level is especially common when working from English into Auslan/NZSL, causing the sign language output to be unnaturally structured (based on the English source) in a way that doesn't make sense to a deaf person. However, more literal interpretation is not always a bad thing, as explained in the next section.

'Literal' interpretation (transliteration) versus 'free' interpretation

Whether they work in a consecutive or simultaneous mode, interpreters can create TL output that is closer to, or further away from, the words/signs and structure of the SL, depending on their skill level, the kind of message they are passing on, and the preference of their clients. This can be seen as a continuum from highly 'literal' (word for word) interpretation (also called 'transliteration') at one end, to a more natural or 'free' interpretation at the other.

Free interpretation

The term 'free' does not imply that the interpreter can take liberties with meaning, or that they don't charge for their work; it simply means that they focus on freeing the interpretation from the actual SL words/signs used. The interpretation should express the intended meaning in a form that may be structured very differently in the TL, but achieves the same overall effect. An interpreter using this approach might hear a sentence in English, listen for the essential meaning, and produce an equivalent Auslan/NZSL sentence that looks nothing like the original English version, but expresses the same meaning, the way a native signer might, for example:

> *English*: I'd like to know the reasons behind your aggressive behaviour yesterday.

> *Auslan/NZSL:* YESTERDAY YOU ANGRY LOSE-TEMPER. PLEASE EXPLAIN-ME WHY YOU ANGRY WHY?

Notice that in this free interpretation, the time sequence has been restructured according to sign language norms, and the speaker's wording and somewhat indirect style have been analysed and restructured into phrasing and style more typical of a deaf signer. The meaning of, 'I'd like to know more', is interpreted as a polite request for explanation, expressed with different wording but equivalent effect in sign language (please explain-me why). The generalised phrase 'aggressive behaviour' is expanded with more specific description of the context or action (you angry lose-temper), as is typical in sign language discourse.

A free approach also applies when interpreting from a signed language to English. In general, a free interpretation approach is the most effective way to convey messages that are meaningful to both parties communicating across unfamiliar languages and cultures. Free interpretation recognises that the same ideas can be expressed quite differently in each language, and that participants bring different life experiences and conceptual frameworks to the communication.

Literal interpretation (transliteration)

In most cases, literal interpretation means the process of transferring a message produced in spoken English into signing which closely follows the English structure (syntax) and vocabulary. It can also be done when interpreting from a signed language into English (for example, when a psychiatrist wants to know each individual sign a deaf patient has used), but this is much less common.

Using the example above, a more literally interpreted version could be:

English: I'd like to know the reasons behind your aggressive behaviour yesterday.

Auslan/NZSL: I LIKE KNOW WHY YOUR BEHAVE ANGRY YESTERDAY?

This version remains close to the English sentence structure or form, does not expand the contextual meaning of 'aggressive', and does not re-structure the speaker's implied question or request for information, except by adding question marking.

In the sign language interpreting field, literal interpretation can be a legitimate practice for deaf people who are bilingual. Deaf signers are surrounded by English throughout their lives, especially in education, which inevitably influences the language structures they use and understand (Johnston 2002). Auslan and NZSL signers may incorporate English word order, lip patterns and fingerspelling into their signing, combining these with other sign language features (such as non-manual signals and spatial grammar) (Lucas and Valli 1990).

Research studies (see, for example, Pollitt 2000, Napier 2002, Napier and Barker 2004) have shown that literal interpreting can be effective, and even preferred, in certain contexts by consumers who want access to English terms. For example, in the university context, students need to know subject-specific terminology or to see the structure of academic English. These deaf people are usually bilingual, and have the capacity and/or desire to receive the signed information in a form that is closer to the original English.

The context and purpose of the communication are important factors in choosing a free or literal approach. For example, a bilingual deaf person may require a more literal interpretation in a university lecture, but prefer a free interpretation in a social setting. Switching between the two styles within a single interaction can also be appropriate; the same deaf person may be comfortable with a combination of the two techniques in a business meeting, where the interpreter uses a free approach to convey the meaning and intent of the discussion, but switches into using English mouth pattern and/ or fingerspelling for technical terms or phrasing of a document that the deaf person needs to follow.

Inappropriate literal interpreting can happen unintentionally and unconsciously, when the interpreter is not able to fully process the English message into a natural signed form. This may be due to time pressure, limitations on sign language proficiency, English input that is too unfamiliar to make sense of, or fear that departing from the words of the original message will be seen as inaccurate by deaf and/or hearing consumers.

Defining an effective literal interpretation is difficult, since the output is a mix of sign language and English features, which varies from one individual and situation to another. However, several research studies have identified common characteristics that make a literal interpretation more comprehensible. (See, for example, Winston 1989; McIntire 1993; Siple 1993, 1995; Sofinski, Yesbeck, Gerhold and Bach-Hansen 2001; Winston and Moni-kowski 2003.) These include using:

- Conceptually equivalent sign vocabulary (for example, using the appropriate sign for 'run', depending on the particular meaning in context);

- Spatial reference to persons and things, and matching use of directionality in verbs and pronouns;

- Non-manual grammar (including facial expression, mouth patterns, head and body position);

- Pauses that signal grouping and phrasing of ideas, marking topic shifts to make the message cohesive;

- Strategic addition of information that is not explicit in the English SL (for example, 'The assignments have been marked' → 'I have marked your assignments');

- Lip-patterns that appropriately link English words and signs.

This list shows that even when interpreters are using a literal approach, they need solid sign language grammatical skills as a basis.

In the US, interpreters are accredited as 'interpreters' or 'transliterators' (or both) through an evaluation process that tests these skills separately. However, in Australia and New Zealand, the focus in training and testing is to ensure that all sign language interpreters meet the needs of a wide range of consumers. Ideally, interpreters should be able to use either free or literal interpreting methods, or combine the two, depending on the client and the situation.

Translating between a signed and a written language

Most sign language interpreting work is done live 'through the air', but sometimes interpreters are asked to translate from, or into, written language. A common example of this is 'sight translation' (that is, spontaneous translation without preparation). Here, the interpreter may be working with a deaf client who needs to fill out a form (for example, in a medical, legal or commercial situation). If the deaf person is not confident with English literacy, they may need the interpreter to translate the meaning of the document, and possibly translate their signed responses into written English. When doing sight translation, take the time to read the written text (or relevant portion of it) fully, to ensure that you have understood its meaning in context, before interpreting into natural sign language. Beware of transliterating sentences into an English influenced form, which may not be clearly understood by the Deaf consumer.

Translation of frozen literary texts between written and signed language is a relatively recent area that has emerged with video/DVD technology and the recognition of deaf people as bilinguals. This area of work includes translating children's stories for sign language videos, biblical translation, theatre interpretation from scripts, signing songs, transcription of letters from dictated signing, and transcription of filmed signed texts for sign language and interpreter training resources, and for television broadcast.

Another growing area is the translation of information from government sources, now increasingly being made available in sign language on websites. Good examples are the NZSL translation of the UN Convention on the Rights of Person with Disabilities (NZ Office for Disability Issues website), and information translated into NZSL on the NZ Human Rights Commission website. Auslan examples include the Education Standards of the Australian *Disability Discrimination Act* (DDA) (available on the DDA website), and 'Auslan Info Bytes' available on the New South Wales Office of Industrial Relations website

Most often, translations of public information aimed at a Deaf audience are presented by a deaf translator (as a first language user of sign language) rather than by a sign language interpreter, although they may work together as a team in preparing the translation. The emerging research on translation into signed languages draws on existing translation theory.

What makes a successful interpretation?

There is rarely one 'correct' interpretation of a message. Interpreters working from the same SL input will invariably create different (but hopefully equivalent) TL output. Also, factors besides the content can be important – such as, whether clients felt comfortable with the way the interaction went. Obviously though, some interpretation is more effective. Who can, or should, judge the quality of interpreting work, and what criteria can they use?

Who can judge?

Because they can't understand the SL input, hearing and deaf consumers can usually only assess an interpreter's performance from the output they receive and the behaviour they observe. Does the message make sense and seem complete? Is it expressed grammatically and naturally? Is it appropriate to the setting? Is the interpreter behaving professionally? Apart from the interpreters themselves, only someone else who is fluent in both languages, and understands the interpreting process, can judge whether the interpretation has fully and accurately portrayed the original meaning. So, apart from seeking feedback from their clients, interpreters need to reflect on their own performance, and where possible, seek feedback from competent colleagues.

What criteria can be used?

There are various frameworks for analysing what makes a successful or unsuccessful interpretation. Taylor (1993) specifies the features of successful interpreting into sign language as follows:

- *Interpretation* – The interpretation accurately conveys linguistic and cultural aspects of the message; meaning should not be added or deleted or changed; the structure of the TL does not inappropriately follow the English SL; speaker's register and affect (emotion) are matched in the TL.

- *Delivery* – Errors are repaired accurately; the interpretation maintains the speaker's pace; interpreter uncertainty about the SL message (for example, not fully hearing it) is conveyed to audience; message is phrased in the first person ('I' for speaker); eye contact with audience is appropriate and utilised for feedback signals; style and size of signing is clear to the audience and matches setting.

- *Composure and appearance* – The interpretation reflects the speaker's meaning and not the interpreter's personal reaction to it (for example, by laughing or frowning); interpreter maintains a composed appearance – free of distracting mannerisms, gestures or facial expressions that are not part of the message; the interpreter appears calm and relaxed, not revealing the mental or physical effort of the interpreting task; grooming is appropriate to the situation and without distracting features (hair, clothes, jewellery).

Taylor points out that any interpretation is rarely entirely good or entirely bad; a sample of work by either a novice or an expert interpreter can contain accurate passages and appropriate features, as well as errors. The novice interpreter might be able to produce a very good interpretation if they have strong background knowledge in a situation, while an experienced inter- preter without that relevant background might struggle with the same material. Most interpreters are able to perform better in some circumstances than in others, depending on their familiarity with the material, the setting, the people, the type of language being used, and the style of interpreting required.

Cokely's (1992) definition of successful interpreting focuses on whether the message is delivered competently in the TL, and the speaker's meaning and intent are conveyed accurately and clearly. He also describes three categories of unsuccessful interpretation, as follows:

- *Deceptive* – The TL message is fluent in form but not equivalent in meaning.

- *Intrusive* – The structure of the TL message contains interference from the language structures of the SL message, making it difficult but not impossible for the audience to understand the speaker's meaning.

- *Dysfunctional* – The TL output contains so many errors of language and/or content that the original message is distorted, confused, and ultimately lost.

Of these three, deceptive is probably the most risky kind of interpreting for consumers, since it can distort communication without consumers being aware of it. Any one interpretation may contain a mixture of successfully interpreted segments and any or all of these three types of unsuccessful interpreting.

Another writer, Gile (1995: 32), discusses evaluating quality in terms of the needs of the message 'sender' and 'receiver', pointing out how difficult it is to satisfy both. He states that the sender of a message generally has an aim in mind, which they want to communicate, although the receiver doesn't always share the same aim. Although his work is about translating, these ideas also apply to interpreting:

> It should be stressed that the Translator is instrumental in helping to achieve the Sender's aims, *but cannot guarantee their fulfilment*: the Sender's statement may be inadequate, and the Receivers may lack the necessary background knowledge, intellectual aptitude, or motivation to receive the message. In fact, they may have strong resistance to the ideas the sender is trying to transmit. Translators are also hampered by their position as 'outsiders' who know less – generally *much* less in most technical and scientific settings – about the subject at hand. Furthermore ... the Translator may know very little about the Sender and the Receiver... It follows that the degree of success in the communication act cannot be taken as the sole

criterion of the Translation quality, though decisions made by the Translator have to be compatible with the aims of the communication actor the Translation is serving, generally the sender.

In practice, sign language interpreters usually feel responsible for making each sender's message comprehensible to the receiver, perhaps because the language, culture and knowledge gap between deaf and hearing consumers is often wide. The point to remember is that even when the interpretation is of good quality, communication might still be unsuccessful for reasons beyond the interpreter's control. Consider this interpreting scenario:

> A deaf man who is a client of the Housing Commission wants to make a complaint about the condition of his unit. He arranges for an interview with a Housing Commission officer and attends with an interpreter. The officer asks them both to sit down, and for the client to explain his complaint. The deaf man describes how rain damage has ruined the carpet and some lounge chairs in his unit, and insists that the carpet and the full lounge suite be replaced. The officer is unhelpful, noting that the premises were inspected recently and that the damage is minor, so if he wants any items replaced he will have to pay for them himself. The conversation is heated and the interpreter voices the exchange accurately. Finally, the deaf man leaves the premises, not sure whether he will take his complaint further.

Even though this deaf client left the interview annoyed with the outcome, he felt his intentions had been communicated to the officer, and that he had understood hers. We can assume the interpreter was effective in matching the communication at various levels: lexically, grammatically, semantically and at discourse level. The negotiation took place as well as could normally be expected in this type of tense exchange. So, even though the deaf man's goals for the transaction were not met, the interpreting accurately reflected the goals of the participants, and enabled effective communication between them. This could therefore be judged as a successful interpretation.

Ultimately, keep in mind that 'effective' interpreting can be measured as successfully conveying the goals, purposes and personal style of the speakers; that is, why they are there, how they relate to each other, and what ideas and feelings they want to exchange. This is sometimes referred to as achieving 'dynamic equivalence': enabling understanding between participants that goes beyond the surface level of words to capture their intended meaning and impact.

This chapter has explained theoretical models and concepts about the process of interpreting, based on broader theories of how communication and discourse works. The next chapter turns to the kinds of competencies and attributes that enable interpreters to perform the task of interpreting effectively.

Thought questions

1. Technical terms and concepts:

(a) How is the task of translating different from interpreting?

(b) Describe how free interpreting differs from literal interpreting/ transliterating in terms of the aims and techniques of each approach?

(c) What circumstances might prompt you to choose a freer or more literal interpreting style?

2. Contextual factors in communication:

(a) Why is it important for interpreters to be aware of the relationship between participants? What difference could this make to the interpretation? Think of an example situation to illustrate.

(b) Why is it so important for interpreters to consider the overall purpose of the communication and speaker's goals? What difference could this make to the interpretation? Think of an example situation to illustrate.

(c) How could the physical setting influence the interpreting process?

(d) What are some ways you could improve and expand your own use of different English and Auslan/NZSL registers?

3. Capturing meaning:

(a) In your own words, explain the distinction between: denotative meaning, connotative meaning and metanotative meaning.

(b) Group the following words under the set of terms in question (a) above: *implied meaning, propositions, innuendo, register, content, delivery, packaging.*

(c) To interpret accurately, what does an interpreter need to attend to? Brainstorm a list.

4. Interpreting processes and skills:

(a) What are four main tasks or stages within the interpreting process?

(b) What are some key mental operations within the phase of 'processing'?

(c) When an interpreter is managing the interpreting process, what is the relationship between 'chunking' and 'lag time'?

(d) Reflecting on your own interpreting skills, which of the 'processing skills' (Colonomos 1992) do you feel you need to strengthen the most, at present?

5. Interpreting effectiveness:

(a) In what circumstances might consecutive interpreting be the most effective technique for a sign language interpreter to use?

(b) In what circumstances might simultaneous interpreting be the most effective technique for a sign language interpreter to use?

(c) Of Cokely's three kinds of unsuccessful interpreting – which kind do you think a novice interpreter is more likely to produce, and which kind is a more experienced interpreter likely to produce? What are the risks inherent in each kind?

(d) What might lead two clients in an interpreted situation to have different views over whether the interpreting was effective or not?

CHAPTER 3

LANGUAGE SKILLS AND KNOWLEDGE

Sign language interpreters face two major language challenges: consolidating their own language skills, and dealing with the variable and unpredictable language use of others. Language skills for interpreters include the ability to understand and express ideas easily in two languages, as well as structural knowledge about each language that can help when problems occur in the transfer of meaning between them. This chapter explores fundamental skills and knowledge relating to spoken and signed languages, which underpin an interpreter's linguistic fitness.

As the majority of interpreters practising now are not native signers, and as there is relatively little information about Auslan and NZSL competencies available elsewhere, this chapter focuses predominantly on sign language (rather than English), and looks at some key differences between Auslan/ NZSL and English.

Language modality (visual-gestural versus auditory-oral) creates differences between the structure of signed languages and spoken languages. New signers are often surprised to find that there isn't a simple one-to-one match of signs to words. Since deaf people perceive and produce information expressed through movement in three-dimensional space, it isn't surprising that meaning is often structured very differently in Auslan/ NZSL than in English. Fluency in both languages is an obvious pre-requisite to interpreting skills, yet the jump from second language conversational fluency to the depth of language adaptability required for interpreting between such different languages can be difficult.

Terms for talking about interpreting

Before looking at specific linguistic skills, it is useful to clarify how we talk about the languages and 'directions' of interpreting. Interpreters are becoming more linguistically aware and work across a broadening range of languages. Naming the actual languages involved (starting with SL and then TL), for example, Auslan to English, or English to NZSL, is more accurate than using 'sign to voice' and 'voice to sign'. Interpreters in Australia used to call Auslan to English interpreting 'reverse interpreting', implying that it was not the norm. This reflected the smaller proportion of interpreting work done from Auslan/NZSL into English; deaf people generally still get less chance to be heard than spoken to. Many interpreters find Auslan/NZSL to

English interpreting stressful; they either don't get the chance to do much of it, or choose not to do it, and their lack of exposure and practice becomes more of a reason to avoid it. However, anyone aspiring to be a professional interpreter needs to work confidently in both directions, to ensure that equal access to expression is available to both consumer groups.

Spoken language skills

Interpreters in Australasia need to be native or highly fluent speakers of English; some might also speak Te Reo Māori or another community language at a suitable level for interpreting. Whichever spoken language is used as a working language, it is essential that interpreters are able to understand and speak it at the level of an educated native speaker. This means having:

- An extensive (and expanding) vocabulary;
- A fluent command of 'standard' spoken grammar;
- The ability to speak appropriately in different registers (levels of formality);
- The cultural knowledge to understand references to places, people, events and concepts in both languages;
- The capacity to hear adequately in a wide range of situations.

When interpreters work from a signed language into a spoken language, their voice not only expresses meaning but also represents the deaf consumer's communication style and impact of their message, so interpreters need good production skills, including:

- A clear, confident speaking voice (with good diction);
- Intonation that is easy to listen to;
- The ability to project their voice confidently in a group or public situation.

These language skills need to be consciously developed and refined.

Te Reo Māori

New Zealand English has always included a considerable number of Māori words, which is now increasing. At a bare minimum, NZSL/English interpreters need to know the meaning of Māori words that are commonly used (without translation) in everyday English in the media and at public events.[1] Interpreters are therefore encouraged to learn enough Māori to be able to interpret predictable greetings and introductions that are frequently used in formal welcomes (pōwhiri) at public events and in educational settings. Because language and culture are intertwined, learning Te Reo Māori even

---

1   See Macalister (2005) for a guide to these.

to a basic level is sure to increase an interpreter's cultural comfort in Māori settings, their understanding of Māori-related topics, and to improve their rapport with Māori deaf (and hearing) consumers. (See further discussion of Māori contexts in Chapter 9.)

Regardless of which spoken language interpreters work with, the process of interpreting from Auslan/NZSL into a spoken TL also requires solid comprehension of the signed language source. Interpreters can improve their Auslan/NZSL to English performance by not only refining their English language skills, but also by getting exposed to, and using, as much Auslan/NZSL as possible, so that their initial comprehension of the source text becomes less of a stumbling block.

Auslan/NZSL skills

The fact that most interpreters are not native signers and have weaknesses in their sign language competence motivated researcher Marty Taylor (1993) to identify linguistic skills for successful English to ASL interpreting. Her findings are transferable to our work, and are summarised below as a checklist of language features and competencies that should be present in interpretation of English to Auslan/NZSL:

Established sign vocabulary (lexicon)

- Signs are clearly formed in all parameters (handshape, orientation, location, movement, non-manual features);
- Production of signs is accurate (for example, differentiating between a noun and verb form);
- Transitions are smooth in compound signs;
- The signs chosen match the meaning of the speaker's intent;
- A diverse range of vocabulary is used to match the diversity of the SL as far as possible;
- Vocabulary choice matches participant, for example, age, regional dialect, and appropriate register for the situation.

Fingerspelling

- Spelling is complete and correct;
- Clearly formed, at a comfortable-to-read pace;
- Used at appropriate times (not over-used);
- Produced with appropriate lip-pattern.

Numbers

- Numbers signs are accurately formed and uniformly paced;

- Numeral incorporation is used appropriately (for example, THREE-OF-US, FOUR-MORE, TWO-WEEKS-AGO, FIVE-YEARS-OLD).

Classifier (depicting) signs

- Are structurally accurate – use appropriate handshapes, locations, movements, and non-manual features;

- Are clearly linked to something previously named in the text;

- Are used where appropriate in the text to represent nouns and verbs in the SL message – keeping in mind how the ideas would be most naturally expressed using classifiers in sign language.

Grammar

- A variety of sign language structures is used, for example, topic-comment statements, role-shift (constructed action and constructed dialogue), and rhetorical questions;

- Sentence structures are accurately formed and complete, including the use of pauses and non-manual signals to mark clauses (spaces between ideas) where appropriate;

- Non-manual features are used to express adverbial and adjectival meaning with signs (for example, large, tiny, fast, dawdling);

- Pluralisation is made clear by use of 'quantity' signs (for example, MANY, FEW), reduplication (repetition of sign), pointing signs and/or classifier signs (creating multiple locations and/or movements);

- Temporal (time) meaning is expressed accurately by verb inflection (for example, changing the sign movement and non-manual features to show duration, regularity, repetition etc) and use of time phrases (for example, THREE MONTH AGO, ME FINISH SEE);

- Clear lip-patterns corresponding to important content words are used.

Making visuospatial sense

When interpreters hear a string of spoken words in English, they reconstruct it into sign language, often using three-dimensional space.[2] For the interpretation

---

2   Borden (1996), Chapter 2, provides a useful introduction to putting some of these principles into practice (Borden and Bennet 1996, *The Art of Interpreting American Sign Language,* Plymouth: Hayden-McNeil Publishing).

to make sense through a deaf person's eyes, it is vital not just to select the right sequence of signs, to produce them clearly, and use appropriate non-manual features, but also to connect these elements effectively in space and motion, by:

- Placing signs for concrete and abstract entities (people, objects, ideas) in reference points in space, and then keeping their relationships to each other consistent;

- Using placement of signs in space to describe actual physical layout (topographic space) as well as indicating hierarchies, contrasts and other relationships between ideas (syntactic space);

- Using directional movement in verbs and classifier signs to show grammatical relationships or to represent physical actions;

- Ensuring directional verb movement and eye gaze correspond accurately to established points in space associated with referents;

- Placing time signs and signs for events on appropriate timelines in space;

- Using close and distant focus in visual scenarios – for example, zooming in and out from a general description to more specific details;

- Allocating non-manual features, eye gaze directions, and sometimes head and body orientation, to specific characters when describing dialogue or actions using role shift.

Making temporal (time) sense

Expressing time (temporal meaning) in signed languages is often different to the way temporal meaning is expressed in English. For example, English uses grammatical words and endings to show tense (for example, *I jumped, I jump, and I will jump*), whereas Auslan/NZSL, and many other languages, do not, so interpreters need to use alternate constructions for establishing the timeframe (for example, *yesterday me jump* or *me finish jump*).

Auslan/NZSL also have a strong tendency to express ideas in the order in which events actually happen, in a natural visual chronology (like the logic of a cartoon strip). This can be seen in narratives where, once the timeframe is established, the story and events unfold in 'present' time. Some word order (syntactic) patterns of Auslan/NZSL follow a visual logic in setting the scene, for example:

- Identifying an object in the signing space before commenting about it or showing what action is involved.

    English: A shark swam into the net.

    Auslan/NZSL: using classifiers, sign a net before showing a shark swimming into it.

- Generally using an 'if' (condition) clause before the result clause.

    English: We'll go to the beach if it's a sunny day.

    AUSLAN/NZSL: IF SUNNY GO BEACH (that is, reflecting natural order)

- Following chronological order with cause-effect relationships.

    English: The koala population diminished after the bush was cleared.

    Auslan/NZSL: TREE CUT-DOWN KOALA CL: group reduce.

- Locating ideas and events in order on timelines in the signing space, to create a visual chronological map of the topic.[3]

These examples of visual and temporal logic in sign languages remind us that an interpreter needs to wait until they can visualise a group of related ideas before re-constructing the message properly in a visual-spatial dimension.

Different discourse styles

Auslan/NZSL and English speakers have differing styles for giving, describing and explaining information, which presents some interesting challenges for interpreters. You may have already noticed the following characteristics of Auslan/NZSL.

High context communication

Auslan/NZSL speakers are used to communicating within a familiar community that shares a lot of contextual knowledge about each other and shared experiences. Deaf signers often assume that their audience (including an interpreter) will understand their references to people, places and events without much elaboration or supporting explanation. Referring to people by name signs is one example. High context communication also shows up in the grammatical structure of Auslan/NZSL, where a deaf person signing a narrative establishes the context of timeframe (when it happened), and person reference (who is involved) at the beginning. The information that follows relies on understanding this initial contextual set-up, because time reference and personal pronouns may be absent or occasional thereafter. An English narrative contains repeated clues through the tense of verbs, and personal pronouns that specify gender (for example, he left, she screamed), whereas information about who and when is embedded in the context of an Auslan/NZSL narrative (for example, via reference points in space, and classifier signs). This is why it can be hard to eavesdrop into an ongoing signed conversation. As deaf people say: *missed bus* (NZ)/*train gone sorry* (Australia), meaning you have missed the context and the point.[4] When

---

3 For further reading, see Sutton-Spence and Woll (1998).
4 Mindess (1999) describes this in ASL, which applies equally to Auslan/ NZSL.

interpreters are working with signed narratives as source or target texts, they need to pay close attention to the initial establishing of context.

Level of detail

In describing objects, people and events, deaf signers tend to give and expect more (and sometimes different) detail about visual aspects and personal information than English speakers do. For example, classifier signs may convey very specific detail about appearance, position, and motion, which might not be included in an English version of the same basic idea (for example, describing an expensive hotel room). When interpreting in either direction, differences in the expected level of detail can be tricky – deciding what information might need to be expanded or condensed, depending on the audience and the purpose of the communication. Deaf signers often describe an incident or piece of information within a very full context; there is a tendency to tell the whole story in a style sometimes referred to in the Deaf world as 'A-Z', whereas an English speaker might give a more condensed version.

First person perspective

Deaf signers tend to 'show' rather than to 'tell' information, using role-shift to reconstruct or enact dialogue, thoughts, action, and behaviour from a first person (present) perspective. An English speaker (except in an informal register) is more likely to report the information indirectly, using the more remote third person, past tense (She said/ He did), taking an 'outside' perspective.

Specific versus general reference

In signed discourse, new concepts are often explained by starting with a practical example or story, working from the concrete to the abstract, whereas English speakers often state a generalisation or main idea before, or instead of, giving examples. This can make explanations in English difficult for many deaf consumers to follow.

Specific items versus general categories

Some English words that refer to a category of related things are expressed in Auslan/NZSL by listing sample components (sometimes after finger-spelling the general term), for example:

Cutlery = KNIFE, FORK, SPOON

Pest (if discussing the NZ bush) = POSSUM, STOAT, DEER, GOAT

This can create translation dilemmas when an interpreter doesn't have enough information to decide how to represent generic terms such as 'pasta', 'abuse', or 'vehicle' in sign language, without choosing a misleading example or definition.

In summary, linguistic competence for interpreters goes beyond having fluent production, accurate grammar, and vocabulary knowledge. It also entails a deeper knowledge of discourse – having a feel for how people in the Deaf community use the language to conceptualise and talk about ideas. An interpreter from a deaf family background explains how she has observed this challenge for interpreters:

> Sometimes we as interpreters develop a false sense of confidence in our signing skills – feeling that because we are proficient, we can interpret well for anybody in the community. But even interpreters who are fluent don't always succeed in expressing ideas in a way that really makes sense to a deaf person. Language skills can be acquired from training, but not the depth of understanding about how deaf people think and naturally express ideas in sign language. There is a lot of interpretation that looks quite acceptable from a language point of view, but doesn't actually convey much sense from a deaf point of view. The only way for interpreters to keep on developing this kind of insight about deaf discourse is by mixing at all levels of the community and observing closely how deaf people talk to each other in different situations.

Variation: Same language, different ways of signing

All living languages are constantly changing and none are therefore completely 'standardised'. But Auslan and NZSL have even more variation in their vocabulary and grammar than Australian and New Zealand English, for several reasons:

- Auslan/NZSL developed in small regional communities around deaf schools that were geographically separated, creating regional (and in some cases religious or gender-based) vocabulary differences. Regional and religious (school-related) differences are particularly prominent in Auslan.

- Historical changes in educational policy on signing in schools have resulted in differences in signing style and vocabulary between different generations of the Deaf community. Younger signers, for example, have been more exposed to the vocabulary of Australasian Signed English. Different generational groupings in school and community settings may also innovate signs that are particular to their peer group, which contributes to lexical variation in the adult community.

- Auslan/NZSL have not been widely used in formal education, in broadcasting, or documented in print, which are the usual routes through which a 'standard' form of a language is promoted. Dictionaries for each of these languages have only recently been created. These are one potential standardising influence, particularly if used as a language learning resource in schools. However, sign language dictionary use seems to be higher for hearing sign language and interpreting students, than for deaf signers.

- As most deaf children are born to hearing parents, few deaf people acquire Auslan/NZSL as a native language from birth – the majority learn sign language at later stages of life, from a mixture of sign language models. This creates a wide range of acceptable articulation, fluency, grammatical structure and discourse styles in Auslan/NZSL. Not all signers conform to the patterns of grammar and semantics (meaning) used by native or fluent signers, which tend to be the ones demonstrated in dictionaries, grammar texts, teaching materials and signing classes.

- The opportunity for transmission, and therefore continuity, of language between generations of signers has been altered by the closure of many deaf clubs, and new patterns of more localised and age-related social interaction

Contact between Sign Language and English

Another ingredient in language variation is the fact that signed languages do not exist in isolation from the surrounding hearing community's spoken and written language. Many linguists have emphasised the independence of signed languages from spoken languages in advocating for signed languages as complete and valid linguistic systems, but in fact, Auslan and NZSL have an obvious interaction with the surrounding English language. Auslan/NZSL indeed have many unique features and structures that are unrelated to spoken English, yet the social reality is that deaf people acquire and use Auslan/NZSL in a 'language contact' situation. Schools, television, books, computers, household items, advertising and so on ensure that deaf people have daily exposure to, and the need to know English in some form. This results in considerable individual variation in their range of vocabulary (drawn from both languages), fingerspelling, syntax (word order) and use of communication behaviours and discourse styles pertinent to each language. Deaf signers' knowledge of English often influences their use of Auslan/NZSL, especially when communicating with hearing people through interpreters.

You may notice deaf people using *code-mixing* – where English words and phrases are incorporated into their Auslan/NZSL signing or *code-switching* – where signers shift the style of their signing, between a more 'deaf' style of Auslan/NZSL and a more English-structured variety of contact signing (or even speaking). Code-switching and code-mixing can be conscious or unconscious and usually happen in response to a particular situation or audience. For example, when signing with hearing people (including interpreters), the deaf person may use more English word order and mouthing, to be better understood. Sometimes deaf people code-switch to a more English syntax, or insert English phrases (code mix), because they are in a formal situation, for example, a meeting or lecture, or are referring to written documents. Code-switching is a signer's instinctive adjustment to the linguistic identity and capability of their audience, or a way of presenting themselves in a particular light through the choice of language used.

Many older deaf people do not identify with the Auslan/NZSL style of younger deaf signers, who tend to be the teachers and language models for trainee interpreters. Younger deaf people who were mainstreamed and acquired sign language as young adults may be less familiar with Auslan/NZSL than English, yet still need access to communication through Auslan/NZSL interpreters. Sometimes the focus on Auslan/NZSL as a TL disadvantages deaf consumers who prefer a more English-based interpretation. A complaint by deaf consumers about the interpreting at a conference illustrates this perspective:

> There were times when we felt 'shortchanged' – language was too simple and too much left out. We are aware that there was a wide range of needs to meet but it was felt that sometimes interpreters are too judgmental in deciding what we can understand. How can deaf people increase our knowledge and understanding of English if what we are given is always limited?

The deaf writers of this letter felt that the interpreters' language choice (to use more vernacular deaf syntax and lexicon) was disempowering – they wanted more literal access to the English source message.

On the other hand, interpreters also risk critical feedback from Auslan/NZSL users who find an English-based interpretation less meaningful. For example, in Australia, many trainee interpreters have learned Auslan from relatively bilingual teachers in Auslan classes, and do not have the skills to work with deaf clients less able to decipher English syntax or 'new' signs.

This section has highlighted variation related to age, region and individual usage in Auslan/NZSL, as well as the prevalence of code-mixing and code-switching, and the impact of signed English or late sign language acquisition on younger generations of signers. It is important for interpreters to recognise that there is a spectrum of signing in the Deaf community and to develop a wide repertoire of signing skills.[5] Good interpreters do their best to provide interpretation in a language style that is acceptable and comprehensible to the particular consumer they are working with. An experienced practitioner advises, 'expect the unexpected':

> Even though I grew up using NZSL at home, and feel that I know the language quite well, I've become more aware through my interpreting work that there is a much wider spectrum of the ways deaf consumers use NZSL – from more 'standard' vocabulary and grammar structures, to some quite idiosyncratic signs and ways of expressing concepts (such as time and

---

5   The significance of linguistic diversity for interpreters in the UK context is discussed by Mairian Corker (1997), and a study of lexical variation in NZSL and how interpreters deal with it, is reported in McKee, Major and McKee (2008).

place). A lot depends on their language and educational background. The variation is huge and can be really challenging to work with.

Bilingual fluency

Ideally, interpreters have equivalent high level receptive and productive skills in each language, to interpret reliably in both directions, but this can be an elusive goal given the backgrounds of most sign language interpreters, and the complex variation within signing communities themselves.

In the spoken language interpreting profession interpreters are referred to as having an 'A' language and a 'B' language (and maybe even a 'C' language). The 'A' language is the first or native language of the interpreter, often referred to as the 'mother tongue'; the 'B' language is a second language that the interpreter knows well and can interpret into accurately, but generally not to the level of native fluency. A true or 'balanced' bilingual is someone who is regarded as having two 'A' languages, which is actually very rare.

As most interpreters are not balanced bilinguals, the general preference in high-level settings is for interpreters to work from their 'B' (second) language into their 'A' (native) language, since they are generally most articulate and confident expressing themselves in their dominant language. A minimum level of bilingualism for interpreters is to have at least equivalent vocabularies (bivocabularism (Bowen 1980)) in each of the languages they use.

Most interpreters working in Auslan/NZSL and English have English as their 'A' language and Auslan/NZSL as their 'B' language, and therefore need to continually work on extending their signing skills. Even those interpreters who have grown up with sign language need to enrich their Auslan/NZSL fluency, to be able to use the language with a broad range of deaf consumers and in a variety of interpreting situations and registers (for example, work meetings, school classrooms, and conference settings).

Because of the necessary focus on Auslan/NZSL skills, English skill development is sometimes overlooked. However, balanced fluency requires the ability and confidence to also be able to use English competently in the full range of interpreting situations and registers that our varied work finds us in. Undertaking higher education is a good way of extending one's vocabulary and use of more formal English.

Fluency in two languages, however, doesn't always equate with being a good interpreter. The following factors hinder many bilinguals from becoming proficient interpreters:[6]

- Unequal fluency in both languages (to a degree that interferes with audience understanding);

- A heavy accent in the second language;

---

6   Adapted from Grosjean (1997).

- Late acquisition or learning of the second language;

- Lack of knowledge of variation in each language;

- Undeveloped processing skills (being able to transfer meaning rapidly between languages);

- Lack of general knowledge;

- Lack of knowledge about how different concepts are expressed in each language;

- Lack of cultural knowledge about the two distinct groups.

So, beyond balanced fluency, interpreters need additional linguistic awareness and skills:

> [R]apid translation from one language to another need not come spontaneously to the bilingual. Indeed many bilinguals who can function extremely well in two languages in clearly demarcated situational contexts often find it difficult to translate spontaneously between their languages without heavy interference. This is one reason why professional interpreters require special training for a task that does not necessarily come naturally, even if they were childhood bilinguals. (Baetens Beardsmore 1986: 106)

This chapter has explored some key linguistic competencies, emphasising the consolidation of sign language skills and knowledge in particular. Bilingual fluency is the foundation of effective interpreting and requires high-level receptive and productive skills in both languages, so interpreters must continually strive to improve and expand their language base. Alongside these essential working tools, interpreters need to develop the cultural knowledge and personal attributes described in the next chapter.

Thought questions

1. Give some examples of how a visual versus auditory language modality affects the way ideas are structured and expressed in Auslan/NZSL and English.

2. When interpreting, what are some strategies for dealing with differences in the way time concepts are organised in Auslan/NZSL compared to English?

3. Explain why interpreting for a deaf consumer who is using 'high context communication' can be challenging. Give an example and describe what strategy you could use.

4. Being bilingual does not guarantee being a competent interpreter. What other linguistic skills are also needed?

5. Identify some strategies that could assist interpreters to become more 'balanced' bilinguals.

CHAPTER 4

INTERPRETER COMPETENCIES AND ATTRIBUTES

Who and what makes a good interpreter? There are many opinions on this subject, but definite answers are hard to pin down. For one thing, the desirable skills and qualities of an interpreter tend to be defined differently by hearing and Deaf consumers, and by practitioners and researchers who are 'inside' the profession. Their perspectives naturally differ because each party experiences the interpreted situation differently, relates differently to the interpreter, and sees the interpreter's role through a different lens. This chapter focuses on interpreter competencies beyond the foundation language skills, and looks at how cultural knowledge and personal qualities also affect the success of interpreting.

Bicultural skills

Using two languages competently also requires being able to navigate socially in two different cultural worlds. But even for bicultural-bilinguals, knowledge of culture (especially our native culture) can be hard to explain because it is mostly unconscious, even though it underlies every aspect of social life. Culture is also personal; it shapes our thinking and regulates our behaviour and our ways of communicating. Cross-cultural encounters between individuals can spotlight differences at this inter-personal level. Sign language interpreters can find themselves in the middle of situations of cultural difference, and need to be consciously aware of aspects of Deaf culture (including attitudes, beliefs, goals, discourse norms) that come into play when communicating with hearing people.[1] Experience in the Deaf world is vital in this respect.

---

1   We recommend Mindess (1999) *Reading between the signs – intercultural communication for sign language interpreters* as a useful source for interpreters on this topic. Although written in an American context, the principles generally apply to Australasian communities. Padden and Humphries (1988, 2005); Lane, Bahan and Hoffmeister (1996); and Bauman (2007) also offer insightful description of Deaf cultural values and perspectives.

Relating to the Deaf community

Deaf consumers need to feel that an interpreter is an acceptable person to trust with their personal business. When deaf people say 'attitude' is a top priority in interpreters, this is shorthand for how well an interpreter relates to people in the Deaf community generally, and on a personal basis. The basis of 'good attitude' is perhaps respect for deaf people, in contrast to the negative or ignorant attitudes they encounter in mainstream hearing society, and personal dispositions such as genuineness, patience, humour, and warmth.

Another expression that deaf people sometimes use about interpreters is 'good heart'. This implies commitment to supporting the Deaf community with a motivation that is not self-seeking or patronising, but empowering. Having 'attitude' and 'heart' also means showing that you like deaf people by being friendly and open. Don't underestimate the extent to which your attitude will be assessed from your face and body language, as well as by your actions and words. Interpreters with good attitude and heart are often valued more than those with excellent technical linguistic skills but weaker relationships with deaf people.

'Attitude' and 'heart' relate to some other core Deaf cultural values:

Involvement in the community

Sign language interpreters differ from most spoken language interpreters who are more often native members of the minority community they interpret for and thus have an automatic acceptance and rapport. As non-deaf people, sign language interpreters don't have this status. Even Codas, who are closely identified with the Deaf world they grew up in, are in an 'other' social category, because they have not experienced being deaf and can participate fully in the hearing world.

Sign language interpreters are paid professionals with private lives, who don't always have the time or inclination to be involved in Deaf community activities[2] and impartiality within the interpreting role requires that interpreters maintain professional distance and not show allegiance to deaf people on the job. However, interpreters will only become trusted professionals if they are seen to have a wider interest in the Deaf world. A 'nine-to-five' attitude doesn't enhance one's reputation – deaf people are often sceptical about interpreters who have no involvement in the Deaf community beyond paid hours.[3] Showing your face at community events from time to time, keeping up with news in the Deaf world, and supporting

---

2   Turner (2001a: 31-32) argues that it is also realistic to acknowledge that there must be limits to the relationship, since interpreters are not Deaf, and 'their professional and personal selves need to have the space to maintain a sense of their own identity ... especially when they spend huge chunks of their waking hours taking on other personas ... in order to do their job properly as interpersonal mediators'.

3   See Mindess (1999) for elaboration on this point.

Deaf causes and achievements are important ways to maintain rapport with the community.

Connection with the community also builds invaluable contextual knowledge of individual people, events, and diverse communication styles and backgrounds, as this deaf person's comment suggests:

> If I get an interpreter that I haven't met socially in the community I feel nervous that they won't have background knowledge of the issues I want to talk about – they won't know my signing style and the kind of vocabulary I use. When someone I've never met shows up to interpret for me, how do I know what their comprehension skills are like?

The same person described an experience of running a mixed meeting in his workplace, where the interpreter could not accurately interpret his signing into English. As a result, he felt that he lost the authority befitting his role as a manager in this situation. He attributed the communication breakdown to the fact that this interpreter had never met him previously in the community, rather than to weak interpreting skills. To him, linguistic ability and accurate interpretation was linked to personal contact and participation in the Deaf community.

Sharing of resources

Most poorly-resourced minority communities expect members to pitch in, exchange favours, and contribute to the group's achievement of its goals.[4] Because deaf people's access to information is limited, personal and general information is freely and directly shared in the community; what hearing people might regard as discretion or privacy can be seen by deaf people as unsociable withholding of information. Access to effective education is also at a premium, so those with knowledge and skills (particularly English literacy) may be called upon to use these on behalf of others. Thus, reciprocity is generally a feature of the community, and this extends to relationships with interpreters.

Reciprocity for interpreters can mean sharing personal information and spending time relating to deaf people (for example, a little chat before or after an assignment), rather than maintaining a rigid boundary between our personal selves and deaf consumers. After all, deaf people have to expose many aspects of their personal lives to interpreters.[5] Reciprocity can mean offering voluntary interpreting occasionally, or contributing other skills or information from the hearing world, in support of a Deaf community activity; for example, making/interpreting phone calls, coordinating other interpreters, or making introductions to relevant hearing world contacts in the organisation of a particular Deaf event or project.

---

4   See Smith (1983) and Mindess (1999), who both discuss expectations of reciprocity in the Deaf world.

5   See Lee (1997) on this point.

Bridging cultural gaps

Experience in the Deaf community develops an interpreter's ability to anticipate when and why cultural misunderstandings are likely to occur between deaf and hearing consumers. Cultural gaps can occur for different reasons:[6]

1. *Differences in form (cultural behaviours)* – Sometimes there is misunderstanding related to *how* communication proceeds, for example, level of eye contact, degree of directness ('straight talk'), giving examples versus generalisations, amount of detail, sequencing of ideas, opening, closing and changing topics, how to ask and answer questions, or politeness conventions.

2. *Differences in content (cultural beliefs and knowledge)* – sometimes there is misunderstanding related to underlying cultural values and assumptions, for example, attitude to being deaf, family relationships, social networks, general world knowledge and educational experiences. There may be different expectations about how a particular kind of interaction proceeds, for example, what kind, and how much, information is appropriate to share in various contexts, and the underlying goals of participants in particular situations.

It is easier for interpreters to make cultural adjustments for differences in 'form' – we can modify our TL output to minimise potential clashes in style by paying attention to expressing the real intent of the communication. A common example of this is adding politeness markers in speech which are not used in sign language, such as saying a person's name or title to address them, or softening a direct request with words such as 'Could I … / Would you mind if…'.

Sometimes cultural difference in content can be bridged by a brief expansion with the interpretation (for example, translating the sign *Oral* along the lines of 'brought up communicating through speech and lip-reading, without sign language', to give an equivalent sense of its meaning). However, bridging content differences can often call for more background explanation of cultural perspectives or experiences than is appropriate to our role, or is possible in the time available.

Beyond linguistic and cultural gaps, interpreters frequently experience tensions between consumers that stem from deaf people's experience of oppression and exclusion from information in hearing society. An interpreter educator comments on this:

> Interpreting students tend to think all deaf people are relatively empowered like their deaf teachers. In fact, even 'well educated' deaf people may have gaps in their hearing-world knowledge, but they are more likely to know how to get information and get their needs met. Whereas out in the wider

---

6   As set out by Mindess (1999).

community, there are many who aren't even aware of the extent of their literacy and education gap, or how differently hearing people do things. That's where cultural mediation, issues of empowerment and judgment around ethical boundaries take on new meaning...Interpreters need to be prepared for that – to know that not all deaf people can articulate their needs and get their rights, and that the interpreter can't do much about that. On the other hand, some deaf people don't want interpreters to do any kind of 'cultural mediation'. I've worked with strong deaf signers who don't want the interpreter to 'change the words' – they want literal interpretation of their signing into English. This is about wanting to retain control, they want it to be exactly like how they've said it. And that's understandable – knowing that they have probably experienced interpreters getting it wrong.

The boundaries of cultural mediation can be murky and putting it into practice takes a depth of bicultural insight, bilingual skill and good judgement. Cultural gaps cannot always be comfortably closed, but as a baseline, Mindess (1999: 182) suggests that:

> Our responsibility as interpreters is to impart each speaker's true intention, making adjustments for differences in communicative style in situations when our failure to do so would result in a misunderstanding of the real meaning of the statement.

This is not always a straightforward task, given the social differences between consumers, their individual preferences and various expectations of how the interpreter should work and the limits of the interpreter's role (as discussed further in the next chapter).

Personal attributes

Are successful interpreters born with an intuitive talent or 'made' by training? Many competent interpreters possess natural aptitude that has been refined through training and experience. Interpreters come from all walks of life with a range of personality types and backgrounds, and naturally maintain their individuality; but there are some common strengths in those who are recognised as successful. Frishberg (1990: 3) proposes that the art of interpretation requires:

> [A]n understanding of the dynamics of human interaction ... an appreciation of social and cultural differences, the ability to concentrate and maintain one's attention, a good deal of tact, judgment, stamina, and above all a sense of humour.

This recipe has three main ingredients: people (social) skills, emotional skills and intellectual skills. All three are essential to the success of an interpreter.

People skills

Interpreters don't work with languages – they work with *people* who are using language to interact and exchange meaning with each other. Skills for understanding and relating to all kinds of people in all kinds of situations are therefore essential. These skills are also important in managing relationships with other interpreters, which can improve our professional motivation and self-esteem. Interpersonal or people skills that serve interpreters well include:

- Being observant of other people (and ourselves);
- Sensitivity to the emotional environment;
- Empathy with consumers;
- Discretion, tact and graciousness;
- Friendliness and cooperation;
- Being supportive of our peers;
- Honesty and assertiveness;
- Advocacy (especially for the use of interpreters);
- Being non-judgmental.

Noticing what people say and do is a good way to learn about them:

> [B]eginning in childhood and continuing throughout life, a translator should be interested in people, all kinds of people – and should take every opportunity to learn about how different people act. (Robinson 1997: 130)

People-watching also helps to stock our mental files with the words/ signs and phrases that people use in different situations:

> The more situational and personal associations you have with a word or phrase, the more complexly and flexibly you will be able to use it yourself … the more complexly and flexibly you use language, the better translator you will be … The goal is to store as many vivid memories of people saying… things as you can. (Robinson 1997: 131)

Emotional skills

Good interpersonal (or 'people') skills rely on a solid emotional framework. According to Daniel Goleman (1996), 'emotional intelligence' is the emotional/ social counterpart to IQ (cognitive intelligence), and is equally, if not more, important. Being able to control our emotional impulses, read others' feelings, and handle relationships smoothly are the basis of emotional intelligence. People with strong 'emotional intelligence' are said to have the following five fundamental characteristics:[7]

(i) Emotional self-awareness (recognising how we are feeling and responding);

(ii) Self-control (channelling our feelings in constructive ways);

---

7   These are summarised by Robinson (1997: 136-138), based on Goleman.

(iii)   Self-motivation (having the drive and initiative to accomplish our goals);

(iv)   Empathy (recognising, understanding, and responding to other people's emotions);

(v)   Maintaining good relationships with people.

Each of these is essential to surviving emotionally and professionally as an interpreter. In fact, the more emotionally stable a person is, the more likely they are to be a successful interpreter (Bontempo and Napier 2009). Other emotional attributes that assist interpreters include:

- Confidence;

- Resilience;

- Humility;

- Reliability;

- Self-discipline and responsibility;

- Independence;

- Enjoyment of work;

- Flexibility and adaptability;

- Sense of humour.

This interpreter reflects on the importance of having a flexible and adaptable approach:

> Adaptability and a thick skin are traits that I've found to be pretty useful in my interpreting career: fitting in, going with the flow, suffering embarrassment and surprising situations with good grace, and being able to let some heavy emotional stuff wash over you … Not to mention the ability to balance on small, unstable surfaces: many a time I've found myself summoning all my poise while interpreting on top of an upturned box, or a rickety chair so that my signing can be seen in a crowd.

A good sense of humour helps, but is sometimes easier to find in retrospect:

> I once had to interpret a tour across the catwalk under the Auckland Harbour Bridge. I had to walk more or less backwards across the bridge, way above the harbour, white-knuckle-gripping the rail with one hand and trying to sign with the other. When I reached the other side my legs were like jelly – and then the deaf person mentioned that, actually, she was an excellent lip-reader and oral interpreting would have been fine!

Extroverts and introverts

What about the performance aspect of interpreting? Does the job really require an extrovert personality? The work of interpreters and actors do have something in common. An interpreter ideally reflects the character and characteristics of other people through their speech or signing, so the ability to 'perform' can be an asset:

> Communication should be lively, with the interpreter changing mood via voice or gesture, and conveying the personality differences between the contributors. Thus, the interpreter cannot be satisfied with being merely a good technician. The interpreter is an actor and must be creative. (Hof 1994: 451)

Poise and an air of confidence or calm are necessary performance elements of interpreting in many situations. There is always a tension between being comfortable at the centre of attention (we are not invisible) and at the same time not detracting from the relationship between our consumers (our reason for being there). A healthy ego can be an advantage when standing up in front of a large crowd, but subtlety and discretion can make or break sensitive communication between two individuals. Interpreters need to balance these attributes as the situation requires.

Intellectual skills

Interpreting is a mentally demanding job and intelligence is obviously important. Individuals entering the field come with different types of intelligence, which is probably a given, rather than something able to be modified through training. Although there is no definitive list of which intellectual skills make an 'ideal' interpreter, a recent study of 28 sign language interpreters' psychological characteristics found that they scored highly in intelligence tests, echoing the results of previous studies. In particular, interpreters performed strongly in tests of problem solving, abstract reasoning, visual and auditory concentration, and attention to graphic detail (Seal 2004).

- Quick witted and able to think on their feet;
- Flexible and lateral thinker;
- Holistic thinker – sees the big picture and inter-relationships;
- Analytical thinker – seeks patterns, organises experience into categories;
- Strong 'verbal' skills – can rapidly understand, manipulate, articulate both languages;
- Good memory – short-term and long-term;
- Enquiring mind – an attitude of life-long learning, collects knowledge of all kinds;
- Observant and reflective about experiences;
- Self-reflective – for example, about own limitations.

A learning attitude

The interpreter's attitude towards their own performance is just as important as the innate cognitive skills they may have; the hallmark of any excellent professional is that they regard themselves as continual learners.[8] It is true to say that most expert interpreters don't just reach 'competent interpreter' level and then relax. Interpreting skills are many and varied, and competence in any one of them isn't a static condition. People cycle through different stages of competence, as shown in the following model:

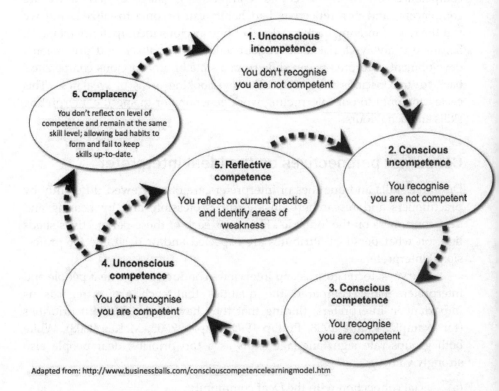

Adapted from: http://www.businessballs.com/consciouscompetencelearningmodel.htm

Beginning at a level of 'unconscious incompetence' (stage 1), new interpreters generally have less awareness of errors in their interpretation or ethical judgement, because they need a certain level of knowledge to detect mistakes. The more training and skills we have, and the more opportunities we have to discuss and reflect on interpreting, the more aware we become of our strengths and weaknesses or need to improve; this allows progression to 'conscious incompetence' (stage 2) – awareness of what we don't know. The ideal progression is to develop this awareness along with our skills – with

---

8   Robinson (1997) elaborates on the importance of a 'learning' disposition in interpreters and translators.

insight into what we are doing effectively; this is the stage of 'conscious competence' (stage 3). Once a skill has been thoroughly acquired, we begin to function so automatically that we become unconscious of what we do know; this is the stage of 'unconscious competence' (stage 4).

We continually move between stages of conscious and unconscious competence as new skills are developed. In the fifth stage – 'reflective competence' – an interpreter is able to reflect on their performance and identify further areas for improvement, which leads them back to stage 2, starting the improvement cycle again. However, if an interpreter bypasses 'reflective competence' they can move into 'complacency' (stage 6). When we are complacent, and non-reflective, bad habits can become fossilized, and we run the risk of moving back to a level of unconscious incompetence (stage 1). So, there is always a risk that without reflection, feedback and professional development, interpreters can slide from a state of 'unconscious competence' back to 'unconscious *in*competence' – overlooking areas of weakness. This cycle can apply to our interpreting work generally, or to specific interpreting skills and behaviours.

Consumer perspectives on the ideal interpreter

Desirable skills and qualities of interpreters are often viewed differently by practitioners and researchers 'inside' the profession, and by hearing and deaf consumers on the 'outside'. However, each of these perspectives sheds light on what personal attributes are expected and/or desirable for professional interpreters.

Surveys, focus groups and interviews conducted with deaf people and interpreters have compared the qualities that each group regards as important in interpreters, finding that they have some different priorities (for example, Kanda 1988; Phillip 1994; Napier 2005; McKee 2008). While both groups rate sign language skills as a top priority, deaf people also strongly value:

(a)   social connection with the Deaf community;

(b)   humility and willingness to learn.

Whereas, interpreters emphasise the importance of:

(a)   maintaining professional role boundaries and distance from deaf clients;

(b)   professional dress and presentation.

Deaf responses were closely tied to values about attitude and connectedness, whereas interpreters focused more on ideas about professionalism. Deaf people's emphasis on 'good attitude' is reflected in this comment from a deaf professional:

I would be most comfortable to work with an interpreter who is a warm, unpretentious person, and is not an attention-seeker. They should look professional, have maturity and be able to make a clear boundary between their personal and professional interests in their job. But at the same time, I expect them to behave naturally in a culturally appropriate way – that is, to be very comfortable in the company of deaf people, show a good attitude towards deaf people and a genuine interest in deaf things.

One of the key issues for many Deaf community members is trust. Research has shown that if deaf people do not know an interpreter, because the interpreter never socialises within the community, they may be suspicious of their interpreting skills, their attitude, and mistrust their ability to do the job (Cokely 2005, Napier and Rohan 2007).

Less research has been done on determining hearing consumer perspectives to our work. Our experience is that they may evaluate interpreters by their perceived 'helpfulness' and their diplomacy in setting them at ease in an unfamiliar communication situation. They may also be more likely to value outward appearances of professionalism (Dean and Pollard 2005). Understanding that there are multiple players and therefore different perspectives on our work in the interpreting interaction is important to our awareness of how we perform our role with consumers from both cultures[9]

This chapter has looked at the types of abilities and personal attributes that underlie competent interpreting. The various skills and aptitudes described here can also be summarised into five essential domains of competence for practitioners entering the field (Witter-Merithew, Johnson and Taylor 2004):

1. *Theory and knowledge* – an academic foundation for understanding the interpreting process, ethics, the Deaf community, interpreting settings.

2. *Human relations* – interpersonal skills for effective collaboration with consumers and colleagues.

3. *Language skills* – high-level competencies that promote effective communication in personal and professional settings, in both first and second languages.

4. *Interpreting skills* – technical competencies for effective interpretation of subject matter in a variety of settings, including consecutive and simultaneous interpreting skills, transliteration skills, and team interpreting skills.

5. *Professionalism* – conforming and contributing to the standards and practices of the profession, including critical self-monitoring, professional development, preparation for assignments, assessment of readiness for

---

[9] See Napier (in press) for a discussion of deaf and hearing consumer attitudes towards signed language interpreters, as compared to interpreters' attitudes.

specific assignments, membership of professional organisations, and ethical behaviour.

Chapter 5 focuses on the final category of knowledge in this list, introducing professional expectations about the interpreter's role and ethics, and some of the practical aspects of carrying out that role in interpreting assignments.

Thought questions

1. Interpreter skills and attributes

(a) 'Interpreters need more than fluent production, grammar and vocabulary knowledge in sign language.' What other types of language abilities does an interpreter need?

(b) Which personal attributes and skills associated with successful interpreters do you believe you have? Give some examples from other areas of your life.

2. Bicultural knowledge and attitudes

(a) Identify two Deaf community priorities about interpreter behaviour and attitude. What are the cultural values underlying these preferences?

(b) In your opinion, do deaf people's expectations for interpreters clash with the idea of professionalism? How could you balance these?

3. Stages of Competence

(a) Describe some behaviour or characteristics that you might observe in an interpreter who is at the stage of:
    - Unconscious incompetence;
    - Conscious competence;
    - Complacency.

(b) How do you think 'professionalism' might be evident to consumers in an interpreter's actual work and conduct?

CHAPTER 5

ROLE, ETHICS AND PROFESSIONAL PRACTICE

Talking to another person through a virtual stranger is an unusual and potentially awkward situation. Interpreters can make or break the success of the interaction in this triangle, depending on how they undertake their role. This chapter outlines different aspects of the interpreter's role, their relationship to clients, and the professional ethics that regulate interpreters' conduct as a group.

What's in a role?

Most people perform multiple roles in their lives: some are social roles (for example, parent, neighbour), some are professional roles (for example, teacher, doctor), while others are situational roles (for example, chairperson, audience member). Each 'role' has two essential aspects: a person's *function* (that is, tasks and responsibilities) and their *relationship* with others in the context (which is expressed through language and actions).

Different roles combine these two aspects in different ways: a doctor may legitimately ask a patient in hospital about their physical functions and touch their body (although not vice versa), yet it would be unacceptable for an accountant to talk and act this way. Most roles depend on a reciprocal, understood relationship between two parties. That is, a host is only a host in relation to someone taking the role of a guest, a teacher is only a teacher in relation to their students; parents only have authority as long their children comply with their authority. Participants in a family, a board meeting, or a sports event, all need to have more or less complementary sets of expectations in order for their different roles to function smoothly.

Expectations about many of our everyday roles are unstated and subconscious. The role of most professionals, however, gives them access to personal information and potential influence over the lives of others. As a result, they are expected to be knowledgeable, objective, honest, respectful and confidential in their dealings with clients. These expectations are usually explicitly spelled out in a code of ethics and/or conduct for the profession, so that consumers know what to expect.

Role tension arises when a person's different roles overlap, and/or where role boundaries blur. A teacher in a small country school whose child is a student in her class is likely to experience role tension around the separa-tion of 'mother' from 'teacher', both at school, and when it comes to homework. When a teacher's aide is unsure how much responsibility to take for disciplining a student, or a taxi driver doesn't load the suitcases that the passenger expects them to, role boundaries are unclear and people may feel uncomfortable or irritated. Interpreters are often expected to be bilingual, able to interpret accurately, and behave professionally. But clients often incorrectly assume that the interpreter's role also extends to friend, advocate, cultural expert, and general information provider. Interpreters may also mix with deaf or hearing consumers outside the interpreting situation, which can contribute to the blurring of role boundaries.

Changing concepts of the interpreter's role

Expectations and beliefs about the appropriate way for an interpreter to operate continue to change with time. Ideas about the interpreter's role have been influenced partly by an evolving awareness of deaf people's status and rights as sign language users, and partly by research that has revealed new understandings of how the interpreting process works in practice. In earlier times, when interpreting was done informally and voluntarily by family members, friends or welfare workers, the interpreter was generally regarded as a helper, supporter or even spokesperson for a deaf person. Since sign language was not recognised as a legitimate language in this era, deaf people were seen to need assistance with a 'communication handicap', and the interpreter naturally filled this helping role. This is referred to today as the 'helper' or 'welfare' model of interpreting and is usually associated with a lack of clear boundaries between facilitating communication and getting involved in decision-making or advocacy. Deaf people in this situation had little control over the quality of interpreting provided, nor assurance that their business would be kept confidential.

While a lot of effective interpreting was certainly provided within the 'helper' role during the pre-professional era, in retrospect, deaf people and interpreters have come to realise that the dependent 'helper-helped' relationship it sets up is potentially disempowering to the deaf person, putting the interpreter in a powerful position in terms of the direction and outcome of situations. In reaction to the drawbacks of this model, the first stage of professionalisation adopted a strict 'conduit' model (also known as 'machine' or 'black box'), based on the role of spoken language conference interpreters, who were heard but not seen in their interpreting booths. During this era, interpreting process models and a new code of ethics emphasising neutrality and confidentiality contributed to the image of the professional interpreter as being virtually invisible, simply processing messages back and forth between languages with minimal personal presence.

As the profession has matured, however, consumers and interpreters have had opportunities to observe and debate how effectively this role works in practice, especially in community interpreting settings. The ideal of total invisibility is contradicted by what we now know from experience and research about the way interpreted interaction works. Research that has analysed how interpreters manage communication and apply the code of ethics in real situations shows that they are neither machine-like nor invisible as participants in the interaction (Metzger 1999; Roy 2000; Tate and Turner 2001; Van Herreweghe 2002; Sanheim 2003; Bélanger 2004). Interpreters make many decisions in response to linguistic and human factors in the specific situations they work in. For example, interpreters may use more or less directive strategies to reduce overlap or confusion in turn-taking between Deaf and hearing participants in a group. The exact nature of the interpreter's role and decisions is shaped by the context, including the participants and how familiar they are with the interpreted situation. Current sociolinguistic models of the interpreting process (as discussed in Chapter 2) recognise the cultural, situational and personal influences on communication, encouraging interpreters and consumers to recognise that they cannot function like translation machines to do the job effectively.

With the recognition of deaf people as members of a cultural-linguistic community, a further model of the interpreter's role therefore emerged: the bilingual-bicultural mediator of communication. This model acknowledges the competencies required by interpreters to bridge cultural as well as linguistic gaps that may arise between deaf and hearing clients. Because the Deaf community is a minority group, much of the cultural mediation that sign language interpreters do is related to explaining or equalising the deaf client's position, rather than vice versa. As a result, interpreters can also be seen as 'allies' in the Deaf community's struggle for empowerment.

In practice, interpreters can and do move along a continuum of more or less interventionist role positions within a single interpreting assignment when necessary, depending on the clients and the situation. The conduit model is still a useful starting point or default position, but is no longer regarded as the sole option. Political and theoretical shifts in thinking about interpreted communication will continue to redefine clear and realistic role boundaries and increasingly effective ways of functioning.

Sometimes it is easier to define an interpreter's role by describing tasks and behaviours that are generally considered to be *outside* the boundaries of the role: providing personal advice, information, emotional or physical support, resolving conflict, teaching. The interpreter's role is to facilitate communication between deaf and hearing people, making appropriate linguistic and cultural decisions in the transfer of messages from one language and person to another.

Specific tasks and behaviours

First person address

Interpreters generally use first person speech ('I'), so that their interpretation of each client sounds as if they are speaking for themselves. Generally, avoiding re-telling in the third person ('She said/ He's asking you') is a very important practice for several reasons. First, maintaining first person speech reminds participants (and the interpreter) that the interpreter's role is to convey what each person has said, without directing the communication as a third participant or editor of the conversation. Secondly, by consistently using first person, the interpreter guides participants to speak directly to each other. This discourages their natural inclination to address each other via the interpreter ('Tell him'/ 'Ask her'). Talking directly to each other, rather than addressing the interpreter as a go-between, has a positive impact on the connection between the deaf and hearing person. Thirdly, taking on the 'voice' of each participant, rather than constantly using 'he/she/they', makes the message easier to follow. Compare the ease of understanding of these two 'interpretations' in a job interview using first and third person:

'Can you tell me about your experience using the internet?'

'He's asking you to tell him about your experience using the internet.'

However, even after an introductory briefing, some consumers are uncomfortable in addressing each other directly, and tend to use indirect address by speaking to the interpreter. This is when a polite and clear intervention is appropriate, explaining that the communication works more smoothly if both parties talk to each other directly, ignoring the interpreter as far as possible. There are some occasions, however, when an interpreter may instinctively feel it is appropriate to use third person reference ('he is saying…'), to clear up confusion about who owns the message; for instance, if the hearing consumer asks a question directly to the interpreter, or if the interpreter feels a strong need to distance themselves from the message (for example, if it is particularly abusive, or emotional, or garbled, and you need to indicate that you are summarising).

Physical considerations

Positioning

Visibility of the interpreter is a top priority and normally means the interpreter being positioned to face the deaf client, and alongside a hearing client, so that the deaf client can watch both faces at once. The other reason for sitting alongside, and slightly behind the hearing person is to discourage them from addressing the interpreter, making eye contact with the deaf client instead.

Layouts

Suggested *layouts* for interpreter positioning in different communication situations are set out in Chapter 6, and also in Chapter 8 where these vary for specialised situations.

Sitting or standing

The choice of *sitting or standing* depends very much on the circumstances: how the other participants are arranged, the space and furniture available, and how long the assignment will be. In interview-type situations where people are seated, the interpreter follows suit. In public speaking situations where the speaker is standing, it is appropriate for the interpreter to stand as well; the deaf audience are likely to be at a distance and so standing also increases the interpreter's visibility. In very large venues, or ones where there is no raised stage – such as a funeral parlour or a meeting room – the interpreter might need to stand on a small dais (or make do with whatever is at hand, for example, chair, box, even telephone books), so that their signing can be seen above the heads of a seated audience. Standing also gives the interpreter flexibility to move, if necessary, between the speaker and any visual aids being shown. However, in a classroom where the teacher might be standing, the interpreter may choose to sit, since the assignment is likely to last for a prolonged period and the student may not want the interpreter to appear so prominent.

Whether seated or standing, aim to be positioned as close as possible to the main information source (hearing speaker, overhead projector, TV screen). In a meeting or group situation, try to ascertain who will be doing most of the talking or facilitating, and sit next to them, as the deaf client will probably want to keep that person in their peripheral vision.

Invading people's space

Be aware that most venues where interpreters work have implicit cultural rules about who is permitted or expected to sit or stand in a particular place. This is most obvious in formal, ritualised settings such as a church, court-room, lecture theatre, or marae (see Chapter 9). In these places, only those in a recognised authority role normally occupy or speak from areas like the pulpit, judge's bench, or the whiteboard. But even in a professional's office, service agency, shop or doctor's surgery, clients instinctively know which side of the desk or counter they should occupy and which space belongs to the 'establishment' or host.

Interpreters need to recognise these boundaries, and must remember to politely negotiate when it is necessary to breach these 'territory norms', to give the deaf person visual access to interpreter and/or speaker. So, before going ahead and re-arranging chairs in someone's office, or standing on stage next to the speaker's podium, or taking up a position in a teaching classroom, the interpreter should explain the need for sightlines to the interpreter and speaker, and politely, but assertively, ask permission to position themselves appropriately. In less familiar and more formal or complicated settings, (for example, church, marae, court, graduation ceremony) find out in advance about the 'spatial rules' that apply to categories of participants (that is, who goes where), and about the movements of participants during the activities. Checking in advance allows the interpreter to make strategic decisions, or at least identify options, about best positioning, and provides an opportunity to discuss this with participants beforehand.

Deaf clients often express definite preferences about the best positioning for the interpreter; they usually have prior experience of using interpreters and know what works best for them. Always check with deaf consumers, whether an individual or a group, to ensure that they are happy with your placement, and the physical set-up (for example, whether you are high enough, close enough, the background is acceptable, etc).

Lighting and background

Following sign language interpretation takes more effort than either conversing directly in Auslan/NZSL, or the effort needed by a hearing person to listen. Using the eyes to take in information, especially for a sustained period, from one signer, takes more physical effort and focus than getting input through the ears. For these reasons, it is important to try to optimise the visual conditions for deaf consumers in terms of lighting, background, and interpreter appearance.

Lighting

Maximise the visibility of face and signs. Ensure that there is enough light on the interpreter, by requesting adjustment to lighting (if possible in the situation), or by choosing the best-lit spot if there are only 'fixed' options available. It is ideal to also have a comfortable level of ambient lighting in the whole room; if there is interaction with deaf participant(s), the interpreter needs to be able to see them clearly as well.

Avoid backlighting from a window, or another source of strong light. Sitting in front of a window that is not shaded causes visual strain for the deaf consumer from the glare, and also puts the interpreter's face into relative shadow. If this position is unavoidable (for example, in a confined office), ask if the blind or curtain can be drawn to reduce glare. The interpreter themselves will also find it a strain to be facing a source of light such as a large window in a meeting room, especially over a long period, and should try to re-position, or shut out bright light.

Background

Minimise visual distraction behind or near the interpreter. Be aware of what is behind you when you choose a spot to stand or sit – particularly in platform or large group situations. (Placement choices may be more limited in a small room situation, and the communication is likely to be shorter in duration anyway). If there is 'visual noise' in the environment such as busy posters, ornaments, geometric patterns in the décor, or a bright whiteboard, try to stand/sit to one side of these; any of these backdrops require visual 'filtering' by the deaf consumer, and can increase strain in the communication (even at a subconscious level).

Interpreter appearance

The interpreter's torso and face form the primary backdrop for signing and these should also minimise visual distraction. Interpreters need to wear plain clothes that contrast with their skin; clothes in dark shades (for example, brown, navy blue, green, black) for people with light skin, and lighter clothes (for example, white, pale blue, yellow) for people with dark skin. It is less of a strain to watch the interpreter's hands against a contrasting plain background than against patterned fabric.

For the same reason, avoid wearing jewellery (especially 'loud' earrings, rings, bracelets and pendants), as this can be distracting for the deaf person watching. Long or brightly coloured fingernails are also inappropriate. Hair needs to be tidily groomed, and off the face so that non-manual features are not obscured.

In selecting styles of clothing, consider the impact on a deaf consumer who has to look continuously at the interpreter. This issue is probably more relevant for female interpreters (since there are more of us) interpreting for male clients. It is easier for clients to concentrate without distraction from low necklines, stray bra-straps, prominent tattoos, or piercings; these create visual and psychological 'noise' for the viewer.

Professional presentation

It is also important for interpreters to present a professional persona by dressing appropriately for the situation. Dressing professionally doesn't necessarily mean wearing a suit, however, 'smart/casual' is usually the minimum dress standard. Think about how other people will be dressed, and dress to blend in. If working in a university or other informal context, jeans may be acceptable. Comfortable and appropriate shoes are a must – you may need to be on your feet for long periods, or you may end up at a muddy building site.

Managing visual-aural modality differences in interaction

As well as developing specific language skills, sign language interpreters need to manage what happens when two different language modalities (visual-gestural versus auditory-oral) come into contact:

Responses to signing

Visual-gestural communication strikes hearing people as highly unusual, because it uses the body and face in ways that conflict with strong cultural inhibitions (for example, Anglo-Celtic reserve). Discomfort, distraction or fascination are common reactions of hearing people in a sign language interpreted situation. Despite trying to keep a low profile as the interpreter, the visibility of sign language sometimes attracts unwelcome attention to both interpreter and deaf person, especially in formal settings such as classrooms or public events. Interpreters therefore need to be sensitive to hearing consumers' possible reactions to sign language and to try to reduce the 'fluster factor' by giving prior information, tactfully negotiating interpreter placement, and responding to consumers' questions or comments with empathy, respect and patience.

Turn-taking in conversations

Deaf signers' behaviours for listening (attending) and turn-taking are different from those used by hearing speakers, which complicates the 'rhythm' of cross-language interactions. The ears are passive, multi-directional sensory organs, so hearing people can listen to another speaker without having to watch them. For deaf consumers, getting information through the eyes requires sustained visual attention and consciously directed eye gaze. When hearing and deaf people interact, part of the interpreter's job is converting auditory conversation cues into visual cues, and vice versa. Sign language interpreters need to develop their visual concentration span and be alert to visual cues such as a deaf speaker lifting their hands to make a comment or expressing a subtle facial response. (A more detailed discussion of turn-taking can be found in Chapter 6).

Information sequence

Because signers cannot watch more than one information source at a time, deaf groups tend to organise talk and action sequentially rather than simultaneously. However, in mixed situations the eyes are needed for more than one task, such as following a paper in a meeting and watching the speaker via an interpreter, or reading the whiteboard in a classroom and following the teacher through an interpreter. Although a deaf participant can't effectively get information from the interpreter and another visual input simultaneously, the interpreter can maximise the deaf person's opportunities to alternate their eye gaze by negotiating with the speaker for some 'catch up' pauses, positioning themselves close to the visual input, or switching to consecutive interpreting mode.

Incidental sounds

Facilitating communication with deaf people in auditory environments also includes conveying incidental sounds that hearing participants would notice during the communication – a phone ringing, a knock on the door, a catch of emotion in the voice, sudden rain on the roof, footsteps approaching the room, a noisy whiteboard pen that is bothering students, the foreign accent of a speaker, a fire alarm, etc. Conveying these sounds is not just a matter of passing interest or safety, but provides information that helps the deaf person make sense of hearing people's actions, facial expressions, sudden topic changes, and sometimes why the interpreter might appear distracted or have difficulty understanding. All these factors are part of the communication context.

Professional ethics

All established professions have codes of ethics that guide the conduct of the profession. These codes set out standards of behaviour based on moral principles designed to protect clients from possible abuses of power or incompetence. Medical, legal, educational, and financial professionals routinely give advice or treatment or make decisions that directly affect the well-being of their clients – their respective codes of conduct provide them with a basis on which to make these decisions. Agreed behavioural standards not only help practitioners, but also provide their clients with clear expectations about how people within the profession will operate. A code of ethics can also act as a benchmark for enforcing high standards of practice, usually through registration requirements and grievance procedures.

In 2007 ASLIA updated its code of ethics to better reflect our current understanding of, and aspirations for, the role and behaviour of sign language interpreters. The new code has been adapted from another sign language interpreter association's model, AVLIC (Association of Visual Language Interpreters of Canada), and is included as Appendix C. The following sections explain the key principles that underpin both the ASLIA and AUSIT codes of ethics. As with any guidelines, these are not provided as absolute rules, rather, they are the starting point for ethical practice. Their application requires integrity and judgement, taking into account the competing demands and complexity of any given situation.

Impartiality and neutrality

Impartiality, neutrality, objectivity and faithfulness are related concepts that are essential to the interpreting function. Their application ensures that messages will be transferred accurately, without influence or bias from the interpreter. When sign language interpreters in Australia and New Zealand started adopting a code of ethics and establishing professional organisations during the 1980s, the dominant model for spoken language interpreting was the conduit style. As the political consciousness of the Deaf community changed towards a more self-determining agenda, the earlier interpreter beha-viours of what we now call the 'welfare/helper' model, came to be seen as out of date, potentially patronising, and unprofessional. At this point, many sign language interpreters took the principles of impartiality and professional neu-trality as a directive to function in a more impersonal, machine-like manner.

The pendulum has since swung to a more interactive model of inter-preting (as explained in Chapter 2), which recognises that while impartiality is important, it is not always possible or appropriate; the meaning and boundaries of the 'detached interpreter' role are now being challenged. Melanie Metzger (1999) discusses the 'myth of neutrality', showing through analysis of interpreted interaction how it is virtually impossible for interpreters to remain invisible; they automatically influence and shape the interaction just by being there as a participant.

There are many potential challenges to a purely neutral position:

- As human beings, some interpreting situations evoke strong personal responses that are unrealistic to ignore, for example, strong beliefs about cochlear implants, abortion, or politics. Or, the interpreter may have a conflict of interest, such as a personal relationship with a client, or standing to gain from the information exchanged. In such cases, ethical practice is to either decline the assignment, or if this is not feasible, to inform both parties of any personal involvement, and to make a concerted effort to put any biases or conflicting interests to one side while interpreting.

- Immediately before or after an assignment, clients may attempt to draw the interpreter on-side (perhaps unintentionally), or to seek the interpreter's opinion. Without seeming cold or rude, interpreters need to re-establish the neutrality and distance that makes them trustworthy in the eyes of both parties.

- Sometimes it is difficult to separate reactions to clients (for example, liking or disliking a particular person or group of people) from the interpreting work. This requires self-awareness of prejudices or stereo-types, recognition of one's own emotional responses, and the self-discipline to restrain spontaneous emotional reactions.

- Neutrality can be difficult to maintain for political reasons too: in choosing sign language interpreting as a profession, most interpreters ally themselves with deaf people as members of a minority and oppres-sed community. Interpreters commonly find themselves defending or explaining deaf people and sign language to unaware hearing friends, colleagues, clients, and the general public. The reality that interpreters do generally care about outcomes and access for deaf people, and are often motivated in their career by a sense of caring, is a perennial subject of ethical discussion within the profession and with deaf consumers.[1]

---

1   See for example, Ben Karlin's (2005) paper on whether interpreters should care.

One way to look at the competing demands of being a trustworthy communication facilitator and a human being is to distinguish between being an interpret*er* versus the task of interpret*ing*. As an interpret*er* you can advocate for the needs and rights of deaf people in many different ways: by ensuring that interpreting access is provided at a public event, correcting outdated labels for example, 'deaf and dumb', explaining that signed languages are not universal, signing a petition for more captioning on television, etc. However, when you are interpret*ing*, you need to remain as impartial as possible by not interjecting your opinion or influencing the outcome inappropriately. You may have an impact on the dynamics of an interaction just by being there, but you should be careful not to let your own perspective interfere with the interpreting process.

Despite the challenges and dilemmas involved in aiming to be impartial, it is still an important goal, encouraging interpreters to minimise any interference with the message as it flows between participants. The following interpreter's comment illustrates the restraint required:

Should interpreters laugh out loud?
If you interpret a joke and the speaker is not laughing, do not laugh while interpreting. When the joke is completed and the audience is laughing, I see nothing wrong with a smile and light laugh from the interpreter. Make sure, though, that you are at the ready to resume the speaker's spirit and mood. What is not appropriate is when the interpreter begins to giggle (react) *during* the interpretation. That is inserting a personal response into what should be a faithful interpretation. Also, continuing to laugh or react when resuming interpreting is not appropriate ... Controlling one's personal reactions is truly about dealing with the role and responsibility of being an interpreter. Controlling one's laughter, or eye-rolling, or disgust, pleasure, anything, is simply a function of being an interpreter. (Powell 2004)[2]

Invisibility versus blending in

Related to the idea of impartiality and neutrality is the profile of the interpreter in an interpreting assignment – how much should they stand out? Although machine and conduit have been powerful metaphors emphasising the detachment and speed necessary for effective interpreting, the interpreter is, in fact, a visible and potentially influential participant in interpreted communication. Even the most unobtrusive interpreter must speak for herself or himself during introductions, briefing, clarifications, and sometimes to coordinate turn-taking in dialogue situations.[3]

Bill Moody, a highly experienced interpreter, comments on the reality that the interpreter's role is dynamic and responsive to the situation:

---

2   Powell (2004) on <www.terps-1majordomo.valenciacc.edu> 18 November 2004 – email posting on an interpreting list.
3   See Angelelli (2003), Metzger (1999), Roy (2000), Wadenjso (1998), as examples of studies that focus attention on how interpreters participate in interpreted interaction beyond simply transferring speakers' words.

The interpreter's role is seldom rigid. While it may be important to distance oneself from the proceedings in one situation, it may be just as important to be fully involved in another, depending on the goal of the participants. The involvement or detachment of the interpreter may change from minute to minute as the feelings of the participants evolve. (Moody 2007: 212)

'Blending in' is probably a more realistic goal for interpreters than invisibility. Apart from conducting the interpreting task efficiently, interpreters should aim to be inconspicuous in the way they dress, talk, and behave, in a given situation. A Deaf community representative going to a government meeting needs a smartly groomed, well-mannered, and well-spoken interpreter to blend in with setting. A deaf student at university would probably feel more comfortable with a casually-dressed interpreter who takes a few minutes for some relaxed chit-chat on the way in or out of a lecture. 'Blending in' behaviours require the confidence and flexibility to step outside the 'strictly interpreting' box, and respond to customary politeness conventions, as the following comments suggest:

A deaf friend remarked to me how interpreters make a spectacle of themselves when they do things like refusing morning tea at a catered meeting, believing that it's not part of their professional role. This deaf person's feeling was – 'For goodness sake, have a cup of tea and a biscuit and just *blend*!' Interpreters need to put themselves in the deaf person's shoes, and think about what they'd want from an interpreter if they were in that situation.

I was challenged by a Pākeha (non-Māori) deaf person at one *pōwhiri* (Māori welcome) I interpreted, because at the end of the speeches I joined in with the deaf people and took part in the *hariru* (shaking hands and pressing noses between each member of the host and visitor parties) at the end. This deaf person said to me afterwards, 'Why did you do that? You're the interpreter: you're impartial, you're not supposed to take part'. But culturally, it was appropriate. Probably in a Pakeha workshop or church setting where the deaf people all went to shake hands with the presenter or the minister, I would just step back and leave them to it. But because I'm Māori, I know that in a *pōwhiri* situation, unless I do the *hariru*, I'm not considered truly part of the process. It's to do with being connected to the group. Once I've connected in that way, I become part of the setting, and my presence is accepted.

Accuracy and faithfulness

The ethic of accuracy requires an interpreter to deliver the message in the same spirit, intent and manner of the speaker, with no additions, deletions, or alterations to the meaning. As discussed in Chapter 2, accuracy in content means conveying not just the main ideas or information, but also how that information is expressed to convey the speaker's underlying intent, attitude, and certainty.

Accurate interpreting is important in every situation, but in some settings there is more at stake. For example, in medical emergencies and court cases, an inaccurate interpretation can affect a client's life or liberty. Generally, when an interpreter has not heard or understood what has been said, it is ethical to ask for a repeat or clarification, rather than to bluff, guess, or omit information. In some cases (for example, a graduation speech or funeral eulogy) this is not appropriate because it is the ritual and sense of occasion that is more important, and accuracy in terms of completeness may be lost.

Since neither client in an interpreted interaction knows exactly what the other party is saying, the interpreter is in a unique position of trust. They decide how and what information is passed on, and, especially for interpreters working alone, have minimal accountability. The interpreter is usually the only one who knows whether they have missed, misunderstood or misinterpreted the message. Sometimes deaf and hearing clients judge interpreters who ask for repeats or clarifications as less competent than interpreters who never ask. But, within reason, checking is desirable and demonstrates a commitment to high standards of accuracy.

Competence

This ethic is related to accuracy and honesty; it obliges interpreters to only undertake jobs they are skilled enough to do. In theory, if an interpreter feels they are unable to interpret accurately in a particular situation for linguistic, technical, physical, or emotional reasons, it is unethical to accept the assignment, even if pressure is applied. However, in practice, the shortage of sign language interpreters and the lack of widely-recognised standards for interpreting, means that sign language interpreters are asked to accept difficult interpreting assignments for which they have inadequate knowledge and skills.

Often, organisations book inappropriately skilled interpreters with good intentions but faulty judgment.[4] A poor interpreter *can* be worse than no interpreter at all, since their presence creates the false impression that full communication access has been achieved, when in fact it hasn't, often with problematic consequences later on. Consider, for example, a deaf student enrolled in a tertiary course, with an interpreter who cannot adequately deal with the vocabulary or the speed of processing required in theoretical subjects. The likely outcome is that the student will not be able to participate and learn effectively, jeopardising their chances of graduation from the course, and future employment, even though educational 'support services' have apparently been provided.

In order to be aware of the limits of their competence, interpreters need well-developed critical analysis and reflection skills, as well as honesty

---

4   Stewart, Schein and Cartwright (1998: 176) cite two Canadian surveys that found evidence of widespread 'flexibility' about applying the competence ethic.

and assertiveness in declining jobs. Opportunities to team interpret with a more experienced colleague can provide models of what competent interpreting looks like and useful feedback about strengths and weaknesses. Beyond preparing for specific jobs, the ethic of competence also implies a commitment to taking part in continued professional development.

Confidentiality

Confidentiality is a fundamental ethic in many professions. Sign language interpreters are privy to conversations, activities, and personal information that would generally not be known if the two parties could communicate with each other directly. How interpreters treat this information is an ethical issue that is of concern to members of the close-knit Deaf community. The following quote reminds us of our obligations:

> In all these situations, the information is the by-product of the professional interpreting function, and the interpreter is not the intended recipient of such information. The interpreter must maintain *confidentiality* about the information that is the possession of the other professional and is the accidental or incidental possession of the interpreter. The interpreter must never use this incidental information for personal or financial gain or in any situation where its use will create a *conflict of interest*. (Gentile et al 1996: 59)

As well as not divulging what was said and done *within* an assignment, confidentiality also extends to information *about* an assignment, including names, place, setting, time, and date. In a small community, mentioning even general information, such as, 'I was interpreting for a young deaf couple at the family court yesterday', can be enough to identify a family in domestic strife, and to give away information that rightfully belongs only to them.

Sometimes interpreting experiences need to be discussed within a professional supervision or mentoring relationship, for debriefing and/or advice. Even then, it is preferable to discuss the issue without identifying the participants. Interpreters owe it to their clients and their professional reputation not to reveal details about the content of interpreting assignments, even to their colleagues.

As with all ethics, there are exceptions; if you are interpreting in public, for example, at a town hall meeting, performance, conference, or media interview, then you can usually safely acknowledge that you were present as the interpreter. Similarly, it is acceptable to tell someone in your family where you are going to work and how long you will be. You can still maintain confidentiality by saying 'I have an interpreting assignment in the city from 9am to 5pm'. With this information, your partner or family member can estimate your travelling time and your approximate time home. This interpreter explains the need for flexibility and commonsense in applying ethics:

I used to know one interpreter who took her code of ethics so seriously that she wouldn't tell her husband anything about her interpreting assignments. She wouldn't say where or when they were for fear of breaking the confidentiality ethic. Only problem was that one time she broke down and couldn't get in touch with her husband (it was before mobile phones). She was stuck in the middle of nowhere, it was getting dark and she was frightened. Her husband was frantic with worry as he had no idea where she was, or whether there might be something wrong or if in fact she had taken a late interpreting job. I learned my lesson from her – don't take the code of ethics to the extreme.

Professional conduct and integrity

Adhering to the Code of Ethics is not the only evidence of professionalism; appropriate professional behaviour is also a requirement. The professional conduct of a sign language interpreter includes:

- Reliability and punctuality – this is a professional obligation when clients are paying for your time and more importantly, cannot start their 'business' until the interpreter arrives;

- Negotiating fair payment – based on your qualifications, expertise and the current range of rates in the field. Interpreters often provide their services for no cost (pro-bono), for example, to deaf friends as a favour, or for community events with no budgets;

- Honouring commitments and contracts: in other words, once an assignment is accepted, it is unethical and unfair to withdraw your services if a better paid, or more interesting assignment is subsequently offered. (Medical or legal emergencies may be an exception to this rule, when no other interpreter is available);

- Support and respect for colleagues – including encouraging newly qualified practitioners, working collegially in teams, and discussing ethical dilemmas together. By asking for and offering support to our colleagues, we can learn from each other and improve our decision-making. Do unto other interpreters as you would have them do unto you;

- Ability to maintain professional boundaries – distinguishing between social and professional interactions, and maintaining socially acceptable behaviour when mixing with deaf (or hearing) consumers.

Continuing professional development

Interpreters need to keep up-to-date with trends in professional practice and knowledge so that they can continue to improve their skills and do the job to the best of their ability. One way to access developmental opportunities is to join the local professional sign language interpreting association (in Australia, ASLIA; in New Zealand, SLIANZ). Membership of interpreting associations promotes professional solidarity, encourages high standards and accountability, and provides opportunities for training.

Professional development can include formal training courses, workshops or seminars, informal discussions, reading books and journals related to interpreting, language or the Deaf community, keeping up with developments in the field by reviewing previous and current research, and attending interpreter association meetings. Interpreters should strive to be 'reflective practitioners' (Bergson and Sperlinger 2003). As detailed in Chapter 10, Auslan/English interpreters accredited by NAATI from 2007 are required to undertake ongoing professional development as part of their accreditation conditions. In fact, many professions and trades require their members to undertake continuing education after becoming qualified (for example, medicine, law, education), for good reason:

> Interpreters cannot deliver effective professional service armed only with their technical knowledge of source and target languages, Deaf culture, and a code of ethics. Like all practice professionals, they must supplement their technical knowledge and skills with input, exchange, and judgment regarding the consumers they are serving in a specific environment and in a specific communicative situation. (Dean and Pollard 2005: 259)

Many interpreters have not had the opportunity to attend formal training, or feel that their interpreting qualification is enough to rely on. According to Gile (1995), training enables interpreters to better achieve their potential for effective performance. Training speeds up the learning process by passing on proven strategies and knowledge, which is more efficient than only learning by trial and error.

Having a system of formal training also raises professional standards for selection and assessment of candidates, which screens entry to the profession at a minimum level. As professional standards of competence are established and linked to qualifications gained through study, this raises public recognition of interpreting as a profession. Ultimately this awareness can generate better working conditions for interpreters and better standards of expected service for consumers. Training programs also provide a pathway for new interpreters to be introduced to professional networks and mentors who offer knowledge of the working environment and employment opportunities.

Ethical decision-making

Making ethical decisions in real situations is not as easy as just following rules, or selecting from a menu of responses that are either 'right' or 'wrong'. It takes well-honed critical thinking skills to recognise and analyse an ethical dilemma, and then determine a course of action after weighing up the options and considering the consequences. Interpreters also need confidence and mature judgement in situations where their personal moral beliefs and the code of ethics collide. Ethical decision-making involves choices, so practitioners need to accept responsibility for the choices they make, and be able to justify them.

One way to improve ethical decision–making is to critically reflect on the reasoning behind our interpreting choices, and outcomes. This maintains our ethical fitness levels:

> New practitioners should enter the field with the understanding that the journey toward ethical fitness is career-long and must be continually assessed, as the market/consumer demands change and become more complex. Consumers of interpreting services are at risk when interpreters, novice and veteran alike, lack a solid foundation in ethical fitness and decision-making. Enhancing the ability of practitioners to make well-informed and reliable ethical decisions is central to the professionalisation process and integrity of the field, as well as central to consumer trust. (Stewart and Witter-Merrithew: 5-6)

Ethical problem solving is required by interpreters at all stages of their career. Usually we need to make on the spot decisions, which rely on experience and refined judgement. In order to develop that capacity, we can reflect on and discuss past or theoretical dilemmas.

A useful framework for analysing our ethical decision-making is to begin by focusing on the consequences of our actions, rather than starting with the values and principles laid out in a code. Dean and Pollard (2005) describe this as a shift from a deontological (rule-based) approach to a teleological (outcomes-based) approach. They suggest that interpreters learn to identify a comprehensive range of demands (conditions that require a response) for a particular situation, and then consider a broad range of possible responses (controls), in order to expand and refine the choices they make. Once possible responses are identified, they can be analysed in terms of further positive and negative consequences – leading to more thoughtful, precise and responsible decision-making. (Chapter 6 examines interpreting demands and controls in more detail.)

Fenton (1988) developed the five steps below as a model for deciding how to respond in a situation that is ethically challenging.

1. *Define the problem*

   Which ethical principle is at stake in this situation? What are the conflicting interests or demands on the interpreter that create the problem?

2. *List the options for interpreter action*

   What are some alternative ways that an interpreter could respond to this problem? Some options may not fit with professional ethics, but they should still be identified so that all the choices can be fully considered before eliminating some.

3. *Visualise the consequences of each option*

    What would be the likely outcomes of each course of action you have identified? Consider the impacts on and possible responses of each of the parties involved, including the interpreter.

4. *Act according to the option which gives the best match between professional ethics and personal ethics*

    Decide which option is most ethical within the professional definition of the interpreter's role, and also fits with the interpreter's conscience, or human ethics (such as the universal ethic of doing no harm).

5. *Evaluate the decision*

    Growth and ongoing fitness in ethical behaviour are the result of practice plus critical reflection on experience. We can't undo poor decisions, but we can learn to make better informed decisions by evaluating the basis for previous decisions made by ourselves or colleagues, and considering the consequences in relation to ethical principles and the impact on consumers.

Beyond the code of ethics

We rely on professional ethics as a basis for guiding our decisions and conduct as interpreters, but there are some situations which call for moral judgement that goes beyond the professional code. In cases where an interpreter becomes aware that a client is in danger of harming themselves or others, or that criminal activity is happening, the interpreter has an ethical responsibility as a human being and citizen to pass on that information to an appropriate person. For example, if a depressed deaf client in a clinic waiting room confides to us that they feel like killing themselves, but does not reveal this to the medical practitioner, it would be morally ethical to let the professional know that this has been said, so that intervention can occur. Similarly, if you become aware that a deaf student you are interpreting for in an education setting is at risk of harm (such as physical or verbal abuse, or illegal behaviour with drugs), your legal duty of care and protection as an adult overrides the professional ethics of impartiality or confidentiality. Commonsense applies when a client is unwell and about to faint, or needs immediate physical assistance, and you are the closest at hand. This is probably not the moment to stand back and cite impartiality: straightforward human responses are more appropriate in an emergency.

The ethics of non-intervention (impartiality) and accuracy are not meant to be used as an excuse for failing to act. Often we are the only ones who can see miscommunication occurring (because of cultural or linguistic differences). Moody (2007) argues that it is sometimes necessary for the interpreter to make proactive choices that bridge the different 'thought-worlds' of participants:

Conversational strategies which are perfectly appropriate in one culture but might be face-threatening or awkward in the interpreted situation can be adapted by the interpreter to the circumstances, permitting the participants to comfortably get on with achieving their goals. When the goals of the participants include cooperation and efficiency, then the interpreter's fidelity to their intentions will include tasks that are not strictly linguistic renderings. (Moody 2007: 204)

The extra tasks that Moody refers to might include strategic omission of a detail that does not transfer meaningfully across languages and would be more confusing to include, expansion of a reference or concept that would otherwise mean nothing to the recipient, or matching culturally appropriate politeness (for example, acceptable degree of 'directness').

Preparing for interpreting assignments

One of the marks of a good interpreter is the ability to reflect on experience as a way of increasing readiness for future similar assignments. By thinking about assignments beforehand, and reflecting on them afterwards, interpreters can develop a greater sense of control through self-awareness about their performance and level of competence.

Once you have accepted an assignment, there are some strategies you can use to better prepare for the assignment. For example, by finding out information contained in the handy acronym – *www.terp.co* as follows: [5]

WHO – Who are the participants? (deaf and hearing). What are their roles? Who is going to be speaking/signing? Who is my team interpreter? Who is the contact person?

WHAT – What type of event is it (meeting, presentation, class)? What is the content? What is the context?

WHERE – Where is the venue? How will the room be set up? Where will I sit/stand?

TECHNICAL LANGUAGE – is there specific terminology or jargon I need to know?

EQUIPMENT – Will there be overheads or PowerPoint presentations? Will any videos be shown? Will I need a microphone? Will lighting be appropriate?

READING MATERIAL – Is there be any written material that I can prepare from? Will any quotes be read out?

---

5   Hendersen, Mandy (2002) 'In depth preparation', unpublished manuscript Newark UK (cited by permission of author).

PRACTICAL POINTS – Travel tips, supplies (for example, water bottle, notepad), agreed team interpreting strategies, etc.

CONTRACT – Have I clarified working conditions (payment, hours booked, breaks)? Do I have invoice details (who to send it to, any reference numbers to quote)?

As useful as any checklist is for interpreters when they are booked for an assignment, they are not always given all the information they need at the time. An alternative preparation strategy is for interpreters to draw on their own knowledge and understanding of language and discourse, and previous interpreting experiences, to create a 'discourse map' for the assignment.

Discourse mapping

Through our life experiences, we develop sets of knowledge (schemas) and perspectives (frames of reference) about different people and events. We also develop standard 'scripts' for social interactions – as a guide to know what to say and do in different situations. All of these frameworks give us an inherent understanding of typical language use and behavioural norms in our culture that we can tap into when preparing for an interpreting assignment.

Interpreters can create a mind map of the discourse setting by brainstorming what they expect from the context (setting, discourse type, participants, venue, etc) and the content (vocabulary, grammar, pace of delivery, volume, etc) (Winston and Monikowski 2000). An example of a discourse map prepared before an interpreting assignment can be seen in Figure 5.1. All the interpreter has been told is that it is a social services agency appointment. A range of factors can still be anticipated, based on the interpreter's existing knowledge and experience.

Discourse maps can be used to both prepare for and reflect on interpreting assignments, in a cycle of continuous learning. For example, once an interpreter is booked for an assignment, they can create an initial discourse map. On completion of the assignment, they can review the map and check what had been predicted accurately, as well as noting unexpected issues that arose. When the interpreter is booked again for a similar interpreting assignment, they can revisit the original discourse map, and fine-tune it for the new booking. Interpreters often automatically engage in this predictive process mentally, but writing it down clarifies and consolidates their preparation and reflection.

Establishing your role at an interpreting assignment

The way that introductions and briefings are handled can set the tone for the rest of the interaction; remember – 'you never get a second chance to make a first impression'.

Figure 5.1: Example discourse map for interpreting assignment

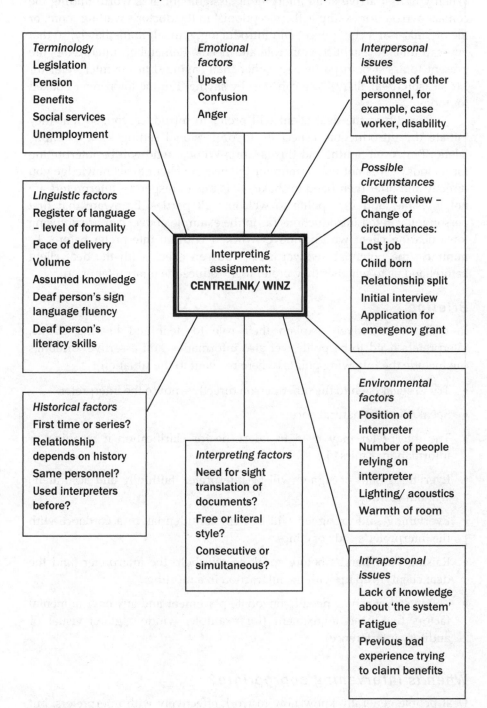

Introductions

When you first arrive at an interpreting assignment, it is worth finding the contact person (for example, the receptionist in the doctor's waiting room, or the organiser at a conference) and introducing yourself immediately, so that you can quickly establish your role and needs. Remember, interpreters are present to assist both parties, so rather than saying 'I'm the interpreter for Mr Jackson (deaf client)' you can start by saying 'I'm the interpreter booked for today …'.

Sometimes the deaf client will prefer to introduce you, so that they initiate the introduction, especially in professional settings. For example, 'Hello, I'm Anna Smith, and this is Chris Woods, who will be interpreting for us today'. It is not uncommon for the hearing client to acknowledge you directly and offer their hand to shake – it is fine to respond – interpreters are not invisible, and it is polite to welcome all parties. Be aware that first person interpreted introductions (as in the example above) can be confusing for a hearing client who has never worked with an interpreter before. To minimise the potential awkwardness, you can check with the deaf client beforehand as to whether they prefer to introduce the interpreter or not.

Briefing

In order to effectively explain their role to deaf and hearing clients, interpreters need to be polite, yet also informative and assertive. Briefings can include the following points (where relevant to the situation):

- Try to speak/sign to the other person directly – not to the interpreter.
- Speak/sign at a natural pace.
- The interpreter may need to intervene for clarification if meaning or information is missed.
- Everything said or signed will be interpreted faithfully and accurately, without editing.
- Everything said or signed will be kept confidential, in accordance with the interpreter's code of ethics.
- Raising your hand/s before speaking will help the interpreter (and the deaf client) keep up with the interaction in a meeting.
- The interpreter may need to negotiate placement and any environmental factors that need adjustment (for example, window glare, visual or auditory interference).

When is intervening appropriate?

Deaf people generally know how to work effectively with interpreters, but as most hearing clients have never communicated with a deaf person via an interpreter before, they are unfamiliar with the 'rules' of interpreted interaction, and don't always remember to follow these suggestions.-Sometimes interpreters need to gently intervene to get communication back on track; for example, where a speaker consistently uses indirect, third person address ('Ask him/tell her ...'), or asks for the interpreter's input into the conversation, or speaks too quickly or quietly. A good rule of thumb is to intervene the *first* time a problem occurs, rather than hoping that the difficulty will resolve itself; it usually just compounds. An intervention should be:[6]

- *Clear* – state what you need to happen, rather than just indicating a problem.

- *Assertive* – don't be overly apologetic or vague – you are only intervening so that you can perform your job and make their communication work better.

- *Brief* – stick to one point and don't hold the floor for so long that the parties get distracted from their business.

- *Polite* – follow cultural rules for a polite interruption, softening with a hedge – 'excuse me', 'would you mind', or focusing the problem towards yourself – 'It will make it easier for me to interpret effectively if you could ...' If the interpreter's intervention uses words, tone, and body language perceived as polite and constructive, rather than critical or controlling, it will achieve a better outcome for the communication and for the interpreter's professional reputation.

Looking and sounding professional, yet also being warm and responsive to clients' concerns or questions can make both parties feel more at ease with the interpreted situation and each other.

Showing respect

Respecting the protocols of the people who belong in the setting, is very important. This applies across cultures-and settings; formal or informal. To some hearing clients, a sign language interpreter can seem like a 'space invader'- an extra body in *their* particular space, creating visual distraction, changing the normal flow of things, and detracting from their control of the interaction. To deaf clients, an interpreter can be a necessary accessory whose presence will affect the hearing person's impression of them.

This experienced interpreter suggests:

> It's important to bear in mind how everyone else feels with you (the interpreter) there; you may be really comfortable because you do this every day, and it's a very normal situation for you – but it's unnatural for everyone else. So if the hearing person forgets and looks at the interpreter instead of the deaf person, they don't want to get barked at; they're already feeling uncomfortable and may be nervous about having a deaf person there at all.

---

6   Thanks to Daniel Cheng, Training Manager, of Interpreting Wellington for this guideline.

Or, if the interpreter is clarifying something with a deaf client and the hearing person is left out, they start to feel like an idiot. They've lost control and they're used to being in control in this situation. Treat people gently and guide them in a nice way. This is also about being an ambassador for the profession. Otherwise you can step on people's toes, and they think, 'I don't ever want to get an interpreter again because it was really uncomfortable for me'.'

This chapter has highlighted the complexity of the interpreting role in different contexts. The application of the code of ethics to interpreting work has been explored, and strategies have been suggested for the preparation and reflection required in interpreting work. The next chapter looks at the demands placed on interpreters by different discourse situations: one-way, two-way, and multi-directional settings.

Thought questions

1. Interpreter role and preparation:

(a) The interpreter's role can be seen as a rather 'unnatural' one, compared to the way people normally relate to each other.

    – In what ways does the interpreter's relationship with clients differ from 'normal' interaction?

    – What are the reasons for interpreters to maintain this restricted role?

(b) Complete these three sentences in as few words as possible.

    – The interpreter's *function* is to …

    – The interpreter's *relationship* to parties in an interpreting situation must be …

    – The *manner* in which interpreters should conduct themselves is …

(c) In relation to the interpreters role, can you identify advantages of using first person 'I' when interpreting a speaker, rather than third person 's/he'?

2. Preparing for assignments:

(a) Can you remember and explain the elements of the mnemonic: *www.terp*.co?

(b) Create a 'discourse map' for an assignment interpreting:

    – driver's licence test (written and oral) for a deaf person with only a basic literacy level

    – visit to GP, 19-year-old female client, with an unplanned pregnancy.

(c) Identify factors that might increase the difficulty of any interpreting assignment.

3.   Code of ethics:

(a)   What is the main reason that all professional groups have ethics?

(b)   Why is it important for interpreters to be consciously aware of their personal and cultural values as well as understanding professional ethics?

(c)   Give an example of a situation where an interpreter's personal values or beliefs could conflict with professional ethics. What are the interpreter's options in this situation?

(d)   What is the link between *trust* and the code of ethics?

(e)   What are some potentially negative outcomes of an interpreter inter-jecting personal opinions or advising clients?

(f)   What are some potentially negative outcomes of an interpreter *disclosing information* about interpreting assignments?

(g)   Can you think of a situation where basic human ethics or safety considerations might override the interpreting role or ethics?

4.   Ethical scenarios:

Practice ethical decision-making by reading the problem situations below and responding to these four questions:

- Nature of problem? (Which ethic is compromised?)

- Options for responding?

- Consequences of each option?

- Action? Which option will you choose and why?

(a)   You are the regular interpreter for a deaf high school student. The mother of the student calls you at home and says she suspects her daughter and a deaf friend have been wagging the period after lunch over the last few Fridays. She asks if you can confirm this.

(b)   You have just interpreted a medical appointment at a hospital out-patient's clinic, where the deaf client has been treated for several months, with you interpreting. You also know the deaf client quite well through social contact in the Deaf community. As you leave the appointment room and are walking along the corridor, the friendly clinic nurse asks you casually, 'How do you think [deaf client] is coping generally with her health and managing things at home – is she getting some extra support with the children?' How will you respond?

(c)   When you arrive at an interpreting job at a doctor's appointment, you discover that the client is seeking advice about an abortion for an unplanned pregnancy. You feel strongly opposed to abortion because you were adopted yourself, and believe this is a much better option.

(d) You are interpreting for a deaf person applying for a job as a storeman in a warehouse. The interviewer asks if the person has a police record, in particular convictions for dishonesty. The deaf person replies no, but you have previously interpreted for them in court on a charge of shoplifting some clothing, for which they were convicted.

(e) You arrive for an appointment at the oncology clinic of the hospital to interpret for a young deaf man who has come along with his hearing mother. When you arrive, the mother takes you aside and tells you that you should be careful about how much you try to interpret of what the doctor says, because the son has limited ability to understand his condition and the treatment, and besides, she doesn't want him to get unnecessarily anxious, because his father previously died of cancer. The mother says that she will explain the important points to him again when they get home. Before you can discuss it with her, the doctor arrives and the session begins. You are feeling uncomfortable and haven't yet decided how to respond to the mother's request.

(f) You are an interpreter for three deaf students in a high school deaf unit. You accompany the students to mainstreamed maths, geography and science classes. You are now attending the weekly staff meeting, and the deaf unit teacher and the science teacher ask for your opinion about how one of the deaf students is getting on with group-work assignments, and whether you feel she is capable of managing the written national science assessments at the end of the term.

(g) You are contacted directly by a deaf man asking you to interpret for his deaf son in an upcoming court hearing on a drug charge. The family has approached you because they know and trust you, and do not want to involve an interpreting agency. You know the defendant, understand his signing well, and are aware of his illegal activities and how much this upsets the parents. You have only interpreted in a traffic court matter before, and are not sure whether you have the skills appropriate to this situation – but you can see that the father is stressed, and that the family are pinning their hopes on you to assist.

(h) You are a male interpreter called out by police at 2 am to interpret an interview with a deaf woman who has reported a violent assault. When you get there and the interview begins, you realise that the assault was of a sexual nature. The superficial and vague answers that the woman is giving and her body language indicate to you that she is quite uncomfortable about describing the physical details to a male. Her hearing sister, who knows basic sign language, is also present at the interview, supporting her. The police officer is female.

(i)   You go to interpret at a parent/teacher interview at school. The deaf parents do not arrive. The teacher understands that the parents may be uncomfortable about communicating with school staff and asks you to drop off the student's report to the parents on your way home, check that they understand what has been written about their child's progress, and encourage them to make another appointment at a later date.

(j)   While you are waiting for a young deaf client to arrive for a social work appointment, the social worker greets you, and informs you that she strongly suspects that the client is suffering abuse within the family. She asks you what you know about the communication between the deaf girl and her hearing family members. You have previously interpreted for this client and know that she experiences communication problems that are typical for deaf people in hearing families who can't sign. The social worker wants to know these details so that she can think about a possible course of action in the situation, including placing her with extended family members who are also non-signers.

(k)   On Friday, you interpreted at a Disputes Tribunal between a deaf couple and their neighbours, over a boundary dispute. It is likely that there will be a follow-up meeting of the two parties at later date, for which the court will probably book you to interpret. On Saturday night, you see the couple at a Deaf community function, and they give you a gift of chocolates to express their gratitude for your interpreting.

(l)   You are a young female interpreting at a police interview for a deaf man who has been arrested for disorderly behaviour in a pub after some drinking and brawling. When the police officer asks if he knows why he has been brought into the station, he starts signing, 'Police are all bastards! Fuck them all! Arseholes! Always picking on deaf', etc. You feel embarrassed at having to repeat this language, and besides, you know this kind of language is not going to help his situation because it will all go into the evidence submitted to court.

(m)   At an appointment for a welfare benefit application, there is a break in communication while the deaf client fills in a two-page form. The hearing interviewer turns and says to you, 'It's so amazing what you do with your hands. How did you learn sign language? My mother's cousin was deaf and dumb, but I don't think they did signing in those days, did they?'

(n)   You are the regular interpreter at a monthly staff meeting for a deaf employee. The meetings are always just before afternoon tea, and so you often stay on to have a cup of tea afterwards and facilitate the deaf employee's conversations during this time. You have noticed that over the last few meetings, one of the managers has shown a lot of interest in talking to the deaf person during afternoon tea, and is becoming increasingly friendly and flirty with you, asking you about your personal life. On this occasion, they ask for your phone number, to talk about meeting up after hours. You rather fancy the person, but know that you will have ongoing professional contact in your interpreting role.

CHAPTER 6

COMMUNICATION DYNAMICS AND DEMANDS

How is interpreting a medical appointment different from interpreting a university lecture, or a police interview, or a committee meeting? Interpreters instinctively know that the patterns of communication in particular situations and settings are quite different, creating specific demands and challenges. Chapters 2 and 3 unpacked some of the communication issues that impact on the process of transferring equivalent meaning between sign language and spoken language. Chapter 5 explored some of the logistical and ethical aspects of managing communication through the interpreter as a third party. This chapter highlights a slightly different dimension of the discourse situations: the direction of interaction between participants and how this affects communication management.

The number of people involved in an interaction, and whether the talk is mainly two-way or one-way have a significant impact on the interpreter's task. Other features of discourse situations include: subject matter, the physical setting, the formality of the context and how much the interpreter can predict or prepare content. All these aspects shape the way the interpreted interaction progresses, the emotional tone, linguistic choices in the interpretation such as register and delivery style, and how much pressure the interpreter feels within the situation.

Discourse situations (for example, an interview, lecture, or meeting) can be categorised by the direction of communication and participant roles in the interaction. We outline three types of discourse that interpreters mediate, and consider the specific challenges of each type:

(a) *Monologic* – one-way communication (for example, a speech, sermon, or instruction) where the speaker controls the flow of information and the audience is mainly passive.

(b) *Dialogic* – two-way communication between two people (for example, a conversation, interview or consultation) where both parties contribute – alternating between speaking and listening.

(c) *Multidirectional* – communication between a group of people (for example, a meeting or group discussion) where many people have speaking turns.

Monologic discourse

Monologic discourse is usually a 'one-to-many' communication situation, where the speaker holds the floor for an extended period of time, and the audience role is to listen. This is the kind of discourse that interpreters relay in lectures, public meetings, presentations, tours, church services, performances, and conferences. The settings are usually quite public and formal, ranging from school classrooms to platform interpreting in large venues. These are the interpreting situations most often visible to the public, which sometimes inspire other's interest in learning sign language and perhaps even an interpreting career. Not all monologic interpreting is high profile, but this situation does spotlight the interpreter because the speaker and therefore the interpreter are visually prominent to the audience for a prolonged period of time. Poise, competence, and good grooming are essential attributes in this situation.

Interpreter positioning in monologic interpreting depends on whether the speaker is deaf or hearing, as shown in Figures 6.1 and 6.2. Notice that these diagrams include a suggested position for a team interpreter; in fact, the team interpreter position as shown in 6.1 may differ according to the room layout and how practical it is to make smooth changeovers from this position (for example, whether there is a stage, whether seats are moveable, the distance between the audience front row and the working interpreter). See Chapter 8 for further detail on teamworking arrangements.

Figure 6.1: Interpreter positions for monologue – hearing presenter

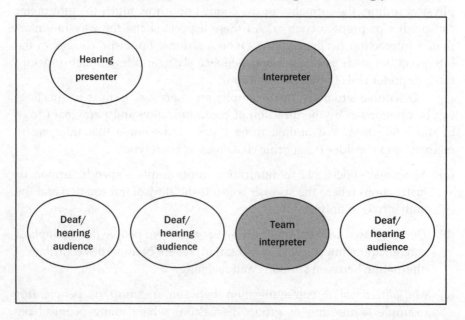

Figure 6.2: Interpreter positions for monologue – deaf presenter

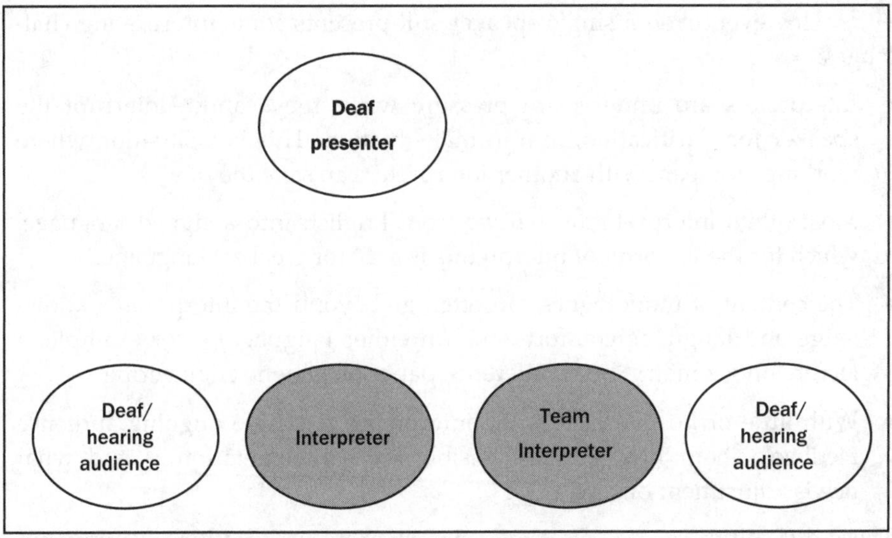

In selecting a position in a monologic situation, try to enable the deaf audience to comfortably see you, the speaker, and any visual aids being used in the presentation. For example, if a speaker is positioned at a distance from the visual display that he or she is referring to (eg, a powerpoint screen), it may be more useful for the interpreter to stand near the screen rather than the speaker, as deaf clients will need to alternate their visual attention between that and the interpreter.

Monologic discourse is often more formal in register than dialogic discourse; this means that speakers use more complex grammar and vocabulary, and generally follow a pre-planned structure in their text. Speeches are often prepared in written form, with the advantage that prior access to written notes can improve the interpreter's comprehension and translation of the content. A disadvantage is that when speakers (deaf or hearing) read from a written text, the pace and structure of delivery generally becomes more difficult to interpret than spontaneous speech. This is because written sentences tend to be longer and more grammatically complex, there is less redundancy ('filler' material) and hesitation in the delivery, and speakers often read quickly, with fewer pauses for breathing. Pauses in natural speech are valuable to interpreters for two reasons: they often signal and shape chunks of related meaning, and pauses build in some lag time which the interpreter can use for processing and delivery of the TL message.

As monologic discourse involves one person speaking or signing for an extended period of time, with minimal audience interaction, a simultaneous interpreting approach is normally used. Minimal interaction can make communication feel more manageable since the interpreter doesn't need to attend to different contributors; one person usually speaks/signs at a time and any turn-taking is quite controlled.

However, even a single speaker still presents some interpreting challenges:

- Interpreters are under extra pressure when they cannot interrupt the speaker for clarification, in a formal situation. This is a situation where working as a team with another interpreter can save the day.

- Most often, interpretation will be from English into a signed language, which for the majority of interpreters is a 'B' (or weaker) language.

- The content of monologues can often go beyond the interpreter's knowledge and language comfort zone (in either language) – for example, a lecture on geometry, or a conference paper on genetic engineering.

- With little or no interaction, the interpreter gets little ongoing audience feedback about how comprehensible their interpretation is and what needs adjustment or repair.

These difficulties can be offset to some extent by preparation, teaming and critical self-monitoring.

Dialogic discourse: Interviews and consultations

'Dialogic' or two-way communication between individuals comprises the bulk of community interpreting work. Spoken and signed language interpreters regularly interpret in public service, legal, medical, mental health, employment and other interviews and consultations. Community interpreting in the spoken language field is known as 'dialogue' or 'liaison' interpreting, which describes the interpreter's function in these two-way interactions (Gentile et al 1996).

In an interpreted dialogue, all three parties can be described as 'participants', since they all take an active part in constructing the communication. But, in fact, their roles and relationships to each other differ. In a public service interview or commercial transaction, usually one party is the professional or service provider and the other is their client or customer. But the interpreter is also a professional who relates to both parties as clients, since speakers of both languages are consumers of their interpreting service.

Ideally, the two consumers in an interpreted dialogue are communicating 'directly' with each other, but since they don't share a language, in reality they both need to communicate with and through the interpreter, in a 'triangle' (triadic) relationship. In any dialogic interaction, the interpreter's role has two aspects to it:[1]

- *Relaying* people's talk – transferring messages from SL to TL;

- *Coordinating* their talk – managing the timing of turns and interaction.

---

1   These aspects of the interpreter's function are identified by Wadenjso (1998).

While the control of an interview or consultation (such as a doctor-patient appointment) must remain with the professional, interpreters in this situation do influence the flow of information from one person to another. They make decisions about the timing of interpretation (simultaneous or consecutive delivery), the interpreting approach to be used (free and/or literal), and might intervene to clarify meaning or to co-ordinate turn-taking more smoothly, if needed. There is also opportunity for the interpreter to repair or adjust their delivery of the target message in response to audience feedback or self-awareness of an error.

The fact that we sign and need to have sustained eye contact with the deaf client makes the relaying and coordinating roles of sign language interpreters more physically obvious than for spoken language interpreters. Also, because hearing people sense that the deaf person is not 'listening' to their voice, and are not accustomed to watching signing, they may be uncertain where to look in a dialogue with a deaf person.

Figure 6.3: Interpreter position in a dialogue

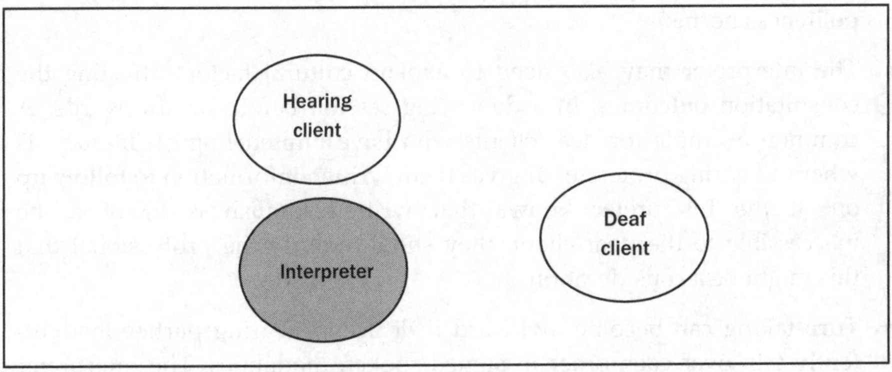

As shown in Figure 6.3, strategic positioning can help minimise the potential physical intrusion of the interpreter between clients. The first guiding principle is to stay close enough to the hearing speaker so that the deaf person can see the interpreter and the hearing speaker in their peripheral vision, switching their gaze between faces as they choose. The second goal is to encourage the hearing person to look towards the deaf person rather than fixing their gaze on the interpreter, by positioning yourself alongside the hearing client.

This set up is not always achievable, for example, if the hearing client is behind a counter or a desk. In that case, the interpreter should aim to sit or stand as close as possible to the hearing speaker, or in a triangle, with their body and gaze angled towards the deaf client rather than the hearing client.

Although one-to-one dialogue situations tend to be the most manageable for interpreters, challenging factors can and do arise:

- The content of private appointments can be highly personal, potentially arousing strong emotions; this sometimes makes the interpreter feel like the 'meat in the sandwich'.

- Deaf and hearing participants might be complete strangers to one other, which adds tension. Or, on the other hand they might know each other and share a background of previous conversations and shared context that the interpreter knows nothing about.

- Participants might express differing expectations of the interpreter (helper, conduit, supporter) which interfere with the interpreter's relaying function.

- Bilingual fluency is tested in two-way discourse by the need to switch back and forth between languages quickly, using each one receptively and expressively.

- The interpreter must decide where cultural adjustment in the interpretation is needed for comprehension or effective interpersonal communication (for example, adjusting for differences between deaf/hearing politeness norms).

- The interpreter may also need to explain cultural factors affecting the consultation outcomes, in a debriefing session before or afterwards. A common example for deaf clients who have limited English literacy, is where a hearing professional gives them written information to follow up on. If the interpreter knows that written English is likely to be inaccessible to the deaf client, they should advise the professional that this might be a consideration.

- Turn-taking can become awkward if deaf and hearing parties inadvertently talk over each other in signed/spoken modalities. The interpreter must decide how to manage this – by letting the parties know what is happening, or choosing to continue interpreting one or the other. Whoever is chosen by the interpreter assumes more dominance in the interaction than the person who is not interpreted; interpreters need to be conscious of which party they enable to hold the floor most often. Necessary interpreter interruptions for handling turn-taking problems must be managed in a way that is culturally acceptable to both parties – that is, avoiding abruptly cutting off eye contact with the deaf client or talking across a hearing client. [2]

---

2   The cultural implications of interpreter's management of interruptions are critically discussed in Kent and Potter (2005).

Dialogic discourse: Conversations

Interpreters may be required to interpret informal conversations between a deaf and a hearing person in a variety of settings. People use informal conversation to get to know each other better, and in a work context to network, share information and promote themselves. There are many situations where an interpreter may have to facilitate conversations for their deaf client: in a meeting break, at a conference dinner, over coffee at a training session. This 'chit-chat' can play an important part in a deaf person's progress at work, or their inclusion in a social group such as a sports team, church congregation, or family gathering.

Conversational styles are absorbed from other people, so everyone has a different style depending on which social group(s) they grew up in and currently participate in (Tannen 1984). Different styles show up in how people turn-take, listen, keep a conversation going, and what they talk about. Styles are influenced by social characteristics including gender, ethnicity, nationality, age, language group, socio-economic status and, of course, whether they are deaf or hearing. Styles can also change according to who someone is talking to, and where. When preparing to interpret conversations interpreters can think about these questions (as per Eighinger and Karlin 2003):

* Who are the *people* involved in the conversation? Is it the deaf person and his/ her boss or another peer? Is one person more in control of the conversation?

* Where is the conversation taking *place*? Should it be interpreted discretely?

* What is the *purpose* or function of the conversation? To exchange office gossip? To congratulate on getting a task completed on time?

* What is the *point* of this conversation? To warn someone about another person in the office? To drop a hint about promotional opportunities?

An experienced interpreter reflects on interpreting informal conversation:

> Some of the hardest interpreting situations are professional networking situations – for a whole host of reasons. Usually they're at the end of a long event so people are tired – there's often alcohol involved – you've got to somehow negotiate if you're going to eat at the same time as your consumers. But most importantly that highly informal but essential communication that helps people to bond – deaf people might not be as practiced in that so that's where cultural mediation really kicks in – in terms of cues and turn-taking. People use humour to network, and they name-drop and story-tell. It's quite easy for an interpreter to feel like a fish out of water in those situations.

Multi-directional discourse: Groups

Where several people are talking in a group, the conditions for interpreting change significantly. Multi-party situations often involve one or more deaf participants in a larger hearing group (for example, at a board meeting or a workplace), or a more balanced mix of deaf and hearing participants (for example, at a Deaf community forum involving parents of deaf children). Occasionally the mix involves hearing individuals in a small deaf group (for example, a hearing consultant or a notetaker at a Deaf committee meeting). When various people in a group take turns at talking and listening, addressing different people at different times, the discourse becomes 'multi-directional' and harder to manage.

An experienced interpreter with a deaf family background remembers the horrors of her first paid job – a large meeting:

> I've been interpreting for nearly 20 years, but my career nearly ended the day it began. My first paid interpreting assignment was a high level meeting – a state sports committee with two deaf and eight hearing representatives from different organisations. I was thrown in at the deep end, and I drowned. Firstly I'm not a sports fan, so I wasn't clued in to the content. Secondly, they were using acronyms and making references to things that had come up at previous meetings – I didn't know I could have asked for an agenda and previous minutes. Worst of all, I had never inter-preted a meeting before and had no idea how to manage everyone talking over each other. I felt *so* bad for the deaf clients – I was battling to keep up with interpreting all the spoken comments and didn't know how to make space for them. I wasn't assertive or experienced enough to take some control – I wanted to give up after that job. I don't think that would happen these days – interpreter training and better booking systems mean that I either wouldn't have been asked, or would have said 'no thanks'.

Although the interpreter in this vignette was a competent bilingual and had plenty of informal interpreting experience, interpreting the complicated discourse of a meeting placed unexpected demands on her ability to relay the content and coordinate the turn-taking within her interpreting role.

In a multi-party situation the interpreter's presence is less prominent than in a two-way interview, so people often give less consideration to the interpreter's needs; they just proceed with their business. Challenges in multiparty interaction include the following:

- Same-language communication can happen between group members without depending on the interpreter. For example, two deaf people may sign to each other while a hearing member of the group is still speaking – the interpreter needs to decide whether to change language direction or to continue signing.

- The interpreter has little impact on the regulation of speaking turns (which frequently overlap in spoken discourse) and less choice about the timing of the delivery of interpretation; simultaneous interpreting with minimal time lag is expected so that deaf participants can keep up with and contribute to the discussion.

- Spoken multi-party discourse is often rapid and people interrupt each other or talk over the top of one another. Many interpreters find themselves requesting, 'Can you please speak one at a time as I only have one pair of hands!' as people often forget the difficulties for the interpreter in trying to keep up with group discussion.

- Even with competent simultaneous interpreting, this interpreting situation presents particular logistical difficulties for deaf people participating in a hearing group, especially around judging when, and how, to take the floor in a rapid stream of discussion.[3] Since there is always a slight time-lag with interpretation, and because deaf and hearing people have different signals for turn-taking, the interpreter (without becoming a 'communication cop') can facilitate interaction by cueing each party as to when the other is beginning or ending a speaking turn. For example, when a deaf person in a meeting lifts their hands to signal that he or she wants to say something, the interpreter needs to verbalise that visual signal so that hearing participants will receive the appropriate auditory cue. This could be a short phrase, such as 'Can I just say …' or 'Excuse me …', or sometimes just an intake of breath and leaning forward will be enough to cue hearing participants to the deaf speaker bidding for a turn.

- As speakers change, the interpreter needs to consistently identify for deaf participants who is talking, by pointing in their direction or using a name sign before interpreting what they say. Without this cue, the voices of the various participants blend into a single stream of talk channelled through the interpreter, and it is impossible for deaf participants to know who is saying what, and how the turn-taking is working within the group.

Pressure on the interpreter (and deaf participants) in group situations can be reduced by briefing the group facilitator and/or members about the need to establish an system of speaking turns to avoid overlap, (for example, raising a hand when ready to contribute), and seeking permission for the interpreter to request clarification (or crowd control) through the facilitator, when necessary.

Working with a team interpreter in multi-party situations is also ideal: the team interpreter can feed any information that is missed or misheard, and provide respite from being in the 'hot seat' for too long. Another possibility is to split the load with each interpreter working in just one language direction – one doing all the signing and the other doing all the voicing. The potential drawback of this is that there is usually more communication in one language direction than the other, and neither interpreter gets a real break. (Team interpreting is discussed further in Chapter 8).

---

3   For research on turn-taking in an interpreted meeting, see Van Herreweghe (2002).

Apart from managing the flow of multi-directional discourse, another challenge in group situations is the background contextual knowledge that participants bring to the communication. Groups that meet regularly, such as committees, staff meetings, or classes have a shared history prior to the meeting. The interpreter might be the only 'outsider' present, and may find that some of the content doesn't make sense because they were not party to previous discussions or the events referred to, and don't understand the relationships between participants. Although the need for background knowledge also applies to dialogue situations, the problem is magnified in group discourse; more participants naturally bring a greater diversity of information, knowledge, assumptions, goals, perspectives and feelings to the communication – all of which the interpreter must try to make sense of on the spot.

One way to reduce this context gap is by prior consultation with clients to obtain the agenda and relevant background information or papers. A brief conversation with a member of the group is often the best way to find out what issues might be important in the meeting and any background story. Working with a team interpreter can again be an advantage. For example, if you are booked to interpret for a board meeting for the first time and you are working with another interpreter who has interpreted previous meetings during the year – that interpreter will have the required background knowledge and be able to support you. It can be useful to ask them to take the first shift, since they will be familiar with the context and can demonstrate established signs to ease you into the picture.

Interpreting multi-directional interaction can be a handful – not a task recommended for new interpreters. As a rule, the more formally controlled the interaction (for example, by a chairperson or facilitator), and the more explicitly information must be presented (for example, through prepared reports or agenda documents), the easier it is for an interpreter to function. On the other hand, very informal events that are not facilitated (such as a dinner) can prove to be more difficult to interpret, as speakers compete to have their say, make quiet asides, and crack in-jokes. Even the best interpreter can't smooth out an inherently bumpy communication event:

> Interpreters asked to interpret in a situation that is chaotic to begin with cannot be held responsible for any further chaos. (Gentile et al 1996: 53)

Predicting the difficulty of interpreting situations

We have distinguished three basic patterns of interaction that interpreters will encounter: monologic, dialogic and multi-directional. In reality communication situations very often slide from one kind of discourse to another. A lecture can progress into a multi-directional question/answer or discussion session, a consultation between a teacher and student can turn into a teaching monologue, and a committee meeting can include a one-person presentation. This means that interpretation style has to shift between different discourse types and registers within the same situation, and it is not always easy to pigeonhole assignments as one type or another.

To be mentally prepared, it's helpful to contact the person running the event, to get as much detail as possible about the program. Relying on the brief description given in a job booking doesn't always provide a full picture. The more information you can glean before accepting an assignment, the better you can determine whether: (a) it is an easy or difficult assignment, and (b) how many interpreters will be needed, and (c) whether you are the best person for the job.

Experience in different discourse situations, good and bad, helps to predict what will happen in future interpreting jobs. Although any assignment is potentially unpredictable, consideration of the following questions[4] can give some sense of the level of likely difficulty and level of competence needed:

1. Preparation – can material be prepared in advance?

2. Direction – is communication in one, two or multiple directions?

3. Stopping – can the communication be stopped for clarification?

4. Sensitivity – how sensitive/emotional is the situation?

5. Multiple roles – how many different professional roles do the participants have?

6. Familiar language – is the sign language variety/style familiar to the interpreter?

7. Language diversity – is more than one variety of signing being used by different deaf participants?

8. Technical language – how specialised/technical is the vocabulary/topic?

9. Flexibility (of consumers) – how easily can the consumers make allowances for difficulties the interpreter might have in processing the material?

10. Scrutiny – who will be in the audience that might be monitoring interpreter performance?

11. On record – will the interpreting assignment be filmed or a transcript made? If so, how will this record be used?

12. Perceived difficulty – how does an interpreter's background and experience influence his or her perceptions about whether an assignment will be difficult or easy? Individual fears can turn a relatively simple assignment into a worst case scenario.

---

4   Adapted from Turner (2001b).

Balance of 'demand and control' in interpreting situations

Interpreters work in a range of discourse situations, where we face different combinations of pressures and conditions (demands). Our ability to respond to these demands (control), determines the perceived level of difficulty of the task. Looking at the relationship between the level and types of *demand* and the level of *control* (available responses) is one way of understanding why some assignments feel more challenging than others (Dean and Pollard 2001, 2005). Have you ever left an interpreting assignment feeling that it went really well and that although it was challenging, you were satisfied with the overall job? This was probably a 'high demand-high control' assignment – you were under pressure but you were able to manage the situation. Other assignments can leave interpreters feeling as if they did a terrible job, and wondering if the deaf client followed anything at all. These are examples of 'high demand-low control' assignments, where the interpreter is under pressure and feels they can't do much to change or cope with the situation.

No single condition or factor in an interpreting assignment is inherently good or bad, it depends on how it affects us in the circumstances. Dean and Pollard have grouped different demands into the following categories: environmental, interpersonal (factors within the interpreter), paralinguistic and intrapersonal (relations between participants).

The following table (see p 103) gives examples.

Once the demands of a situation are analysed and better understood, it is easier to identify available controls; the responses, resources and choices we can bring to bear. Interpreters can apply controls before (for example, via preparation), during (for example, dealing with self-talk, making direct interventions, particular translation choices) and after an assignment (for example, debriefing, self-care) (Dean and Pollard 2007).

In this chapter we have surveyed some of the generic features and demands of interpreting three different types of discourse: monologic, dialogic and multi-directional. We have shown how the direction and conditions of interaction between deaf and hearing participants (for example, whether turn-taking is controlled by a facilitator or not, and the difference in visual versus spoken language modalities) impacts an interpreter's functioning. The chapter has also set out some strategies for managing the task of interpreting typical communication dynamics. Building on this general foundation, Chapters 7, 8 and 9 go on to look in more detail at specific settings and situations in which sign language interpreters work.

Table 6.1: Demand sources in interpreting assignments

TYPE OF DEMAND	SOURCES (in a particular setting)

Environmental	• Goal or purpose
	• Terminology
	• Personnel
	• Physical surroundings:
	  - Room temperature
	  - Chemicals and odours
	  - Seating arrangements/ sight lines
	  - Lighting quality
	  - Visual distractions
	  - Background noise
	  - Space (people, furniture, equipment)

Interpersonal	• Power and authority • Communication styles and goals • Emotional tone or mood • Role and cultural differences • Communication flow (eg turn-taking) • Relationships (new, familiar, intimate) • 'Thought worlds' of deaf and hearing people
Paralinguistic	• Idiosyncrasies of speakers/ signers • Volume/ size • Pace • Accents • Clarity of speech/ sign • Physical position • Physical limitations

Intrapersonal	• Feelings or concerns about:
	  - Safety
	  - Interpreting performance
	  - Liability
	  - People and dynamics
	  - Environment
	• Physiological distractions (eg pain, hunger, fatigue)
	• Psychological responses or distractions

Source: Adapted from Dean and Pollard (2007)

Thought questions

1.　Discourse situations and interaction:

Discourse situations for interpreting can be categorised as monologic, dialogic or multi-party. Each type of interaction presents particular demands on the interpreter. For each category, think of an example of a situation, identify difficulty factors for the interpreter, and suggest a strategy for coping with those difficulties. Fill in the chart.

	Monologic	Dialogic	Multiparty
(a) Example of situation/setting			
(b) Possible difficulty factors for the interpreter (demands)			
(c) Strategies and resources for coping with demands (control)			

2.　Predicting assignment difficulty:

Imagine you have been asked to interpret a panel discussion on the topic of pre-natal genetic screening for disabilities, including deafness. One of the panellists is a Deaf parent of a Deaf child, another is a geneticist. This event is being recorded for screening on a weekly TV program on science issues. Identify at least six factors about the potential difficulty of this assignment that you should consider in deciding whether you are competent to accept it or not.

3.　Demand and Control theory

The Demand-Control schema explains the tension between situational conditions and the interpreter's capacity to respond to them. Look at Table 6.1: 'Demand sources in interpreting assignments' in relation to the situation above:

(a)　Do you think any of the demand types (for example environmental, intrapersonal) are easier for an interpreter to control than others?

(b)　Choose three examples of specific demand sources from the table and suggest interpreter strategies for addressing them.

CHAPTER 7

INTERPRETING CONTEXTS

This chapter introduces the contexts in which sign language interpreters typically work: education, social services, employment, medical, mental health and legal contexts, and with deaf professionals in workplace and social settings. We have also included contexts that are less common, but still require particular skills and preparation: religious, conference, and performance interpreting. The chapter gives an overview of each domain, focusing on typical interpreting challenges, introducing relevant strategies and knowledge, and providing references to more detailed information.

Education

Educational interpreting is one of the largest employment areas for sign language interpreters (McIntire 1990; Hayes 1992; Seal 1998; Stewart, Schein and Cartwright 1998; Napier and Barker 2003) and many interpreters work solely within this setting. The changing policies of deaf education (from segregated special schools to inclusion in mainstream programs) and the access that human rights legislation has opened up (especially in tertiary education), have created a demand for sign language interpreters at every level of the education system – primary, secondary and tertiary. Educational interpreting has traditionally been a context unique to sign language interpreters; it is rare for other interpreters to work with students in a classroom. However, South Africa is an interesting exception, where spoken language interpreters have been introduced into universities to accommodate students from different language backgrounds.[1]

Primary and secondary school interpreting

The main differences between interpreting in the school and college or university sectors are the job description, working conditions and remuneration for interpreters. In the US, the role of 'educational interpreter' in schools is acknowledged and appropriately remunerated, whereas in New Zealand and Australia interpreting is performed by teaching assistants (also called 'teacher aide', or 'communication support worker'), since there is no

---

1   See van Rooy (2005), Beukes and Pienaar (2009) and Verhoef and Blaauw (2009) for discussion of the emerging need for spoken language educational interpreting in universities due to the recognition of 11 official languages in South Africa.

funded job category for 'interpreter' in the school system. Tertiary education institutions are not bound by the same award system, so the role, conditions and remuneration of interpreters employed there better reflect the professional status of interpreting work.

Employment conditions make interpreting work in primary and secondary schools less attractive to qualified sign language interpreters. This is unfortunate, as deaf children are usually already disadvantaged in terms of their language development, fluency in sign language and English, and their general knowledge.

> Ninety percent of deaf children born to hearing parents will not be fluent during the critical years of language acquisition, so only the best interpreters should be working with them ... Yet, students who are deaf or hard of hearing are regularly subjected to unqualified, non-certified interpreters. (Jones, Clark and Soltz 1997:265)

For those interpreters who do work in school classrooms, a number of additional skills are required to deal with the educational environment, and the fact that the deaf clients are not adults and may not have a fully-developed first language (Elliott and Powers 1995).

Modified signing

In the same way that teachers adjust their speech and language specifically in 'child directed speech' (for example, choice of vocabulary, intonation), interpreters also need to adapt their signing to younger deaf children. Deaf adults provide a good model for some of the sign language strategies that can be used with deaf children, for example, signing more slowly, using more facial expression, stronger eye contact, repeating signs, more role shift, etc.

Role models

Interpreters work with deaf students who have varying degrees of sign language proficiency; the interpreter is often the only signing adult that the children are exposed to, so the interpreter becomes the default language and social role model. School is also the first place most deaf children have ever seen or worked with an interpreter, so educational interpreters also become role models for how interpreting relationships are managed. These are additional, unstated responsibilities that go with the role of educational interpreter.

Language use

Individual schools or education systems often have declared language policies (for example, Signed English or bilingual programs) that are more or less strictly adhered to in the classroom. One difficulty for Signed English programs is the fact that qualified interpreters are trained in Auslan/NZSL and not in Signed English. Regardless of policy, in practice interpreters must balance the need for information to be clearly understood by the student/s (via free interpretation into the relevant sign language), versus the need for students to acquire English words and grammar (via a more literal English-based form). Interpreting modes and directions in classrooms include:

- Spoken English into Auslan/NZSL;

- Written English into Auslan/NZSL; and

- Child-based (often less than fluent or idiosyncratic) forms of Auslan/NZSL into spoken English.

Teachers' use of prosody (intonation, pausing, volume, etc) is used deliberately to control the classroom environment, therefore interpreters must try to represent the vocal prosody in their signing (Schick 2001).

Client relationship and role boundaries

School interpreting work involves many face-to-face hours per day (which can be an occupational health and safety issue) and may also be prolonged in terms of the length of contract (sometimes years) with the same client(s). In many mainstream settings, the interpreter is the only person in the classroom who can communicate with the deaf student, and this can create a close bond (or tension) between the two. As a result, maintaining impartiality and clear role boundaries can be challenging; educational interpreters often feel responsible for the student's learning, and/or get caught up in divided loyalties, for example, when a teacher asks the interpreter to evaluate a child's learning or language competence. Interpreters in schools are commonly expected to undertake duties beyond interpreting, such as notetaking, behaviour management, playground duty, parent liaison, and to take some responsibility for the student's progress as part of an educational team.[2] Negotiating a workable interpreter role in a school context is rather different from working with adults in the community; Seal (1998) offers a good introduction to the issues involved.

Positioning in the classroom

Interpreters generally locate themselves at the front of the classroom during whole-class instruction, near the teacher and close to any teaching media being used, for example, whiteboard, video monitor, wall charts. Since interpreters usually work for long hours (and alone) in schools, they usually sit, either on a stool or chair, rather than stand. When activities change, interpreters need to monitor their positioning so that they have clear sightlines to the deaf student(s), and also don't block other students' (deaf or hearing) visual access to the teacher and/or teaching media.

---

2   McKee and Smith (2003).

Classroom tasks in two modalities

Many learning/teaching activities are designed for simultaneous use of the ears and eyes, since hearing students can attend to both spoken and visual input together. However, deaf students with interpreters in mainstream classrooms are relying on a single visual modality for access to teacher talk as well as other visual inputs. Research by Betsy Winston (1990) has identified how deaf students have to juggle competing demands on their visual attention during many learning tasks mediated through an interpreter. Table 7.1 below is based on Winston's analysis of combinations of sensory channels needed for typical classroom tasks, and whether deaf and hearing students have comparable learning conditions in terms of access to all the input.

Table7.1. Modality demands for deaf students in classrooms

ACTIVITY	Attending tasks: HEARING student		Attending tasks: DEAF student		Comparable conditions with an interpreter?
	Ears to speaker	Eyes to visual source	Eyes to inter- preter	Eyes to visual source	
Teacher lecture	+	-	+	-	Yes
Teacher lecture with visuals	+	+	+	+	No
Q & A (speech based)	+	-	+	-	Yes – modified
Q & A (paper based)	+	+	+	+	No
Reading aloud	+	+	+	+	No
Desk work (with talking)	+/-	+	+/-	+	No

Classroom activities that involve talking plus reading, writing, or watching require the deaf student to choose between watching the interpreter and looking at another source of relevant input. This means information will inevitably be lost. Interpreters, as well as teachers, need to be conscious of such conflicting visual demands, and use strategies to minimise the disadvantage. In many situations it is possible to brief the teacher about working with an interpreter; suggesting that they allow brief reading time (without talking) when giving a handout, or introducing a dense overhead transparency or powerpoint slide. If this does not happen, you can assist by:

- Positioning yourself as close as possible to the visual input – a screen, whiteboard, or in a school situation with younger students even pro- ducing signs closer to the page or worksheet that a student must refer to during a group activity.

- Having a copy of the written source material on hand so that you can cue the student as to where the speaker is up to on the page (for example, by paragraph, line, or number), since it is difficult for a deaf student to keep track of the place when looking up and down between interpreter and page without auditory cues.

- Interpreting consecutively and paraphrasing – that is, building in pauses for the student to read, while you 'hold' a chunk of information to deliver at an appropriate gap in the talk. This allows the deaf student to alternate their attention between written and spoken input.

- Interpreting any quoted chunks of text literally – so that the student can identify word-by-word the passage that is being referred to.

Given the inherent challenges and compromises involved in interpreter-mediated education, a number of people in the interpreting field have begun to question whether signing deaf children can be educated effectively in mainstream schools at all. Even 'competent' interpreting may not result in the full inclusion of a deaf child in the complex communication environment of a school, placing them in a disadvantaged position (Ramsey 1997; Winston 2004; Thoutenhooft 2005).

Tertiary education contexts

The growing number of deaf students entering further and higher education has consequently increased the demand for sign language interpreters in this context. In some respects the role of interpreters in tertiary education is more contained than in primary or secondary schools. The interaction in tertiary environments is typically quite 'controlled' and more often monologic com- pared with communication in school classrooms. Interpreters at tertiary level are working with adults who have made a decision to further their education, and usually have a clearer understanding of how to work with interpreters, and what they want from them. For example, many deaf uni- versity students request a more literal interpretation of lectures so that they can access academic English and/or subject-specific terminology (Bremner and Housden 1996; Napier and Barker 2004).

One of the major challenges for interpreters working in tertiary education is subject matter. In an ideal world interpreters would be matched with deaf students according to their background knowledge of the program content. Given the shortage of available interpreters, and the wide range of subjects studied by deaf students, this is not often possible. Interpreting lectures in a subject you know nothing about can be incredibly demanding and stressful, considering the technical nature of presentations, use of academic English, audiovisual aids, the pace of the presentation, the assumed knowledge base, and the need to negotiate subject-specific signs with the deaf student (Locker 1990; Johnson 1991; Harrington 2000; Leeson and Foley-Cave 2007). For this reason, interpreters who have had a university education themselves, have a better chance of coping with university discourse, even if they don't have expertise in the particular subject being studied by the deaf student (Patrie 1993; Seal 1998; Sameshima 1999; Harrington 2000; Napier 2002).

Preparation

Whether you are working at a TAFE college, technical institute or university, it is important to get information about the teaching program ahead of time to optimise your interpretation. Wherever possible, negotiate with teachers/lecturers to get access to lesson content (for example, readings, overhead transparencies, PowerPoint presentations, Web CT) so that you have the chance to see what will be covered, and to identify and research unfamiliar terminology and concepts. It is usually easier to follow unfamiliar subject matter when you interpret a course continuously from the very first session; that way you are learning and developing subject knowledge along with the student.

Negotiating new vocabulary

The increased participation of deaf people in mainstream education at all levels means that the vocabulary of Auslan/NZSL is rapidly expanding to express concepts and terms that are new to the wider signing community and not yet an established part of the language. Educational interpreters are the interface between new information and deaf students, which creates linguistic pressure. They need to make split-second decisions about finding equivalents for all sorts of English words and concepts they have never seen used in Auslan/NZSL. Sometimes, the sense of an academic English word can be conveyed by choosing a semantically related sign (for example, WORLD for 'global'), accompanied by either fingerspelling and/or a clear lip-pattern of the English term (Napier 2002; Davis 2003). However, where a related sign is not available, it is often necessary for interpreters and deaf clients to co-create new signs; this situation gives interpreters considerable influence on the introduction of new vocabulary, since even 'emergency' signs ('just for this class') can find their way into wider circulation in the community. Interpreters need to be mindful of the ownership of Auslan/NZSL and not assume that the temporary signs they may devise in specific settings with particular clients are appropriate for use in the wider Deaf community.

Comprehensibility of interpreted lectures

How easily can deaf students understand and learn new content by watching an interpretation of the original lecture? Do interpreter's choices and techniques make a critical difference to this? Several studies have investigated these questions (eg, Marschark et al 2004; Napier and Barker 2004). Marschark et al tested deaf students' comprehension of interpreted university lectures under different (for example, transliteration vs free interpreting, and students with and without subject knowledge). They found no clear pattern of factors that increased student comprehension of lecture information. In this study deaf students overestimated how much of the interpreted material they had understood, whereas hearing students who listened directly to the lecture were able to make more realistic estimates of how much information they had understood. Marschark et al concluded that 'effective' interpreting (in terms of well-formed, accurate target language output, and positive consumer perceptions of comprehensibility) does not guarantee effective learning outcomes. However, other studies suggest that the comprehensibility of interpretation in educational contexts can be enhanced by using strategies such as indicating new topics, providing links between concepts, matching register, and finding conceptual equivalence in vocabulary choices (Locker 1990; Winston and Monikowski 2003).

One form of tertiary interpreting which is not yet common in Australia or New Zealand, but which is becoming more prevalent in the US and the UK, is interpreting for deaf academics who present lectures to hearing audiences.[3] In this case, the interpreting demands will vary depending on whether the lecturer is presenting in a signed language or speaking, and how much audience feedback the deaf lecturer needs. Working with deaf professionals is discussed in more detail later in this chapter.

Social services and government agencies

Many community interpreters work with clients of social service and government agencies that provide services relating to income support (welfare benefits), housing, workers' accident compensation, vocational guidance, children and youth services, taxes, and disability support funding. In New Zealand, agencies commonly used by deaf clients are Work and Income NZ, Accident Compensation Corporation, Housing NZ, Workbridge, Children, Young Persons and their Families Service, and Inland Revenue Department. In Australia, agencies commonly used by deaf clients are Centrelink, Department of Families, Housing, Community Services and Indigenous Affairs, Comcare, Commonwealth Rehab Service (CRS), Worksafe Australia, Australian Tax Office (ATO), plus various State government bodies related to Community Services and Housing.

---

3   See Campbell, Rohan and Woodcock (2008).

Communication in these settings often focuses on determining whether a deaf client is eligible for financial or other services, and generally involves standardised forms that need to be completed by the interviewing officer with the client. Questions typically focus on the client's domestic circumstances, employment situation and finances.

Preparation and background knowledge

Interpreters can prepare for work in these contexts by familiarising themselves with standard forms and typical questions (many forms are available online). Background knowledge of the agency's services, particularly the names and criteria for benefits and grants they offer, is useful contextual information. Some terms may require expansion or paraphrasing in sign language, for example, 'expenses' or 'outgoings' are commonly used to inquire about a client's financial situation. A functionally equivalent translation may require listing examples, such as 'rent, food, transport, electricity, etc'.

Employing interpreters

Social service agencies vary in their policies and procedures for the hiring and payment of interpreters. If you have not been booked by an agency, it is wise to confirm with a case manager or senior administrator, prior to arriving for the job, that payment will be authorised. Also find out whether a client's case number or case manager's name is required on an invoice for payment.

Physical setting

Agencies with a high volume of clients (such as WINZ or Centrelink) generally have open-plan offices, where numerous clients are simultaneously talking to staff members at their desks. For the deaf person, this lack of visual privacy may be uncomfortable, while the interpreter may be distracted by the noise – it is not unusual to overhear heated conversations with other clients in the room. Seating arrangements can sometimes be negotiated (by polite explanation and request) to place the interpreter next to the staff member, to enable the client to simultaneously see both interpreter and interviewer, and possibly a computer screen which shows the client's case details.

Cultural mediation

Sometimes the officer/agency and the deaf client have different perspectives or understandings that need to be bridged. For example, when a case manager is trying to establish whether a deaf client is eligible for a supplementary disability allowance they might say, 'Do you have any ongoing costs relating to your disability?' The deaf person may not automatically associate the term 'disability' with their deafness, and might respond in the negative. In this situation, the meaning would be better expressed by substituting the sign for 'deaf' instead of 'disabled'. If the interpreter knows that the supplementary allowance specifically covers hearing aid batteries and fax paper, they could choose to translate 'costs' (which is not often used as a generic noun in Auslan/NZSL) by listing some deaf-related examples of costs, including hearing aids and fax paper. There is an overlap between 'prompting' (verging on advocacy) and bridging a knowledge gap that stems from a deaf person's lack of access to information about available resources and 'the system'.

Employment

High rates of under-employment and unemployment in the Deaf community reflect the communication barriers that deaf people face in training and in the workplace (Dugdale 2000). Historically, deaf people in Australia and New Zealand were mainly confined to blue-collar jobs, but increasing access to higher education combined with technological changes in the job market, anti-discrimination obligations, and the availability of interpreting services have broadened the range of occupations deaf people are entering. 'Employment interpreting' covers a spectrum of work contexts ranging from blue-collar/industrial to white-collar/ professional, and includes the following situations:

- Vocational guidance and job search services;
- Job interviews;
- In-service staff training;
- Staff meetings;
- Disciplinary or dispute resolution situations;
- Union meetings.

Although deaf people still generally work in lower status jobs, deaf professionals and/or business people tend to use a disproportionate share of employment interpreting services (Ozolins and Bridge 1999). Their work environments and responsibilities often require extensive interpersonal communication – such as meetings, consultations, and workshops, and their workplaces are more likely to accept their obligations to provide equal access and reasonable accommodation. Deaf employees in these contexts often expect a very polished level of interpreting (similar to conference interpreting level) that reflects their professional status.

Since the principles of interpreting in workplace training and meeting situations have already been covered in Chapter 5 (interpreting in group situations and meetings), the next section will only focus on issues related to job interviews.

Job interviews

Interpreting in job interviews is a sensitive task, given the importance of the outcome for the deaf applicant. The interpreter needs to pay attention to the content of the interview (information about the job and the applicant's experience) as well as rapport building, since this is the first meeting between an employer and a potential employee.

Preparation

Before the interview, find out about the job, the employer and any important technical terms likely to arise in discussion. To minimise interruptions and misinterpretations during an interview, check with the deaf applicant beforehand for any key names or terminology that they plan to mention, for example, former places of work and employers, job titles, or abbreviations for qualifications. If they have a CV with them, ask to have a look at it as well. Prior knowledge about the experience, background and style of the person you will be voicing for helps you to represent them as competently as possible.

Presentation

Since the interpreter's presence will be associated with the deaf job applicant, consider the kind of impression the applicant might want to create and the dress code of the workplace. As a rule of thumb, avoid conspicuously under-dressing or over-dressing in comparison to the applicant themselves. The physical setting is also a consideration; for example, an interview at a plant nursery or a joinery factory calls for more casual presentation (and sensible shoes) than an office setting.

Introductions and positioning

Taking time for a polite introduction and briefing of the interviewer about the interpreter's role and positioning is an important start; whether this is led by the interpreter or by the deaf client can be agreed beforehand. Job interviews are generally either one on one (employer and applicant) or with the applicant facing a panel. The interpreter needs to tactfully negotiate a position near whoever will be asking the questions. When an interview panel takes turns asking questions, interpreters can decide who the key member of the panel is (for example, the convenor) and stay positioned adjacent to them. As an interpreted interview with a deaf person is usually a new and awkward experience for most employers, and the interpreter's behaviour will affect overall impressions of the deaf candidate, it is important that interpreters include normal politeness behaviours (such as responding to opening greetings and questions directed at the interpreter) and to create as little disruption of the physical set-up as possible.

Intercultural mediation

In any job interview, the applicant aims to present a positive impression of their capability for a job, but many deaf job applicants are unfamiliar with the hearing cultural 'script' for expected questions, responses, and presentation that go with a job interview. At the same time, the interviewer is probably encountering a deaf person, sign language and interpreted communication for the very first time. This communication situation in itself is a potential barrier to a good interview. The interpreter therefore needs to try and maximise participants' understanding of each other's intent, and minimise awkwardness in the dialogue.

Knowing the rules

Job interviews are structured by a 'cultural set' of assumptions about what should be said by whom, when and how (Mindess 1999: 139-142). One basic assumption is that the job applicant should only present themselves in a positive light, and never disclose weaknesses. Successful interviewees are adept at summarising and matching their relevant skills and experience to the specific requirements of the position, rather than offering a complete employment history and life story. Another example of the 'rules of the game' is the conventional closing of an interview by inviting the applicant to ask any questions; this is really an opportunity for the applicant to sell themselves or to look knowledgeable by asking relevant questions about the job, rather than an opportunity to enquire about details such as the timing of lunch breaks, or where the nearest bus-stop is.

If deaf applicants are not familiar with these cultural rules, they may be qualified for the job but not present themselves to best advantage in the interview. Interpreters cannot always bridge this gap, (schools and vocational counsellors have a role here), but they can make decisions about cultural adjustments that will facilitate the interaction, such as:

- Adjusting TL English phrasing to include politeness makers. For example, if the deaf person asks the interpreter to sit next to the interviewer, and for curtains to be drawn for visual comfort, the interpreter should express this with a polite hedge such as 'Would you mind if ...?', and expand on the unstated reason, 'so that I can see you speaking and the interpreter signing at the same time/because the glare from the window makes it difficult to see your face and the interpreter's face clearly'. Politeness adjustments and clarification between cultures are important in facilitating a basic rapport between the clients.

- Interpreting questions in a way that makes it very clear what the real intent is, and provides some guidance as to the expected form of reply.

For example, if an interviewer is obviously seeking a simple yes/no answer – 'Are you a union member?' or 'Do you have your own transport?' – the interpreter can add: YES, NO, WHICH? to the end of the question, to reduce the chance of the applicant launching into unnecessary detail. Where elaboration is clearly expected, the interpreter can use signs that clearly show this expectation for example, EXPLAIN FULL DETAIL – WHAT? If the interviewer is seeking a summary or self-promotion such as 'Why do you feel you are qualified for this job?', this could be indicated by translating the question, then adding SUMMARY, 'ENUMERATE' ONE TWO THREE, WHAT?

In job interviews, as well as many other interpreting situations, it is important to listen beyond the literal surface message, for the function and intent of what is being said by each party. In this way interpreters can convey deeper levels of meaning between the parties, making the interaction more 'normal' and comfortable.

Deaf professionals

As mentioned earlier in this chapter, more deaf students are now entering higher education. Many are studying to postgraduate level and entering the workplace in various professional roles. This means that more sign language interpreters are working with deaf professionals, which provides new challenges in relation to their role (Dickinson and Turner 2008).

Interpreters in these contexts may have to interpret for a range of workplace interactions – office meetings or training sessions, or formal presentations at conferences or seminars – where the deaf professional may be the presenter or audience member. Thus deaf professionals often prefer to work with the same interpreter(s) regularly and closely, to navigate their workplace relationships and career ambitions. This new interpreting partnership has been defined as the *deaf professional-designated interpreter model* (Hauser and Hauser 2008).[4]

As well as interpreting for professional consultations, meetings and presentations, sign language interpreters may also be required to work with deaf professionals in social networking situations, providing *diplomatic* interpreting.

Diplomatic interpreting

'Diplomatic interpreting' (also known as escort or executive interpreting), involves chaperoning one client at an event, and providing a personal interpreting service for their interaction with others. This client may be a deaf person (at a hearing function), or a hearing person (at a deaf function). They

---

4   This volume details a range of deaf professionals working with 'designated' interpreters in ways that challenge the conventional concept of the interpreter's role.

may be a VIP or an executive attending a dinner, conference, or other event. The interpreter's main function is to enable the client to socialise as smoothly as possible. In a work-related social event, the navigation of social etiquette via an interpreter can be critical to the success of the deaf professional (Clark and Finch 2008).

In Chapter 6 we discussed the challenges of interpreting conversations in professional networking situations. In diplomatic interpreting, this type of interpreting is typical. The topics of spontaneous conversations can be wildly unpredictable, and communication can range from formal speeches to relaxed banter and gossip. This demands concentration and flexibility of role from the interpreter, which may challenge their position of neutrality (Cook 2004).

Some issues to consider in 'diplomatic' settings include:

- Where you stand or sit in relation to your client. For a hearing client, the general rule is to stay close – 'at their elbow' – to allow for interpreting at a discreet conversational volume, and also to encourage deaf and hearing participants to engage as directly as possible. With a deaf client, the interpreter should move closer to hearing participants (without invading their personal space).

- If interpreting at a dinner function, it is advisable to eat something before you arrive. Interpreting while eating a full dinner is a difficult manoeuvre, and can distract your attention from your main task. Just as you take a bite, someone is bound to ask your client a question. If you do decide to eat, either because of politeness (for example, the host or client insists), or because you need sustenance, take a small portion and nibble discretely, or it may be possible to negotiate a short break with your client while you eat.

- What you wear is important in this context. You should dress in keeping with the status of the client you are interpreting for, as you will also be meeting all the people that he or she meets, and your appearance will add to or detract from their social impact.

- Diplomatic interpreting events can be long, and it may be difficult to take a break without leaving your client stranded. Although the workload may not be heavy, it is constant, so be mindful of fatigue and its effect on your interpreting. If possible, arrange a team interpreter for assignments longer than two hours.

Medical

Medical interpreting assignments are diverse and unpredictable: they are often one-off jobs, with a diverse range of patients (age, communication style etc) and presenting conditions. Even when the interpreter knows what type of practitioner the client is seeing, they can't always predict the direction or outcome of the consultation. In medical interpreting situations, an incorrect explanation of symptoms to the practitioner or incomplete instructions to the patient can have serious ramifications: the wrong diagnosis or treatment can be life threatening. So, like legal interpreting, medical interpreting is a potentially high stakes context.

Medical or healthcare interpreting includes:

- GP appointments;

- Specialist consultations (in private rooms or in hospitals);

- Allied health practitioner appointments (for example, physiotherapy, optometry, radiography, baby health clinics);

- Hospital procedures (outpatient and inpatient);

- Rehabilitation therapy sessions.

In Australia, medical interpreting outside the hospital system is arranged through the National Auslan Booking Service (NABS); interpreting in public hospitals systems is co-ordinated by State health departments, individual hospitals and/or Deaf Societies. In New Zealand, most healthcare interpreting outside the hospital system is covered by Deaf Aoteroa NZ services, while hospital interpreting booking arrangements vary regionally. Many deaf people choose not to use an interpreter for visits to their local GP, because they can manage the communication themselves (for example, via notes or lipreading), maintaining independence and privacy, however for more critical or complicated medical situations, they will usually ask for an interpreter.

Contextual knowledge

Healthcare interpreters should ideally have a solid grounding in medical terminology, the systems of the body, common illnesses and conditions and their treatments, hospital procedures, the range of specialist medical disciplines, as well as the ability to communicate clearly with the full spectrum of deaf clients. This is a tall order. Many medical interpreters initially rely on their own knowledge and experience of the healthcare system in dealing with the terminology, discourse styles, and physical settings they find themselves in. However, if you plan to take on regular medical interpreting work, it is worthwhile enrolling in a medical terminology course. These are sometimes provided by hospitals or medical interpreting agencies, but are also available as short courses in some tertiary institutions.

Seating position

Often medical practitioners (specialists in particular) are perceived as authority figures by their clients, as well as by interpreters. Doctors also have their own preferred methods of interacting with the client and their records (usually on a computer screen). Consequently an interpreter will need to tactfully negotiate where to position themselves in the doctor's space. In consulting rooms the layout of the furniture and the comfort levels of the doctor mean that a triangle arrangement is more realistic than sitting behind the doctor's desk. Often the deaf patient needs to be adjacent to the doctor, for easy access for routine procedures (injections, blood pressure or temperature checks etc) and/or for physical examination, so interpreters need to work out what seating or standing position is practicable in the circumstances. If available, swivel chairs on rollers can make it easier to adjust interpreting positions quickly.

Modesty

GPs and specialists often need to examine patients on a bed (for example, internal examinations, checking surgical wounds, skin checks etc). Normally a patient would not have a third party present and watching them, so preserving the dignity of deaf clients in these situations is important. The trick is knowing how to maintain sightlines with the deaf client, without embarrassing them. When a deaf patient needs to remove their clothes, the interpreter can ensure the instructions are clearly given beforehand, and then avert their eyes for the undressing. Once the patient is on the bed, the interpreter can usually move to a position where they can see (and be seen by) the deaf client's face, but are facing away from any sensitive body part. When a practitioner examines their patient behind a curtain, the interpreter can ask for the curtain to be drawn back just enough to see the deaf client's face. Occasionally, medical practitioners ask for, or are open to learning, a few relevant signs (for example, cough, breathe-deeply, hold-breath) or signals (for example, tapping on the shoulder to stop and start breathing) so that they can communicate directly with their patient throughout the procedure in privacy.

Eye appointments

Deaf people's sight is particularly precious, and many deaf clients visit optometrists and ophthalmologists (eye specialists). The problem with interpreting in these settings is that some procedures remove light, sightlines, glasses and even vision from the equation. Complicating factors include: the level of the deaf client's vision impairment (especially without glasses), the procedure they are undergoing (for example, eye drops, glaucoma test, field test, lens selection), the layout of specialist equipment and the ambient lighting in the consulting room. In some circumstances the deaf client may not be able to see or touch the interpreter at all. If you are interpreting for a deaf client's first visit to an eye specialist, you will probably need to discuss alternate communication strategies with the deaf client and the specialist beforehand. Some strategies include:

- The practitioner giving ALL instructions to the deaf client before any procedure, so that they know what will happen in sequence.

- Working out signals for advising the deaf client of any instructions or questions while they can't see, for example, being told to open/close eyes, hold breath etc – via tapping on their shoulder, tactile fingerspelling.

- Working out signals for the deaf client to advise of responses to particular tests or stimuli – via using their voice, tapping on the desk, holding their thumb up, etc.

Emotional issues

Healthcare patients (and consequently interpreters) presenting for diagnosis or treatment do not know what the outcome of the consultation will be. In many cases the patient is in pain or may be fearful of the treatment they need to undergo. When medical conditions are treated successfully via an interpreter, the outcome is very satisfying. However, with the good comes the bad; many procedures are painful, and many diagnoses are confronting. It is difficult to watch anyone in extreme pain, let alone need to focus on their experience of it so that it can be communicated to the practitioner as accurately as possible. It is even more difficult to pass on 'bad' news (for example, diagnosis of a patient's terminal illness, notifying a mother in labour that her child will be stillborn).

Accident and emergency departments are particularly stressful places (Crezée 1998: 35). The interpreter has usually been called out without notice and can be confronted with acute medical conditions or gross injuries. The patient (and any accompanying friends or relatives) is usually stressed and sometimes has to wait for long periods before being admitted. This calls for stamina and a cool head, so that information is passed on accurately and the correct diagnosis can be made. Sometimes the patient does not survive, and the interpreter needs to be able to pass on that information clearly, and with dignity.

Despite ideals of professional detachment, interpreters are only human and cannot help but be affected by such emotionally-charged situations. Interpreters need to be emotionally prepared for these types of challenges, and to ensure that they debrief with a supervisor, clinician or trusted colleague wherever necessary. This can help reduce the likelihood of 'vicarious trauma' – where the interpreter is indirectly traumatised because of their exposure to intensely upsetting events and information. A related issue is queasiness – if you are someone who faints at the sight of blood, or over-empathises with others' pain, you may not be ideally suited for the full range of medical interpreting assignments.

Common situations

The following scenarios are common for interpreters:[5]

- Initial medical consultations typically start with a case history; practitioners may ask about the deaf client's family history, own medical and surgical history, diet, drug and alcohol use and general stress levels.

- Physical checkups commonly include checking a patient's pulse, blood pressure, auscultation (listening to the heart, lungs and/or abdomen) and palpation (feeling for lumps/abnormalities).

- In hospital emergency departments, medical staff need to know key information fast, so they will ask specific questions related to the patient's current condition (for example, heart attack, burns, asthma attack, drug overdose etc).

- Whenever a doctor needs to perform an 'invasive' (surgical) procedure, they are legally required to obtain the patient's 'informed consent'. This is usually done via a consent form (which the interpreter may have to 'sight translate') or can be done verbally in urgent situations. The doctor is obliged to explain the procedure, the hoped-for benefits, and the possible side effects or risks, and to clearly determine whether the patient agrees to the surgery or not.

Accuracy

This is *the* critical ethic for medical interpreting; without accurate information, practitioners cannot form an accurate diagnosis and start appropriate treatment. In particular, the interpretation of patient symptoms needs to be very precise, as this information forms the basis for diagnosis and treatment. Take care to accurately translate grammatical markers of time, frequency, duration, and how intensely any symptoms are experienced. Explanations by practitioners need to be conveyed equally precisely, especially when describing side effects and the timing of medication. If you are in doubt about whether your interpretation is clear to the patient, it is acceptable to ask the practitioner to re-phrase or expand their description. For example, if they say 'take this three times a day with food', the interpreter may want to check whether they mean specifically with breakfast, lunch and dinner, and whether it matters if the medication is taken before or after meals. If they say 'you may have a sensation of pins and needles', the interpreter needs to clarify in which area of the body, in order to sign this accurately.

Interpreters are often dealing with clients, situations, medical conditions and terminology that they are unfamiliar with. It is therefore essential that whenever the interpreter is unclear about what the clinician or

---

5   Outlined by Crezée (1998).

the patient means, they take the time to clarify until they are confident that they understand the meaning and can pass it on.[6]

Mental health

Interpreters work with deaf clients in a range of mental health contexts including: psychiatric assessments and consultations, individual counselling, family therapy and case conferences. In Australia and New Zealand most mental health practitioners rely on interpreters to assess and treat their deaf clients since there are few qualified deaf mental health professionals or hearing mental health professionals who can sign.

Mental health interactions are inherently deeply personal and also heavily dependent on verbal communication for methods of diagnosis and therapy. On both counts, the situation is complicated by the presence of an interpreter. The challenges for sign language interpreters working in mental health contexts include the following factors (Harvey 1982; Turner, Klein and Kitson 1998; McCay and Miller 2001; Napier and Cornes 2004; Cornes and Napier 2005):

Physical aspects

Mental health assignments often take place in clinical settings, such as a psychiatric hospital, a clinic, or a practitioner's rooms. But in crisis situations, the interpreter may be working in a non-clinical setting such as someone's home, a police station, or a prison, which can be unfamiliar and unpleasant environments. The home of a person who is chronically mentally unwell may be in a very poor state of hygiene, or there may be a risk that a psychotic client in a custodial setting will become physically aggressive. Before the assignment begins, always ask a member of the mental health professional team or the booking agency to explain the type of setting you are going into, the client's situation, the background to this event, and any physical risk factors. They might, for example, advise you to position yourself near an exit or another staff member, in case of threatening behaviour. Whatever the situation, be alert and flexible in terms of how the communication might work. Keep in mind that a deaf client in a mental health crisis will not always be receptive to communication with hearing 'strangers', and it may be difficult to maintain the necessary eye gaze or turn-taking for communication to progress. If this is the case, you need to keep hearing professionals informed about the difficulty of the communication dynamic.

---

6   See SanheimZ (2003), Angelelli (2003) and Smeijers and Pfau (2009) for discussions of challenges for interpreters in medical consultations.

Interpreting role

Therapy is effective if an 'alliance' can be established between the therapist and their client. When an interpreter is added to the dynamic, the deaf client may focus on the interpreter in order to access the message, so there is a risk that the client will align with the interpreter rather than the therapist or doctor. Physical positioning (that is, sitting close to the therapist) and carefully reflecting the therapist's manner can help to downplay the interpreter's presence and reinforce the therapist's role.

Translation issues

Mental health practitioners assess clients based on they way they communicate, as well as looking at what the client is saying, taking into account both verbal and non-verbal signals. Variation in the patient's volume, rate of speaking, pauses, emphasis, tone of voice, breathing, facial expression and body language all carry potentially significant meaning for the mental health clinician. The interpreter's job, therefore, is to convey these paralinguistic aspects of a signed message as accurately as possible. At times, these features may need to be described to the clinician when they cannot easily be incorporated into delivery of the TL message itself (for example, that a deaf client's sign production is very 'blurry', or that it seems incoherent).

As with many other interpreting contexts, interpreters may encounter specialised English terminology without lexical equivalents in sign language. Very few deaf people work as professionals in the mental health field in Australia and New Zealand, so there has been little chance to develop an appropriate signed vocabulary for all the concepts and jargon used. Specific communication techniques may also be used in diagnosis and therapy, which the interpreter should ideally be aware of in advance. For example, a counsellor may intentionally pose questions in a very confrontational manner, and their goals may be foiled if the interpreter re-packages the utterance in a way that softens it and influences the response.

A psychiatrist may ask the interpreter to translate literally a psychotic client's disordered 'stream of consciousness', in order to assess their mental state. Sometimes the language and thoughts of mentally ill or distressed clients are incoherent and make little sense. This kind of discourse is difficult to interpret accurately, since it is easier to reproduce a message that is connected and meaningful than one that is fragmented. The interpreter here is challenged to distinguish between signing that is grammatically disordered or disconnected, which needs to be conveyed or described to the clinician, versus language that is relatively coherent in form, but nonsensical in content (that is, not reality-based, or jumping from topic to topic in a confusing manner), which should be interpreted as is. In mental health contexts it is important to avoid the natural temptation to make sense of what the client 'means', which is the job of the clinician based on the language 'data' or communication itself.[7]

Emotional factors

When accepting a mental health interpreting assignment, it is difficult to predict what may be revealed during the session. Clients' disclosure of traumatic personal experiences may trigger emotional responses in the interpreter or identification with similar experiences. In a counselling or psychiatric session it is helpful for the therapist and the interpreter to have a quick briefing before the session and to debrief afterwards. In this way, roles and strategies can be clarified from the start and the interpreter can seek assistance if they have been adversely affected by what has arisen during the session or need to clarify aspects of the interpreted communication process itself. In some psychiatric contexts, such as hospital wards or institutions, the interpreter can be faced with a variety of unusual and sometimes upsetting behaviours, conditions and predicaments. Familiarity with these settings and situations helps interpreters to cope but debriefing after specific assignments may also be worthwhile after particularly stressful jobs.

Cultural mediation

Unfortunately counsellors, psychologists and psychiatrists get little if any training about the Deaf community and the range of social-linguistic or educational circumstances that affect the development and lives of deaf individuals. Interpreters may need to explain particular communication behaviours or typical gaps in knowledge that could otherwise be misinterpreted or misdiagnosed by a clinician for example, vocalising, attention-getting behaviours, literacy problems, or barriers to accessing support services. Often there is a wide gap between the conceptual and linguistic frameworks of hearing clinicians and relatively uneducated deaf clients in mental health services. Some researchers suggest that the interpreter work collaboratively with the practitioner to gain the background information required from a deaf client, and to assist with any gaps in understanding or differences in style of communication (McCay and Miller 2001). The consistency of the same interpreter throughout a series of sessions is also important for three reasons:

1. Establishing a rapport and sense of trust between the three parties involved in treatment.

2. Developing background knowledge about the client's circumstances and consistent ways of referring to this in the communication.

---

7   See Gentile et al (1996), Chapter 7, for a useful discussion of the language interpreted in mental health settings.

3. Building understanding in the interpreter of the therapeutic goals and techniques, which in turn affects the way they will interpret and function in the situation

Working with a deaf interpreter or a deaf support worker as part of the team can be very beneficial in addressing some of the communication and cultural challenges in mental health situations. The deaf team member will usually be able to establish rapport and a sense of reassurance with the deaf client, and can relay questions and responses in language that is most accessible to the client in the situation. Depending on their role and training, they may also be able to provide hearing personnel with additional information about matters of culture, language, educational and social background, and deaf support services that the interpreter would not be in a position to advise on.

Legal

Legal interpreting is high stakes work that calls for a solid foundation of interpreting experience and knowledge of legal contexts. Settings for legal interpreting include police stations, courts of various levels and types, disputes tribunals, legal offices, probation, detention and prison facilities. In criminal justice situations, sign language interpreters are employed when a deaf person is arrested, charged with a crime, is the victim of a crime, or provides evidence as a witness to a crime. Interpreters also work in civil law situations when a deaf person brings or defends a civil case in a court, disputes tribunal, family court, or seeks advice from a lawyer.

Given the specialised and important nature of this work, legal interpreters should ideally have training in legal procedures, offences, legal terminology and discourse, and techniques appropriate to court interpreting. The current reality is that sign language interpreters working in legal settings in Australia and New Zealand typically are not assessed for legal interpreting competence, but have a general professional level interpreting qualification (NAATI Professional Interpreter/DipSLI), and some contextual knowledge developed through experience and limited professional development. Two useful publications dealing with issues and techniques in legal interpreting for deaf people are: Brennan and Brown (2004) and Russell and Hale (2008).

Employers

Interpreters are usually paid by the justice system, and are considered 'officers of the court', or, in a police interview, an employee of the police. Sometimes defence counsel in a trial will hire an interpreter to work exclusively for their client, particularly when there are deaf parties on opposing sides of proceedings (prosecution and defence, or in a family dispute). An interpreter hired privately by the defence is not considered an officer of the court, but part of the defence team, and usually provides interpreting and translation between the deaf client and their counsel outside the courtroom. Irrespective of the employer, the appropriate role for any legal interpreter is one of detached neutrality.

Accuracy

Neutrality (impartiality) and accuracy are the cornerstones of a legal interpreter's ethics. Before beginning any work in a courtroom, interpreters swear an oath that they will, to the best of their ability, interpret faithfully (accurately). Interpreting accurately means without addition, alteration or omission (the meaning, the whole meaning and nothing but the meaning) even if the content is uncomfortable for the interpreter, such as obscene language, sexual reference or questions that seem difficult to interpret. Faithful interpretation also conveys the speaker's delivery, such as hesitations, self-correction, emphasis, tone, and register – which are important to the overall impression formed by 'listeners' in a police interview or a courtroom, especially a judge or jury. Errors made by speakers, either intentionally or unintentionally, should never be corrected by an interpreter in court. If the interpreter realises that they themselves have made an error of interpretation, they should advise the judge as soon as possible so that the record, or the communication itself, can be clarified.

Accuracy is equally critical in police situations during arrest and interview procedures. Communication in police situations can form the basis of charges and the prosecution case presented in court; if errors are made at this stage, the risk of miscarriage of justice is high and the interpreter may be culpable (legally responsible) for their part in any miscommunication that comes to light. An experienced legal interpreter suggests:

> Go and observe a lot before you go into court or police work. These are areas that interpreters need to have the fear of god before they go into it! I feel sorry for interpreters in police interviews because I've seen where the interview video has been taken into court and just picked to pieces. Someone will say, 'That was a wrong interpretation, what they should have done was x, y, z.'

The standard practice of videorecording of police interviews is both a protection and a risk for the interpreter as the accuracy of their interpretation is open to scrutiny. This places an increased level of ethical responsibility on individual interpreters to monitor their own performance. The expected standard of accuracy and level of accountability is extremely high in legal interpreting contexts. One strategy to consider when interpreting extremely complex or critical information, is to use a consecutive approach. Research on ASL interpreters in court found that they made fewer errors in this mode (Russell 2002).

Impartiality

Even beyond the interpreting task, interpreters are expected to conduct themselves in a way that maintains their impartiality in the eyes of the justice system. A neutral interpreter is seen as more trustworthy in providing the unbiased interpretation appropriate to the administration of the law. In fact, the 'invisible' conduit model of professional interpreting evolved from the Nuremburg trials of war criminals following World War II, where interpreters played a major role. These interpreters were expected to maintain a strict standard of detachment to eliminate allegations of political bias in the court proceedings. These origins of the interpreting profession still shape the legal system's expectation that legal interpreters should function essentially as a conduit. In reality, the interface of language, power, culture, and interpersonal communication that characterises legal situations makes an interpreter's task far from machine-like.[8]

A potential challenge to impartiality is familiarity with the deaf client from previous assignments or social contact. Deaf clients may naturally see the familiar face of an interpreter as an ally in a stressful situation. Explaining the limits of the interpreting role and the ethics of impartiality and confidentiality to the client as soon as there is an opportunity is a better option than just presenting a 'cold shoulder'. Although it is very important to establish that you can communicate with the deaf client before going into a courtroom, it is also important to be seen to be impartial in legal settings, so it is advisable to distance yourself from the client as well as lawyers and police during waiting times, keeping any conversation minimal and away from the case in hand. Casual conversation can arouse suspicion or anxiety in a deaf person who is unsure what is going on, or in legal personnel who may see you signing with the deaf client and cannot judge the content. Minimise these interactions, and tell any observing parties the gist of your conversations in the other language if they look curious.

Clarifying the role

The role of interpreters in courts is not set out in any one document, and often legal cases which have been interpreted contribute to the definition of the role. In Australia a case involving a deaf woman with an Auslan interpreter (*Gradidge v Grace Bros* (1988))[9] set a precedent for all Australian interpreters and courtrooms to follow. In that case the judge told the interpreter to stop signing while he and the barristers were having a discussion. The interpreter, feeling that it was morally wrong to deny the deaf client access to this interaction, continued to interpret into Auslan, effectively

---

8   The complexities of interpreters' task in mediating courtroom interaction is discussed in more detail by Laster and Taylor (1994) and Gentile and Ozolins (1996).

9   The transcript of the judgment in this case can be found in the *Federal Law Reports*: *Gradidge v Grace Bros Pty Ltd* (1988) 93 FLR 414, and is an interesting decision to read.

disobeying the judge's order. The matter was adjourned and referred to the New South Wales Court of Appeal for a determination about this aspect of the interpreter's role. Fortunately that court found that a deaf person, or anyone else without access to the spoken English of the court, was entitled to have all audible spoken interaction interpreted. Because the interpreter is usually the only person able to communicate directly with the deaf person in a legal situation, and because justice system personnel and clients often lack awareness of an interpreter's role boundaries, interpreters may be asked to provide advice, cultural information, or emotional and practical support. Interpreters need to be assertive in clarifying their role or declining additional responsibilities.

Should an interpreter ever intervene in court?

Legal processes depend heavily on the strategic use of language. When more than one language and culture is involved, the interpreter takes on a crucial role as the only person who understands both sides of the communication. In this sense interpretation has a potentially significant impact on the evidence presented and the outcomes; this is one reason why the interpreter's role is so strictly defined. But what should an interpreter do when they are aware that meaning has fallen through a gap between two languages?

In general, it is the barrister's responsibility to clear up misunderstandings, rather than the interpreter's. In a situation where the interpreter is the *only* person with the linguistic or cultural insight to detect a breakdown of understanding, they should intervene by respectfully seeking permission from the judge to explain the problem.

Although this sounds clear in principle, in practice it leaves the interpreter with considerable responsibility for determining when communication has 'broken down' or 'false assumptions' are being made – which can be more subtle than obvious. As in other interpreting situations, training, experience, and self-monitoring skills are necessary to making good judgment calls about when it is absolutely necessary to intervene, and how to do so without overstepping the boundaries of the interpreter's role or unduly disrupting legal protocols. Any intervention must be directed (politely) through the judge or magistrate ('Your honour').

Even when an interpreter is aware that a deaf client lacks understanding of the legal process, it is not their role to shepherd the client through the justice system. The interpreter can suggest that a deaf client seek support from Deaf community advocates or other legal personnel if necessary.

Preparation

Interpreters can prepare for a legal assignment (in particular, a defended hearing) by asking for access to documents relating to the case, for example, charges, summary of facts, diagrams, written statements to be read out as evidence in court. As with any interpreting work, the opportunity to meet with deaf clients prior to the interview or court appearance will help determine the appropriate target language style and register. One way to become familiar with court and tribunal settings is to visit them before undertaking legal interpreting assignments, to see how the process works without the pressure of being in the 'hot seat'. Any opportunity to watch a more experienced sign language interpreter in a legal context is invaluable.

Emotional factors

Working in legal situations takes self-confidence and emotional stamina. Deaf clients in legal situations tend to feel stressed, and generally find the proceedings unfamiliar and intimidating. People in courtrooms and police cells are often in distressed and depressing circumstances, and can behave aggressively. The emotional impact of these environments can unnerve an unprepared interpreter. Another potential source of tension for legal interpreters is the knowledge that even competent interpretation does not guarantee a 'just' outcome for a minority language speaker, due to social and cultural disadvantages in society and within the justice system.[10] Peer mentoring or formal supervision is important in helping interpreters to address technical, ethical, and emotional pressures faced in legal contexts.

Legal discourse

In adversarial legal discourse all evidence must be presented and challenged through questioning; in this process, language is used tactically to control the presentation of information and character, and to achieve certain outcomes in a case. Broadly speaking, two important types of discourse can be identified (described by Quynh-Du 1996: 105) in which communication is either for the purpose of:

- Genuinely seeking or exchanging information with another party (for example, police or lawyer interviews, judge addressing a jury or giving instructions); or

- Playing out a drama to create an impression on other parties (for example, giving evidence in chief, cross-examination, re-examination in a trial).

The experience of cross-examination can be confusing for witnesses trying to give a straightforward account of their experience; communication proceeds in an unnatural and disjointed way, in order to conform to rules about questioning and because the cross-examining lawyer is aiming to discredit the witness' account. Adding interpretation across languages and cultures to

---

10   Brennan and Brown (2004) report a study of barriers within the justice system faced by Deaf people and interpreters in the UK, which is relevant to Australia/New Zealand contexts. Sources of miscommunication and injustice that commonly befall Deaf people (and other minority groups) in legal interactions are discussed in Lucas (2003).

this mix works against the grain; interpreters can be seen as impediments to legal strategy, since they filter all communication, removing some of the original speaker's control of language by possibly clarifying, re-phrasing, or altering the emphasis of what has been said. Studying the structure of legal discourse, and different types of questioning in particular, is valuable preparation for legal interpreters.

The next section covers some sign language-specific issues pertinent to legal translation.

Translation issues

Differences between the structures of English and Auslan/NZSL present a number of specific translation challenges, including the following examples:

- *Accurate representation of spatial, physical realities in signed languages:* English speakers may describe location and movement with phrases such as 'next to', 'on the other side', or 'approach', whereas in signed languages it is usual to represent position or the direction of movement realistically, through the arrangement and movement of signs in space. If a question is asked in English, 'Did someone approach you?' and the interpreter signs a person approaching from the front (in a face-to-face orientation) when in fact someone had approached from the right hand side, this may elicit an inappropriate, *'no'*, or a correction (to an apparently straightforward yes/no question) from the deaf witness. A similar difficulty arises with verbs such as 'punch', 'touch', and 'penetrate' which are used deliberately in English with as little context as possible, to avoid leading questions or allegations, for example, 'Did he touch you?' In order to transfer meaning accurately, the interpreter needs to either choose a 'neutral' location for the verb (which may or may not exist or be understood), apply prior knowledge of the situation, or seek clarification of spatial/physical details from the questioner. None of these strategies is ideal, but may be a necessary compromise.

- *Untranslatable reference to persons and places:* In the Deaf community, name signs are sometimes used without knowledge of a person's full legal name. In a court or police setting, an interpreter might encounter unfamiliar name signs in a deaf person's evidence, or even recognise a name sign, but not know the person's spoken name. Familiar places, such as a workplace, can be identified in sign language by physical appearance or a partial English reference, for example: 'FACTORY, BUILDING YELLOW, NAME W-R ...' Personal pronouns in signed languages can also present unknown information since they do not indicate gender, which is required for translation into English 'he' or 'she' (and could be very important in a legal context). In this case, the interpreter needs to either use a gender-neutral alternative for example, 'a person', or seek permission from the judge to clarify with the signer exactly who they are referring to.

- *Generic versus specific words*: Auslan and NZSL use fewer 'category' terms than English, which creates translation dilemmas in the legal context. Criminal charges are labelled by generic terms that cover a range of possibilities, such as 'weapon', 'assault', 'disorderly conduct', 'sexual assault', 'resist arrest'. A signer would tend to express these concepts with signs that specify the particular circumstances for example, knife/gun/bat/bottle/cigarette (weapon), punch/stab/kick/slap (assault), or drunk/fight/swear (disorderly). An interpreter has to decide between different options: giving a general meaning by listing a range of examples (which may be irrelevant or leading), using contextual knowledge to select a specific sign (which could be incorrect), choosing one 'representative' sign and using it with generalised meaning (which may not be recognised as relevant by the deaf person), or fingerspelling (which avoids the other problems, but may be meaningless to the deaf client). There is often no simple solution to such linguistic differences, and counsel or a judge can be informed if the dilemma is interfering with understanding or accuracy of communication.

- *Mismatch of question and answer form*: Sometimes the grammar of an English question requires re-structuring into sign language in a way that produces the opposite of the expected answer, which the interpreter then has to adapt to match the original question. For example, 'Is it true to say that you did not know about their plan to sell the cannabis?' could be translated as a leading question – BEFORE, YOU DON'T-KNOW ABOUT THEIR PLAN SELL MARIJUANA, RIGHT?; or as a simple yes/no question – THAT TIME, YOU KNOW ABOUT THEIR PLAN SELL MARIJUANA? Assuming the client was unaware of the plan, either of these translations is likely to elicit a response in the negative. Since the original question was framed as, 'Is it true to say ...?', the negative response either needs to be interpreted fully as, 'No, I didn't know about the plan', or 'Yes, that is true'. The second version may be accurate in meaning, but if people in the courtroom see a deaf person shaking or nodding their head, and hear the interpreter voicing the opposite response, this risks confusion and/or doubt about the quality of the interpretation. Sometimes this 'mismatch' is an unavoidable translation choice, but should be weighed up in terms of its impact, and may need to be explained if challenged by the court.

Religious

Due to the multi-cultural nature of the Australian and New Zealand communities, the contexts for religious interpreting are diverse, and not yet well documented. The details and examples given in this section are predominantly based on Christian forms of worship that generate the most interpreting assignments, however, many of the principles and general features apply to other faiths and practices as well.

Some interpreters work on a regular, committed basis for a particular congregation and build up familiarity with the language, referents, and perspective of their particular denomination. They are often members of the congregation and share the faith, which helps with contextual knowledge, processing meaning and establishing rapport with their deaf clients (in many churches, deaf members of the congregation along with interpreters have developed a set of agreed signs for specific religious terms and concepts). Other interpreters are booked for one-off religious events, for example, weddings and funerals. In these situations the interpreter has a more 'outsider' status, and can feel more challenged by religious content and language.

Common scenarios for interpreters who work regularly in religious contexts include:

• Weekly services;

• Special services, for example, Easter, Yom Kippur, Saints' days, Ramadan, Christmas;

• Prayer meetings and bible study groups;

• Baptisms, christenings, bar/bat mitzvahs and confirmations;

• Weddings;

• Funerals;

• Religious study courses and seminars.

Religious discourse

The style of liturgy (form of worship) in Christian churches ranges from traditional (for example, Roman Catholic and Anglican) to contemporary (for example, Pentecostal). The traditional churches tend to follow more set (frozen) texts with ritual responses from the congregation and hymns that are well established (Borrmann 2004). Traditional and modern style churches often use different versions of the Bible, from the King James Bible with its old English, to very contemporary translations such as the Message Bible (Peterson 1993), either of which can be equally challenging to translate.

Pentecostal or other contemporary style churches tend to use a more informal register and include modern Christian songs. Their biblical teachings use contemporary images and references to the everyday lives of the congregation, and are delivered more in the style of motivational seminars; matching the desired impact of the delivery is an important aspect of interpreting here.

Ceremonies: 'hatches, matches and dispatches'

Christenings, weddings and funerals are usually more formal in register than regular church services. For marriage and christening ceremonies especially, exact details and scripts of the service are normally pre-planned which allows the interpreter to prepare thoroughly. Funerals tend to come at short notice, so it is good to be familiar with commonly sung hymns such as Psalm 23, 'The Lord is My Shepherd', 'Amazing Grace' and 'How Great Thou Art'. Popular readings for weddings include the 'Love Chapter' from 1 Corinthians 13, or 'On Marriage' from *The Prophet*, by Kahlil Gibran. Both weddings and funerals frequently include poems and songs that need prior translation.

Eulogies and tributes at funerals cover personal history, mentioning the names of family and friends, locations, places of work, hobbies, important events and achievements. Where possible, find out about the person's life history to avoid mistakes in interpretation. One experienced interpreter heard the term 'bowling', and used the sign for 'indoor bowling', only to learn later with embarrassment that the deceased was actually a cricket bowler. Another interpreter misread the fingerspelled names of the deceased's hearing family members who were sitting nearby and were distracted by hearing their names mangled. The funeral director is usually a good first point of contact to seek out preparation materials for the service.

Speeches at wedding receptions can be a minefield of personal information and innuendo that may be familiar or hilarious to the wedding guests, but make no sense to the interpreter. Finding the speakers (usually between the service and the formal part of the reception) and asking for a brief run-down, especially jokes and anecdotes, is a wise precaution.

Positioning

The configuration of different religious events varies, but a basic rule of thumb, as for any platform interpreting, is to stand near hearing speakers and any other visual input or actions that deaf participants need to see. Obviously a more expansive, public-speaking style of signing is also appropriate to this context.

At a funeral, it is also preferable to stay close to the speaker, as deaf people want to see the speaker's emotion, as well as the interpreter; however, a key consideration is where the main target audience are seated (for example, the deaf family members of the deceased). You need to ensure that you are visible to them, even if this means positioning yourself further from the speaker. Try to keep a respectful distance from the casket. The interpreter may be expected to stay on for refreshments after the funeral service, as this can be an important time for people to express condolences to the family of the deceased.

For weddings and christenings, ensure that you attend any rehearsals – seeing where the celebrant and the main participants will stand and move from and to. That way, you can negotiate where to position yourself so that you are visible to the main participants as well as the rest of the congregation. Choice of attire needs to be considered – discuss colour or style preferences with the clients, but aim to dress respectfully. For an outdoor wedding, consider where the sun will be at that time of day, and try and avoid standing with it behind or just above you. It is also worth considering how to control hair and clothing in a strong wind. There is considerable choreographing of movement and communication to be worked out in advance.

Demeanour

The interpreter's overall demeanour at funerals and weddings should complement the event; conveying a sense of grace, poise and an emotional tone that is appropriate to the atmosphere and dignity of the ceremony. Emotions often run high at funerals and weddings, and even the most professional interpreter can be affected. Some strategies that we have used for regaining composure include breathing slowly and deeply through your nose for a moment, looking at your shoes, diverting your eyes from any crying audience members, or visualising a calm scene. There is often a fine line between showing empathy and exposing personal emotion that creates extra stress or distraction for the participants, and interferes with the interpretation.[11]

Specialist knowledge

Whether a church member or not, an excellent command of English and sign language and strong translation instincts are needed, as are performance or platform interpreting skills. Knowledge of the language, content and symbolism of the authoritative text used by a particular church or religion is essential to making sense of readings, liturgy, and references in sermons, for example:

- Christian church – the Holy Bible (and sometimes knowledge of Latin);

- Jewish synagogue – knowledge of Hebrew, the Tanakh and the Talmud;

- Mosque – knowledge of Arabic, the Koran, the Haddith, the Torah, Psalms of David, and Gospel of Jesus;

- Jehovah's Witnesses Hall – New World Translation of the Holy Scriptures and Watch Tower publications;

- Church of Jesus Christ of Latter-day Saints – The Holy Bible (King James Version), Book of Mormon, Doctrine and Covenants, and Pearl of Great Price.

---

11   A useful discussion of the fine line between empathy and over-involvement, in relation to any interpreting situation, is presented in Harvey (2003).

Remuneration

With regard to compensation for religious interpreting, there is no standard scenario. It is quite common for interpreters to donate interpreting services for weddings or christenings if asked as a friend of the deaf family, while in other cases families will book and pay for an interpreter directly or through an interpreting agency. At funerals, the interpreter is generally paid by an interpreting agency or by the family but where there is no funding offered, they may choose to do this work voluntarily. Most regular church interpreting is done on a voluntary basis as a contribution to the church community.

Conference

Conference interpreting is usually performed by highly educated and experienced interpreters. This domain is certainly challenging in terms of content, and is seen as high status work, however it is important to acknowledge that community interpreting can be equally demanding in other ways. Sign language interpreters in Australia and New Zealand do not work exclusively as conference interpreters because there is not sufficient work available in this region, however, the types of assignments available include:

• Deaf-specific conferences – for example, World Federation of the Deaf Congresses (WFD), International Congresses for Educators of the Deaf (ICED), Deaflympics ceremonies, Australian national deafness conferences and symposiums.

• Professional conferences – for example, academic, organisational.

• Political events – for example, party political launches, union rallies.

• Public events – for example, corporation AGMs.

Conference interpreting careers are more available to spoken language interpreters, who can choose to specialise in conference interpreting, and even in particular types of conferences – such as political, trade, scientific, academic.

Working conditions and profile – In conference settings, spoken language interpreters typically work simultaneously, based in a booth at the back of the conference venue; they are heard (usually via headphones) but not seen. This is where the initial image of the 'conduit' model came from: interpreters in a 'black box' invisibly relaying information to multiple delegates with minimal impact on the interaction. In some cases, where only a few delegates need interpretation, an interpreter may work consecutively, using a technique called chucotage (whispering in the ear, or into a microphone linked to a headset system). This technique is sometimes seen in television coverage of high profile political meetings where interpreters are working.

For signed language interpreters, the majority of conference work involves interpreting from English into Auslan/NZSL. For deaf-specific conferences there is usually more of a balance of deaf and hearing presenters, and therefore interpretation in both language directions. When interpreting from English into a signed language, interpreters are usually positioned at the front of the conference venue and are therefore highly visible. It is easier for sign language interpreters to adopt a more conduit approach in this context, as they are usually positioned on one side of the stage and have little direct contact with the speaker/s or audience. Sometimes interpreters are booked specifically because deaf people will be attending; at other times they are booked to provide access just in case deaf people turn up, or because the event will be televised.

Preparation

Wherever possible request that copies of all papers are made available prior to the conference. When papers are not available, interpreters can still prepare by doing general research on the topics to be presented (for example, via internet searches). Sometimes it is possible to meet with the presenter beforehand, to clarify any questions arising from the preparation, and to get a sense of the style of the presenter and their pace. If the presenter is deaf, it's useful to meet with them to gauge their signing style, and to check their sign choices for any specialist terminology.

Traditional welcome

Sign language interpreters working in Australia often interpret at conferences which begin with a 'Welcome to country' or 'Traditional welcome' ceremony. This is conducted by a representative of the traditional Aboriginal owners, giving their blessing for the event to take place on their land. When interpreting for a traditional welcome, interpreters need to be familiar with the name and spelling of the relevant indigenous nation, and the protocols of the ceremony. Conference interpreters in New Zealand are often involved in interpreting a Māori welcome (powhiri). This is discussed separately in Chapter 9.

Positioning

When a presentation is spoken, one interpreter is usually on stage, as close to the presenter and/or screen as can be practically negotiated. Where possible it helps to meet with whoever is stage managing the event beforehand and check that sufficient lighting will be available on the interpreter, even when the house lights need to be dimmed for any audiovisual presentations. If PowerPoint, overheads or other visual aids are being used, the interpreter needs to be in a position to see them (at least in their peripheral vision), as well as allowing the deaf audience to take in the interpreter and the screen in their sight-line. The team interpreter is generally seated directly in front of the working interpreter, and with a clear sightline to their colleague, and the screen, in case prompting (in sign) is needed.

When the presentation is signed, interpreters are usually seated together in the audience, directly in front of the presenter, with clear eye-lines to their face and hands. In this situation, interpreters use a microphone, and should check that the sound system is working beforehand.

Presentation

Conference interpreting situations tend to be formal events where the inter-preter needs to present themselves professionally and in keeping with the other people on stage. It is useful to have an 'interpreting suit' available for these occasions. Keep in mind that if your image is being projected onto a screen (as often happens in large conferences) any distracting features like jewellery or unkempt hair will be magnified.

Performance

Performance interpreting generally refers to the signed translation of a dramatic text performed in English, for example, stage plays, musicals or concert songs. In this language direction, interpreters are up on stage, in the spotlight and very conspicuous. Occasionally interpreters do 'perform' in the opposite direction, interpreting a signed performance (for example, a deaf theatre production) into English, but they are usually heard and not seen. This section will focus on English to Auslan/NZ renditions, because of the particular skills, preparation and presentation required. There are few opportunities for interpreters to work in this area and not everyone wants to, but for those who do, the chance to express yourself artistically (and the adrenaline rush) can be addictive.

Process

Performance interpreting differs from most other contexts in one key respect – there is usually time to prepare a 'translation' of the source text. Although translation and interpreting are usually seen as separate processes, prepared performance interpreting can be seen as a hybrid of both; interpreters usually prepare a translation, but the actual performance is an interpretation because it occurs live and in real time (Turner and Pollitt 2002; Leneham 2005). For stage plays and musicals, the director, actors and singers are generally obliged to follow a script or lyrics as written, so the source text is fixed, predictable, and available ahead of time. One temptation therefore is to start as soon as possible, preparing a signed interpretation from the written text, however this is often a waste of time. Scripts and lyrics cannot be effectively translated until they are in a 'live' form, that is, the actual performance (or rehearsal) is recorded on video/DVD/CD. This is because you need to know how the performers have 'interpreted' the source text first; you need to work off their version. They will have made decisions about the pace (particularly important), subtext, emotional tone, light and shade, character details, and how the characters relate to each other and the audience – all of which can impact on the message, even though the words of the script have not been changed.

Research

One thing the original script is useful for, is to check the meanings of individual words or references that may be unfamiliar (and sometimes, to figure out what the singer or actor is actually saying). Often playwrights and songwriters incorporate layers of meaning into their texts, so it can take time to analyse and understand what the intended message really is. Once you know how much time the actors are taking for each utterance, have a clearer understanding of the meaning of each line and how it relates to the full text, you can start working on the translation. Some interpreters write a rough 'gloss' (written signs) alongside the English script, as a record of their translation ideas.

Teamwork

Where there are a number of characters in a play, there are usually at least two interpreters employed who then share the interpreting load. Both interpreters need to feel comfortable working together, since their delivery needs to be synchronised tightly, and they spend long hours rehearsing and supporting each other. Although it might seem logical to allocate characters according to gender, or to just allocate half to each interpreter, the script needs to be analysed at a discourse level. To ensure that one interpreter doesn't end up signing to themselves for most of the night, it is important to pay attention to what the main relationships are, whether there is a central character, who ends up talking to whom, and how often. Character allocations may need to vary from scene to scene, depending on who features in each scene.

Once the character allocation is determined, each interpreter needs to practise their translations of each line so that they are synchronised to start and finish with the actor's delivery. Otherwise, the interpreters will overlap on stage, which is very confusing and ineffective for the deaf audience. This often requires interpreters to 'prune' their translations to get to the most essential message within the time available and without rushing their delivery, often by moving to very free interpretation choices. Another issue related to characters, is how to avoid using fingerspelling of names (too hard for the audience to see) when characters are referring to each other, either on or off stage. Obvious name signs for each character can be created, but somehow need to be introduced so that the audience knows who's who. One way of getting feedback on the effectiveness of the translation is to video a rehearsal, and then play it back without sound (a very humbling process).

This will reveal any sections that seemed like good ideas but need more work to make visual sense. Another common practise is to ask for feedback during rehearsal, from a deaf consultant.

Songs

The translation of songs follows a similar process to that for theatre scripts, but also needs to incorporate rhythm, and sometimes choreography. The interpreter has the task of devising a translation that not only makes visual sense, but can also reflect the beat of the music. Where more than one interpreter is involved, the interpreters need to work out if the signed rendition should be produced identically (in stereo) or divided up according to the lyric structure.

Style

Interpreters on stage are often at a distance from the deaf audience, so, just like the actors, need to 'project' their signing via sharp and clear sign production and by expanding their personal signing space. Often, in preparing the translation, theatre interpreters will choose to use double-handed or more dramatic signs over smaller or initialised ones. Theatre interpreting also requires interpreters to have strong role-shift and characterisation skills, so that characters can be clearly distinguished and their moods and emotions can be accurately portrayed. Although interpreters need to be careful not to take over the show, innate acting skills are a valuable asset.

Stamina

For theatre productions, interpreters must stand in the one location for the full show, switching quickly between characters, under the public pressure of the spotlight. Although adrenaline helps, it is physically and mentally demanding work. Doing rehearsals of the whole play standing up, can build up stamina prior to the night of the performance.

Position and technical issues

Generally, interpreters are located on stage to the far left or right of the actors/ performers. The specific location will depend on: the constraints of the theatre and set design, the willingness of the director (and performers) to allow the interpretation to be incorporated into the show, and the location of the deaf audience members. Usually it is a compromise, negotiated with the stage manager as soon as possible once rehearsals have begun. Lighting for the interpreters needs to cover the full range of their signing space, and to be left on for any auditory cues (for example, voices on or off stage) even when the rest of the stage is in darkness. Another consideration is the relative positioning of interpreters to each other, that is, who stands on the left or right side in the pair. Sometimes this is determined by character stage location (if consistent or dominant on either side throughout the performance), or whether the interpreters are left or right handed signers (especially for any signed songs).

Some theatre companies are now using captioning technology for stage productions, as in the opera, where translation of dialogue is displayed above the stage. These captions are called sur-titles, and allow deaf and hearing impaired audience members to follow the original text in English as it is played out. This innovation could mean that the art of theatre interpreting has a limited future, relegated to performances by smaller mainstream theatre companies and Deaf theatre company productions.

Summary

The various interpreting contexts canvassed in this chapter highlight the need for interpreters to build up a repertoire of contextual knowledge and language skills wide and deep enough to accommodate the demands of diverse topics and clients. This overview has provided a brief and generalised introduction to the dynamics of communication and content in each of these settings; some areas clearly require more specialised study and training than others in order to provide consumers with a high standard of interpreting access. The issues highlighted in this chapter will at least give interpreters a general framework for approaching assignments and assessing their readiness to work within each of these contexts. For those interested in studying these areas in more depth, we have provided a list of context-specific recommended readings, included as Appendix A.

The next two chapters extend this guide to work contexts with a focus on more specialised or less often encountered interpreting settings, skills and client groups.

Thought questions

1. Education:

(a) As the regular interpreter for a mainstreamed primary school student aged seven years, what might be some additional responsibilities within your role? (Think of duties that would not be part of your role with a tertiary student, for example).

(b) Managing relationships within an educational context is an important consideration for the interpreter. Why is this so?

(c) What are some different ways that an interpreter can improve their ability to deal with the content matter in educational interpreting?

2.   Social service agencies:

(a)   Of the common social service settings listed in the chapter, which ones have you had dealings with before? How could you familiarise yourself with the ones you have no personal experience of?

3.   Employment:

(a)   Create a discourse map for a job interview, where a 30-year-old deaf woman (mother of two young children) is applying for a mail sorter's job (shift-work) at a postal service.

(b)   You are booked to interpret a two-day training session for a tertiary qualified deaf employee starting work at the tax department. The training will be with their work team. How will you prepare for this job, and what demand sources should you anticipate?

4.   Deaf professionals:

(a)   From a deaf professional's point of view, try to identify three desirable attributes for an interpreter working in an ongoing role in their workplace.

(b)   Can you think of one potential advantage and one challenge of working as a 'designated interpreter' alongside a deaf professional?

5.   Medical:

(a)   If you became ill overseas, and had to take an interpreter with you to see a doctor, how would you want the interpreter to behave? Make a list of qualities, skills, behaviours you would want in this person.

(b)   From a medical practitioner's point of view, what do you think they would expect and need from an interpreter in a consultation with a deaf patient?

6.   Mental health:

(a)   Why is the impact of an interpreter in a mental health situation potentially so significant? Explain at least two reasons.

(b)   In terms of interpreting accuracy, what are some particular considerations to be aware of in the mental health context?

7.   Legal:

(a)   To interpret in legal contexts, what kinds of knowledge and skills would you consider essential? (Considering deaf clients as well as the legal setting.)

(b) What are two crucial ethics in the legal context? For each one, think of an example of a problem that might arise for the interpreter in maintaining that ethic.

(c) Language is an important tool in all legal proceedings. Can you think of an example of where an interpreter's choice of translation could have an important impact on altering the communication?

8. Religious and ceremonial:

(a) Based on your personal experience and knowledge of religious contexts, predict what you think would be challenges for you in interpreting a religious service.

(b) Imagine this scenario: at a funeral of a hearing relative of a deaf person, the celebrant invites people to come forward and make spontaneous tributes to the deceased. A gentleman comes forward and announces that he will recite a poem. The poem is in rhyming verse, is quite lengthy (about three minutes), and is recited rather rapidly. The interpreter makes a decision not to interpret this, given the difficulty of impromptu translation, instead explaining to the five deaf people present that a poem is being recited, and that it is difficult to translate the meaning. The deaf relative says to the interpreter, 'Don't worry, no need to sign it'. Discuss the pros and cons of the interpreter's decision, and decide whether you think this is a reasonable course of action in this situation.

(c) In religious (and other contexts), is it possible to interpret anything and everything simultaneously?

(d) In a ceremonial situation such as a wedding (decide whether it is traditional-religious, or modern-secular), would you expect to use a more free or more literal style of interpretation? Discuss the reasons for your response.

9. Conference:

(a) If you were asked to interpret a conference, what working conditions (before and during the conference) would you need to ensure to make your performance as effective as possible? Brainstorm as many factors as you can.

10. Performance:

(a) What would attract you to the opportunity to do performance interpreting?

(b) What would daunt you about the prospect of performance interpreting?

(c) If you were interpreting a play, list at least four aspects of your preparation.

CHAPTER 8

SPECIALISED INTERPRETING SKILLS

This chapter looks at the specialised techniques and knowledge needed by interpreters working in situations that have an additional dimension to the communication, over and above 'everyday' interpreting circumstances. Some of these knowledge areas are related to specific consumer groups, while others involve technology or special communication techniques. In general, the situations and *skills* covered in this chapter are less frequently encountered than those described in Chapter 7. For each of the following topics, we provide an overview of the particular features and challenges of working in this area:

- Team interpreting;
- Telephone interpreting;
- Video (remote) interpreting;
- Relay interpreting and deaf interpreters;
- Working with minimal language clients who have 'minimal language competence';
- Working with deafblind clients;
- Oral interpreting;
- International Sign interpreting.

Team interpreting

Team interpreting (also called teaming) means working with an interpreting partner, so that each interpreter alternates between responsibility for active interpreting and responsibility for providing support during 'off' times. The chief reasons for team interpreting are:

(a) To reduce the risk of overuse injury (or OOS) to interpreters who undertake prolonged assignments (more than one to two hours); and

(b) To reduce the effects of interpreter fatigue on the quality of the interpretation.

Occupational Overuse Syndrome (OOS) is a particular hazard for interpreters who spend prolonged periods doing monologic (one-way) interpreting (as discussed further in chapter ten). In settings where this type of interpreting is common (education, conference and extended meetings), team interpreting is a particularly valuable technique for reducing physical and mental stress.

Research has shown that mental fatigue in interpreters dramatically reduces accuracy and 'intactness' of the TL output. Moser-Mercer, Kunzli and Korac (1998), for example, found (for spoken language interpreters) that the more prolonged the interpreting task, the higher the number of errors, with omissions being the most frequent. They recommend shorter turns to be taken by conference interpreters to ensure a consistently high quality of output. Other research has indicated that a period of 20 to 25 minutes is the optimum span for interpreter concentration, before fatigue begins to affect the message. For sign language interpreting, team interpreters generally switch every 20 to 30 minutes. In some situations, where the material is very dense and/or the team has been working for a long time, they may choose to shorten the turnaround time to 15 minutes – to keep fresh.

When a team works well together, they support one another and enhance each other's interpretations. Although it might appear that one interpreter is 'on' while the other is 'off', both interpreters are working. The interpreter who is 'passive' is still responsible for supporting their partner's work, rather than switching off completely. This means being alert to 'prompt' for any information that is missed or unclear to the active interpreter. Effective cooperation within interpreting teams is essential to maintaining the quality of the interpreted message and the trust of the deaf consumers (Russell 2008). Strategies for effective team interpreting, before, during and after the assignment, include:

- Deciding where to sit/ stand in relation to each other, ensuring clear sightlines to each other if feeding or prompting with signs is required. Usually the team sits adjacent to each other if they are working from Auslan/NZSL into English or if they are in a round-table meeting (where constant position changes would be too disruptive). Where the team is interpreting from English into Auslan/NZSL in a more formal setting, the active interpreter usually stands in view of their team interpreter and deaf audience (as discussed in monologic interpreting in Chapter 6)

- In more formal settings – allocating responsibility for checking lighting and sound, or taking the lead for liaison with the organisers.

- Deciding how to divide up the work. In some meeting scenarios, it may be more effective for one interpreter to focus on English to Auslan/NZSL interpretation, while the other interpreter is responsible for the other language direction. The interpreters can also switch these language directions at agreed times, to even up the workload.

- Deciding who goes first. This can depend on who has most familiarity with topic or speaker. Where one interpreter is more confident or experienced than their co-worker, they may start first, to set up concepts and sign choices for the less experienced partner to follow, or, if the presentation begins with more straightforward housekeeping and introductions, the less experienced interpreter may prefer to start off and warm up.

- Discussing how best to give and receive prompts when information is missed. This requires each interpreter knowing what form(s) of prompt they prefer to receive and how they tend to ask for it – what we do and what we think we do are often different things (Cokely and Hawkins 2003). Prompting strategies need to be learned through practice and feedback. For Auslan/NZSL to English teaming (side by side), requests can include: leaning, tapping, silence, direct request, or even passing the microphone. Prompts (or feeds) in this language direction can be done by: whispering, signing, one word or a whole sentence, reference to written scripts etc. For English to Auslan/NZSL teaming, requests can include: eyegaze to interpreter or direct request (signed or mouthed). Possible prompts in this language direction include: signing, fingerspelling, reference to an AV source, one sign or a whole sentence.

- Using note-taking to assist each other, with the passive interpreter writing down items that are difficult to retain, such as names and large numbers, for the active interpreter to glance at and retrieve (or be fed) without interrupting the flow of the interpretation. If both interpreters are willing, the passive interpreter can also take notes about the interpretation for constructive feedback at the end of the session.

- Negotiating the length of active interpreting segments and when to change over; the passive interpreter usually keeps time, but the active interpreter usually decides the precise moment for changing over (that is, when they have finished interpreting the current utterance or concept). Many interpreters prefer to have some warning before the actual change time, so it is worth advising your team interpreter what works for you, for example, one minute's notice, or an agreed signal to let you know to start winding up your turn (so you become alert to logical places to stop).

- Agreeing how changeovers will be 'choreographed' to minimise disruption to other participants (that is, not tripping over each other or nudging each other off the spot). This is easier when both interpreters are seated together. Where interpreters are signing and the swap is more prominent, it is useful to agree on the 'move' beforehand – depending on the physical distance between the two interpreters. Whether the relieving team member moves into position alongside their active colleague on a podium, or steps up from a nearby chair, the team will look more professional if the changeover action is consistent.

- Discussing agreed choices of signs for specialised terminology beforehand. Having the speech or paper available beforehand allows this to be done in detail.

- Monitoring each other's establishment of referent locations in space and maintaining logical continuity in the TL text if there needs to be a changeover during a presentation.

- In a conference where there is a range of presenters, dividing up the speeches between the interpreters in a way that takes advantage of individual knowledge of the subject matter and/or familiarity with the presenter.

Given that so much interpreting work is done solo, team interpreting is a unique opportunity for peer support and feedback. Interpreters provide constructive feedback to each other (as mentioned earlier – via note taking when in the passive role) as a basis for sharing ideas, expanding their repertoire, and reflecting on their work. Less experienced interpreters teamed with more experienced colleagues often find it a valuable learning experience.

Telephone interpreting

For many interpreters, early interpreting experiences involved making phone calls for deaf friends, family or colleagues. Telecommunications are increasingly accessible to deaf people, with more options for instantaneous contact (sms, e-mail, chat-lines, and telephone relay services). These options allow deaf people more autonomy in their contact with the hearing world, however many deaf clients still request interpreted calls. One reason for this is that even though many telecommunication options (including relay services) are not sound-based, they do rely on English literacy skills. Another reason deaf people prefer interpreted calls, is for expedience; via an interpreter, they can more quickly and directly make contact with the other person, and get more information about their mood and responses from the interpreter's non-manual features.

Although it seems a simple task, interpreting telephone calls can be very challenging depending on the purpose and content of the call, and because telephone use is based on hearing cultural protocols. When two hearing participants make a telephone call, they rely exclusively on sound. Most people have used a telephone all their lives, so they know the 'scripts' for introductions, conversations, transactions, etc. If a spoken language interpreter (for example, English/Arabic) is introduced into the dynamic, the interpreter needs to mediate any cultural differences between the parties, but assumes that each party is familiar with the basic turn-taking rules of a phone call. Even though they may not understand each other, both clients can hear how and when the other participant is talking.

Things can be more complicated when a deaf person contacts a hearing person via a sign language interpreter. For one thing, deaf people generally lack personal experience of voice telephones and therefore don't always know the 'script' for typical calls. Furthermore, although the deaf client can see the interpreter, they cannot see the person on the other end of the phone, and must rely heavily on the interpreter to know when to speak, and how their message is being received. From the hearing client's perspective, this is often the first time they have received an interpreted call, and generally expect that the usual rules of telephone interaction apply.

Interpreters therefore need to bridge the cultural gap between deaf and hearing participants in telephone interactions (Dickinson 2002; Pollitt and Haddon 2005), for example, how you start and end the phone call, how you cue the turn-taking, and how to deal with silence on the telephone (which is not comfortable to hearing participants). In phone conversations, there is less tolerance for pauses and silence than in face-to-face discourse. If you have ever interpreted a telephone call, you have probably heard the phrase 'Hello, is there anyone there?' as the hearing party waits for an interpreted reply.

Who takes the lead?

Where the hearing recipient of a call from a deaf person either knows the caller or is used to interpreted telephone calls, the 'conduit' approach where the interpreter is not briefed, and the deaf person takes the lead from the first 'hello' can work well. Unfortunately many calls are not so simple. The very beginnings of telephone calls are important in establishing communication and rapport and we need to tread carefully to make them work. For example, when calling a business or organisation, the first person who answers the call is often a front line receptionist, rather than the person you actually need to speak to. Hearing callers are used to explaining their question in general terms, or just asking if a specific person is available first. Many deaf people have no experience of this filtering system, and as soon as the phone is answered, start explaining their status as a deaf caller with a sign language interpreter, and/or telling their 'story' in great detail, to someone who doesn't understand or want to know. Another complicating factor is the increasing computerisation of telephone calls, where callers must respond to a series of digitally recorded prompts or questions, before being connected to a human being.

These beginnings can be awkward and confusing for all participants (including the interpreter). In order for an interpreter to better navigate the initial connection between the parties, one option is to seek permission from the deaf caller to 'locate' the right person or section in an organisation if necessary, first.

First person versus third person

When hearing people make a telephone call, and find the person they need to speak to, they introduce themselves in the first person. For deaf people calling via an interpreter, introductions are not so straightforward. Although interpreters generally speak and sign in first person, in telephone calls, especially when the hearing client is unfamiliar with the situation, this can sometimes be counterproductive. The hearing client cannot see what is happening, so cannot know that there are two people on the end of the phone and that one of them is signing. Gender differences between the interpreter and the deaf client can further exacerbate the potential confusion. For example, imagine a female interpreter working with a male deaf client as he signs 'Hello, my name is Mark Scott. I am deaf and I'm calling through a sign language interpreter. I'm calling to inquire about ...'. This may seem clear to us, but for the hearing client it's a lot of information to take on board, and they may spend the next few minutes of the call trying to figure out why Mark has a female voice, how he can be deaf if he is speaking, and what a sign language interpreter is anyway – rather than paying attention to what is actually being said.

As noted earlier, we need to negotiate with the deaf client the most effective approach to use in the circumstances, to avoid miscommunication. Deaf clients who are experienced in using telephone interpreting, will often choose to introduce themselves and explain the process in ways that make sense to a hearing person. However, when it is left to the interpreter, it is appropriate to step out of first person address, to introduce the caller and the set up. For example, you as the interpreter speak directly to the hearing person first: 'Hello, my name is Lee Collins, and I'm a sign language interpreter. I'm here with Mark Scott who is deaf, and I'm going to interpret the conversation between you both. Whenever he signs something, I'll speak to you, and when you speak I'll sign back to him. There might be short delays in responding, while I pass the message on, so don't worry if things go silent every now and then. Ok? So, now over to Mark. Hi, I'm, calling to inquire about ...', and so on.

Another option for calls that are not life important is to retain the first person, but not to state that the deaf person is speaking through an interpreter – to avoid the initial confusion and miscommunication. For example, 'Hello, my name is Sarah Scott and I'm calling to inquire about ...'. For this approach to work, the deaf caller and the interpreter, need to be familiar with interpreted calls and work as a tight team. Otherwise, things can become awkward if the timing is not exactly right.

Filling the gaps

During an interpreted conversation there may be a number of gaps, for example, when a deaf person is checking their diary to confirm the date and time for an appointment. The deaf client may not be saying anything, but the hearing person at the other end of the phone will expect to hear something. One strategy is to think about what you would normally say in the same situation 'Ok … let me just check my diary … here we go … Tuesday 12th March … 10.00am … yes, that seems fine.' Because deaf people may not be aware of the need to fill the sound gaps, you may need to do this to keep the conversation flowing.

In reverse, the interpreter needs to let the deaf person know of any sound cues on the other end; for example, after dialling the number at the beginning of the call, indicate each time the phone rings at the other end, or if there is a busy signal. This is all 'information' that relates to the call. If there is background noise at the other end that makes it difficult to hear, or it sounds as though the person on the other end is looking for something on a computer or looking through papers as they speak, these are also relevant auditory cues to relay.

Video (remote) interpreting

The term 'video remote interpreting' or 'video relay interpreting' refers to the process of interpreting via video technology, where the interpreter is in a different location to one or both clients. In the US, the term video *relay* interpreting is used where the interpreter is in a different location to all parties, and video *remote* interpreting, where the interpreter is in the same location as either the deaf or hearing person. We will use the term video *remote* interpreting (VRI) to refer to any situation where an interpreter is working via video.

Figure 8.1: VRI – two different locations

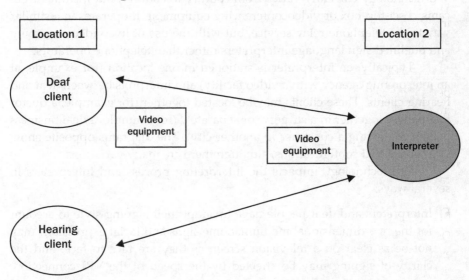

Figure 8.2: VRI – three different locations

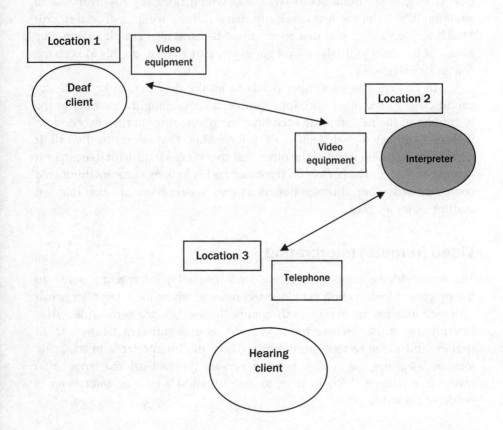

VRI technology currently varies from country to country, but includes web-cams, a set-top-box or videoconferencing equipment. It operates in a similar way to the telephone relay service, but with the use of live video streaming and qualified sign language interpreters rather than telephone operators.

Typically, an interpreter is stationed in one location (for example, at an interpreting agency with a video facility) and interprets between deaf and hearing clients. These clients may be located together (for example, a doctor and patient together in a surgery) or separately (for example, a deaf business person contacting a customer in another city). The diagrams opposite show two typical VRI configurations, although there are many variations.

VRI technology impacts the interpreting process and interpreters in several ways:

- Interpreters and deaf people have to adapt their signing style to account for the two-dimensional medium. Some signs and facial expressions may not be as clear on a television screen as they are face to face, and the clarity of signing may be affected by the speed of the VRI connection.

Therefore the pace of signing needs to be slightly slower, especially fingerspelling.

- Because of the TV medium, it is even more important for interpreters to wear appropriate clothing of contrasting colour. This also applies to deaf clients, as interpreters need to read their signing from a television screen. Another complication is reflection; shiny clothing causes reflections which also make signing difficult to read on screen, so should be avoided.

- The VRI set-up prevents interpreters taking the opportunity to assess their client's language needs before the assignment begins (if the deaf person calls into the service from elsewhere).

- There is less chance of a briefing with the hearing person beforehand, to explain your role, protocols for talking directly to a deaf person, etc, so the interpreter may have to make allowances for this and intervene accordingly.

- It can be difficult to get the deaf person's attention if you are in different locations and they look away from the screen.

- As with telephone conference calls, when using VRI in a meeting situation, it can be hard to distinguish the voices of people off screen.

- Turn taking is affected by time lag in VRI settings because of a slight delay in video transmission. So interpreters need to use similar strategies for 'filling gaps' in telephone calls.

- Interpreters employed to work for a VRI service may be booked for block sessions, reducing the need to travel to and between assignments. This is potentially more appealing and may attract more interpreters to VRI work at the expense of face-to-face community jobs.

- Interpreters deal with different ergonomic issues in VRI work – as well as the possibilities of OOS, they also have to be aware of the possibilities of eye strain from looking at a computer/television screen and back pain from sitting in a chair for longer periods.

- Due to the increased daily variety and number of assignments that can be fitted in, interpreters may also experience greater fatigue, now known as 'contact fatigue' (Dion 2005).

- Interpreters may be booked to interpret for deaf people in any part of the country, exposing them to a range of sign variation that they may not be familiar with.

- The relationship between deaf people and interpreters may become more superficial if they are not having any direct contact.

At present, deaf people are using VRI services in order to organise short meetings at the last minute, and to make phone calls. With further advances in technology, it is likely that more deaf people will use this service regularly for personal communication, and that an increasing proportion of well skilled interpreters will therefore be employed within this type of service, following trends already established in the US.

Relay interpreting and deaf interpreters

Relay interpreting encompasses a whole range of scenarios where a single interpreter is unable to bridge the communication gap between the clients. In relay settings, the usual triad of one interpreter working between two clients, is extended to include two or more interpreters in the communication chain. Relay interpreting occurs between spoken languages as well as in signed language settings. Examples of relay interpreting set-ups using sign language interpreters include:

- A deaf client who is not fluent in NZSL, but uses ASL, needs to see a medical specialist. If there is no local interpreter who knows ASL, a deaf relay interpreter who does, can work between the deaf client and the hearing interpreter.

- A family counsellor needs to talk with the family of her client – a young deaf woman of Lebanese background, whose parents don't speak English. A spoken language interpreter (Arabic/English), as well as a sign language interpreter (Auslan/English), is needed to ensure communication occurs between all the parties.

- A Deafblind Association meeting has a visiting hearing guest speaker. A hearing interpreter provides the English to Auslan translation, and a number of deaf and hearing relay interpreters pass the message on to individual DB clients.

- A deaf client who is not fluent in any sign language, needs to attend a court hearing. A deaf relay interpreter is booked to work with the NZSL/English interpreter, because the deaf client and the hearing interpreter cannot understand each other.

- A representative of the Japanese Federation of the Deaf is presenting at an International Deaf conference. A deaf interpreter is up on stage ready to interpret into International Sign. The relay chain is: Japanese Sign → Japanese → English → Auslan → International Sign.

Since interpreting strategies for working directly with clients who are deafblind or have minimal language competency are discussed later in the chapter, this section will focus on working in a team with deaf interpreters.

'Deaf relay interpreters' or 'deaf interpreters' are relatively new terms for a role that has been around for a long time; there is still debate around the appropriate term to use. Deaf interpreters act as an intermediary communicator between a hearing interpreter and a deaf client, a deaf presenter and a deafblind client, or a hearing interpreter and a deafblind client. Deaf people's experience of making themselves understood non-verbally, their first-hand knowledge of diverse communication and personal backgrounds in the Deaf community, and their ability to conceptualise experiences and ideas through the eyes of a deaf person can give them a repertoire of visual communication skills that most hearing interpreters envy.

Typically, a deaf interpreter is employed along with a hearing interpreter, when the hearing interpreter is unable to communicate effectively with a deaf client, for example, where the client:

- Uses idiosyncratic signs or gestures, or 'home signs' which are unique to a family;

- Uses a foreign sign language;

- Has minimal or limited language skills; (see later section in this chapter);

- Is deafblind or deaf with limited vision; (see later section in this chapter);

- Uses signs particular to a given region, ethnic or age group that are not known by the hearing interpreter;

- Is in a mental state that makes ordinary interpreted communication especially difficult.

The Registry of Interpreters for the Deaf (RID) gives this definition of the task (CDI refers to Certified Deaf Interpreter):

> In the CDI/hearing interpreter team situation, the CDI transmits message content between a deaf consumer and a hearing interpreter; the hearing interpreter transmits message content between the CDI and a hearing consumer. While this process resembles a message relay, it is more than that. Each interpreter receives the message in one communication mode (or language), processes it linguistically and culturally, then passes it on in the appropriate communication mode. In even more challenging situations, the CDI and hearing interpreter may work together to understand a deaf individual's message, confer with each other to arrive at their best interpretation, then convey that interpretation to the hearing party'. (RID 1997).

Figure 8.3 (see next page) represents how this process may occur (NB the exact process and positions may vary, depending on the number of deaf and hearing clients and their communication needs).

Every interpreter likes to work differently, so if presented with the opportunity to work together, deaf and hearing interpreters should negotiate a system that works for them as a team. Some of the things to keep in mind include:

Figure 8.3: Relay interpreting steps

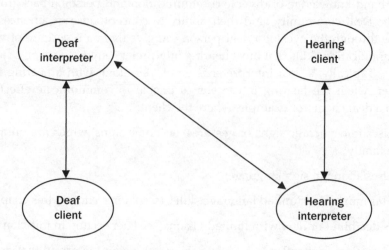

- Does the deaf interpreter want the hearing interpreter to complete the first stage of the translation as freely as possible into Auslan/NZSL, or do they prefer a more literal interpretation of the English source message, to allow the deaf interpreter to do most of the translation? This often depends on how bilingual the deaf interpreter is.

- Does the deaf interpreter prefer to receive the information simultaneously (for example, when working with a deafblind client who requires minimal re-structuring of the source message) or do they need the hearing interpreter to pass on the information in consecutive chunks (for example, when the deaf client has limited language skills, and requires substantial unpacking of the information).

- Does the deaf interpreter want the hearing interpreter to monitor their output and let them know if they have misinterpreted or missed anything?

- How will the deaf interpreter advise/interrupt the hearing interpreter when they judge there is a communication breakdown?

- When and how will breaks occur?

Sometimes, the deaf interpreter can assist the hearing interpreter to develop strategies for improved communication with a deaf client. If there are ongoing appointments, the hearing interpreter may, over time, be able to take the lead in interpreting between the clients, with the deaf interpreter acting in a back-up role.

The demand for deaf people to work as interpreters with specific clients is increasing, especially in medical and legal situations. In the US, deaf people can become accredited as a 'Certified Deaf Interpreter' (CDI). In Australia and New Zealand, there is currently no formal accreditation system for deaf people working as interpreters. In Australia, training has been sporadic. Western Australia TAFE offered a one-off Diploma of Interpreting course in 2000-2001, however only short unaccredited training courses, at TAFE and Deaf Societies, have been offered since then. In 2007 ASLIA created and administered a national pilot testing program funded by NABS: the Deaf Relay Interpreter Certification Project. The test assessed skills for working with deaf clients who have limited Auslan fluency, and is recognised by NABS and some Deaf Societies in lieu of any other qualifications. The testing process revealed a strong demand and need for formal training of deaf interpreters and has led to negotiations with NAATI about possible future accreditation of DRIs under their testing regime.

We are now seeing deaf interpreters working more frequently at conferences either in their own sign language or International Sign. The deaf interpreter is positioned on stage, with a hearing relay interpreter 'feeding' the message coming from the conference presenter. Relayed interpreting of monologues, such as conference presentations, creates time pressure difficulties. In a dialogue situation (such as a police interview), deaf and hearing interpreters can work consecutively to control the flow of information. When interpreting a monologue, however, the speaker will continue to talk, so the hearing interpreter and deaf interpreter need to consider practical issues in relation to feeding chunks of information and maintaining eye contact to non-manually signal 'stop', 'go' or 'hold' as necessary.

Working with a skilled deaf interpreter (particularly with clients who have limited language skills) is a rich opportunity to observe, learn and expand your own interpreting skills.

Deaf clients who have minimal language competence

Some deaf individuals have been so socially and linguistically isolated during their lifetime that they have not fully acquired either a sign language from deaf peers, or a spoken language. Currently there are a variety of terms used for people in this predicament: minimal language competence (MLC), minimal language skills (MLS), high visual orientation (HVO), and special linguistic needs (SLN). As yet there is no agreement on a preferred term, but for the purposes of this book, we will describe these individuals as having 'minimal language competence' (MLC). These individuals tend not to be socially connected to a Deaf community, but may be encountered by interpreters at an assignment. These deaf clients have received little or no education, and their actual intelligence, knowledge, or ability to absorb new information is often masked by their language deficit. They generally lack standard (commonly understood) ways of referring to concrete things or experiences, and have difficulty with understanding and expressing abstract concepts.

Occasionally, a deaf person is described as MLC when they are actually an immigrant with knowledge of a foreign sign language, and perhaps some literacy in the language of their home country. In these cases, using a local interpreter who also knows the client's sign language is an ideal but rarely available solution. Alternatively, you can work with a deaf person who is skilled at 'foreigner talk' and can act as a relay interpreter.

MLC clients often have an idiosyncratic system of communication, based on gestures that they use within their limited familiar social world (family, caregivers, or workplace). They may also have a smattering of local sign language vocabulary. However their limited language development will show up through gaps in their comprehension and expression of abstract information: time concepts, identifying family relationships, grammatical pronoun reference (who's doing what to whom), cause and effect, emotional states, and moral concepts. Within this group, there is a range of communication abilities and styles, and working with an interpreter is not always a realistic approach. Sometimes it is more appropriate to arrange long-term language development work with a deaf coach or a language therapist, to build some common conceptual knowledge (Solow 1996).

Where the need for interpreting is unavoidable (such as in a medical or legal situation), working with a deaf interpreter can bring invaluable communication skills – using mime, gesture, pictures and body language. Solow (1996) points out that the presence of a deaf interpreter who shares the basic experience and identity of being deaf can make the client feel more at ease, which helps communication in a stressful situation.

Working with deaf interpreters who are experienced in MLC communication techniques is ideal, but there are many occasions where this is not practical or available (for example, when identifying a MLC client for the first time, or in remote settings). Interpreters who do work solo with MLC clients can draw on the general strategies and resources described below.[1]

Communication strategies

Communication props

Communication props are invaluable for making ideas visible and concrete, including:

- Paper and coloured pens for drawing scenes and identifying colours;
- Calendars for clarifying time concepts;
- Picture dictionaries;
- Photographs of relevant people, places and objects;
- Index cards for drawing actions and assembling a sequence of events;

---

1   These suggestions draw on strategies described by Frishberg (1990), Solow (1996) and Turner (2005).

- Anatomical dolls for medical/sexual matters;

- Maps and globes for locations.

Linguistic adjustment

Strategies for restructuring information can include:

- Reducing the vocabulary range, and increasing use of mime, gesture, role shift and non-manual expression – for example, using pantomime to 'act out' rather than using signed verbs to describe action;

- Learning and using whatever signs or gestures the client knows and understands;

- Finding out about the background to the person's experience and daily life and co-creating some shared signs or symbols to refer to through a conversation;

- Expressing concepts as concretely as possible;

- Repeating ideas in different ways and continually monitoring understanding;

- Using all available 'real world' cues to point to, such as objects, pictures, and actions in the environment.

A common worry for the interpreter is whether communication difficulties are due to their own interpretation skills, or to the clients' language skills and/or mental state (Solow 1996). Since confusion is between the two parties trying to communicate, Solow suggests that it is best to describe difficulties in terms of the interpreter's problem – for example, 'I don't seem to be getting through, can I try a different way?', or 'I'm not clear about what they mean', to reduce negative focus on the client themselves. Even with the most skilled resources, interpreters and hearing clients must acknowledge that there is no guarantee of satisfactory communication outcomes given the inherent limitations. Solow recommends that, 'Interpreters be assertive about getting resources, assistance and time such that these communication problems can be dealt with thoroughly and responsibly' (1988: 21).

Deaf clients with MLC in legal contexts

MLC individuals sometimes fall foul of the law, getting into situations without understanding the consequences. Their communication limitations may go unrecognised by police, or even initially by an interpreter (especially where the deaf client is adept at mimicking signs and facial expression to give the appearance of reasonable sign language skills). The 1990 case of a New Zealand deaf man with limited language who was wrongfully accused of murder and imprisoned as a result of miscommunication was dramatised in a TVNZ documentary, 'The Remand of Ivan Curry'.[2]

Living in a small rural town amongst hearing family, but relatively isolated from a Deaf community, Ivan Curry was a profoundly deaf man with limited formal sign language skills and education. Based on two police interviews – the first without an interpreter, and the second assisted by an itinerant teacher of the deaf (without training in NZSL) – Curry was said to have confessed to killing his infant nephew by punches to the chest, and was held on remand in prison for 22 months awaiting trial for murder in the High Court. He was eventually acquitted in the trial, when it came to light that the infant had actually died as a result of another family member applying adult CPR to the baby's chest after finding him lifeless in his cot. Curry himself never gave evidence in court, but during the 22 months between arrest and trial, interpreters and deaf persons experienced with communicating with MLC individuals were consulted as expert witnesses and used to facilitate further interviews with Curry. As a result of a more informed picture of his actual communication abilities (as well as the weight of new evidence from family members), the two original police statements containing Curry's 'confessions' were ruled as inadmissible evidence by the trial judge on the grounds that valid communication was unlikely to have occurred. He was acquitted after a lengthy process of three full-scale hearings including the Court of Appeal. Some people close to him claimed that during his extended period of imprisonment on remand, he did not fully understand why he was in prison.

In some cases, the comprehension and communication skills of a deaf person with MLC may be so limited or inconsistent that they are deemed linguistically incompetent to stand trial (McKay and Miller 2001). Given that trials are based on questioning – a form of communication with which persons with MLC client have little experience – and that any conviction must rest upon evidence 'beyond reasonable doubt', the level of communication and certainty of facts required in legal proceedings may well be beyond the capability of some MLC clients, even with skilled relay interpreting support.

Clients who are deafblind

As with clients who have MLC, deafblind (DB) people are a very diverse group. Many have not always been deafblind; they can be:

- Congenitally deafblind;
- Congenitally deaf and have lost their vision;

---

2   Hunter (1992). This dramatised documentary is an interesting reference material for interpreters, because the real defendant (Curry) and the interpreters played themselves in re-enactments of trial and interview scenes. The accuracy of the facts portrayed in this documentary is substantially acknowledged in the subsequent report of the Police Complaints Authority investigation (Jeffries 1992).

- Congenitally blind and have lost their hearing;

- Born with both hearing and vision intact, but have lost both (to varying degrees).

Sign language interpreters generally work with clients from the first two groups, since they rely more on sign language and/or fingerspelling as their primary language input. There are many different causes of deafblindness, and not all DB people have completely lost their vision (or hearing). There are medical standards which determine when a person is legally blind, relating to the amount of effective vision they have left. People with Usher Syndrome often fit into this category of a DB person.

Usher Syndrome

Usher Syndrome is the most common cause of deafblindness. The most common form of this syndrome (type II) causes children to be born deaf, and then lose vision as they get older (sometimes over years, sometimes over decades). Vision loss is due to a condition known as retinitis pigmentosa and starts with peripheral vision; the first stages include 'tunnel vision' and night blindness. Over time the deaf person may lose all of their sight or may retain a small central fragment, like a keyhole. This means that their access to signed communication, independent mobility and socialisation reduces as their sight diminishes.

Communication methods

Each DB client will have their own communication preferences; these may change over time, or according to lighting conditions. Deafblind clients who have lost effective vision, may be unfamiliar with more recently introduced signs, simply because they have not seen them. It is important to remember that although DB clients may need specialised communication inputs, they are able to express themselves in the usual ways (for example, finger-spelling, signing, using their voice). The following methods are therefore 'inputs' from the interpreter, and are the most commonly used techniques:

Visual frame

Visual frame is a minimally adapted form of signing, used with DB clients who have some vision (for example, the Usher 'keyhole'), where the interpreter sits in front of the DB client and signs 'small'.

- Because the client's range of vision is reduced, they need to see signing in a restricted signing space (at chest height) otherwise they miss the details of signs made too far away from the face. Interpreters need to check their seating distance with the DB client, so that their face and hands fit within this window of vision.

- Signing in a smaller space needs to be clear and not too fast, to minimise eyestrain for the client.

- Lighting and glare can also be a problem for DB clients with limited vision, so the interpreter should check with the client about positioning in relation to lighting levels on the interpreter, and background lighting.

- Even more than usual, clothing needs to be contrasting and 'modest' – black is preferred against fair skin and lighter colours against dark skin. Low necklines are out, because the client's eyes have difficulty registering an interpreter's hands against skin, and excessive jewellery needs to be removed as it can create glare problems.

- Sometimes visual frame clients request (female) interpreters to wear dark lipstick, as an aid to picking up lip patterns and other non-manual features.

Hand over hand (also called 'tactile signing')

The hand over hand technique is used with DB clients who have no vision, or cannot see in a particular environment, but have previously seen well enough to acquire sign language, so that they are familiar with signed movement in space, and can recognise individual vocabulary items. It usually requires sitting (or standing) close in front of the DB client, who places their hands on top of the interpreter's hands/wrists and 'rides' the signing:

- It is very tiring (for both parties) and often done on a special padded split table that can be adjusted to the different elbow heights of the interpreter and the DB client.

- Variations of hand-positioning include the client holding on to the interpreter's wrists, or just using one hand on top of the interpreter's hand.

- Personal hygiene is particularly important because of the close proximity to the DB client – interpreters need to ensure that they have clean hands and arms, wear clothing (especially sleeves) that is comfortable to touch, avoid strong perfumes and smoking, and have fresh breath.

- Interpreters need to remove any heavy or sharp rings – to avoid scratching or stabbing the DB client's hands.

Tactile fingerspelling (also called 'in the hand DB alphabet')

Tactile fingerspelling is used with DB clients who have no vision, or cannot see in a particular environment, and who, for various reasons, choose not to use hand-over-hand (tactile signing). Tactile fingerspelling requires the interpreter to sit next to the client and manually spell each letter onto their hand:

- Uses a slightly adapted version of the fingerspelling alphabet, so that some letters are easier to 'receive' on the hand: b, c, f, g, p, q, s, w, x, y, z. (See Appendix D – DB Alphabet Chart.)

- Some interpreters who work with regular DB clients develop short-cuts to speed up the information, by incorporating more sign-like formations or visual details.

- The amount of fingerspelling of individual English words depends on the client; some prefer complete English sentences, while others prefer a more abbreviated 'TTY' English style or a mix of some fingerspelled words plus signs.

- Because of the sensitivity of DB people's hands, interpreters need to cut their nails short, and as with hand over hand (tactile signing), personal hygiene is important because of proximity between interpreter and client.

Environmental/visual cues

An additional task for interpreters working with DB clients is to brief them with supplementary information on the visual cues that they cannot pick up themselves (just as we are used to doing with auditory cues):

- Describe the environment you are in – locating doors, furniture, obstacles, steps.

- Name and locate the other people in the room.

- Indicate relevant behaviours (for example, 'the speaker is angry', 'the person on your left is leaving', 'the interpreters are changing over now', etc).

- Indicate the turn-taking in a group discussion (for example, by using name signs).

Guiding and transport

An extra task required of interpreters working with DB clients relates to mobility. Usually deaf clients arrive, move around and depart independently of the interpreter. For a deafblind person this is not possible; even when they have some sight, unfamiliar environments can be dangerous. Occasionally interpreters are booked to collect and return the DB client to their home. More commonly the DB client is brought to the interpreting venue by someone else (for example, a carer) but needs guiding assistance while they are there (for example, finding their seat, locating the toilet, meal breaks). Always offer guiding assistance (your arm), even when the client has a guide dog.

Occupational Health and Safety

The interpreting techniques used with DB clients are more taxing on the interpreter than regular signing; back, arm and neck strain are common. It is therefore important to ensure regular breaks and/or to work with a team interpreter wherever possible. The deafblind client may also need breaks for the same reasons and because of eye strain.

Deaf interpreters

Deaf people are often called on to interpret one-on-one with DB clients, at conferences, in meetings, at social events, and for appointments. In this case, the deaf interpreter will either watch a deaf speaker, or a hearing interpreter (if the speaker is hearing), and relay the message to the DB person using one of the communication techniques described above. If the source message is coming from a deaf person using Auslan/NZSL, the deaf interpreter needs to sit facing the speaker so they can take in the message, while the DB client has their back to the speaker as they receive the TL from the deaf relay.

Oral interpreting

Oral interpreting (also called oral transliterating and lipspeaking) involves facilitating communication between hearing speakers and people who are deaf or hearing impaired and who use speech and lipreading as their preferred mode of communication. Lipreaders may want communication facilitation in group situations where it is difficult to follow all the parties, or where an individual speaker is difficult to lipread due to distance, acoustics, or physical features (such as bushy facial hair or indistinct lip patterns). In some situations, interpreter voice-over also assists hearing participants who cannot understand the speech of a hearing impaired or deaf person.

The oral interpreter's task is to relay a spoken message in the form of silent mouthing. Since the output is very close to the source language form, this process is more akin to transliterating than interpreting. Performing this task effectively requires the interpreter to have:

- Accurate understanding and production of the spoken message;
- Clear enunciation and phrasing of English;
- Facial expression that matches message meaning;
- Appropriately selected natural gestures;
- Good lipreading skills (to understand speech of deaf/hearing impaired person).

The following techniques can enhance the clarity of the message for a lipreader:

- Rephrasing (for example, breaking a long sentence into two smaller parts, or simplifying structure of a disjointed or unusually complex sentence);

- Word substitutions to enhance clarity on the lips – choosing words that are more familiar and visible while maintaining the original message meaning;

- Adding natural gestures to clarify difficult-to-lipread words;

- Emphasising a new name or term by pausing briefly immediately after the word, and using slower pronunciation that clearly shows the number of syllables;

- Showing the end of phrases, or silences, by closing the lips. Breaking eye contact with the lipreader can also signal that the interpreter is waiting for the speaker to continue;

- Indicate who is speaking in a multi-party situation – by discrete pointing, name, or description;

- Printing numbers, proper nouns, or easily misunderstood words, in the air or on paper;

- Team interpreting is appropriate as oral interpreting requires intense concentration; repeating a message verbatim can sometimes be more taxing than interpreting from one language to another;

- If the speaker is speaking very quickly or indistinctly, let the consumer know, and allow them to request adjustment of speaking style.

As with sign language interpreting, it is it appropriate to check beforehand if the client has any preferences or suggestions for how they prefer you to work, and also to keep an eye out for non-verbal consumer feedback about their comprehension while you work.

There is currently no specific training or accreditation for this type of communication assistance in Australia or New Zealand; these skills were more widely used in the past, but are now only occasionally called upon.[3]

International Sign interpreting

Over the past 20 years, it has become common for international deafness conferences and sports meetings to include interpreting into International Sign (IS). The aim of 'International Sign' interpreting is to provide some communication access for deaf participants who don't have on-site interpretation into their own sign language.

---

3   For further information on oral interpreting, see the Registry of Interpreters for the Deaf (USA) *Standard Practice Paper on Oral Transliteration* or the Council for the Advancement of Communication with the Deaf (UK) *Factsheet Number 19 on Lipspeaking*, available at the websites of those organisations <www.rid.org>, <www.cdcap.ork.uk>.

IS interpreting is a rather unique phenomenon in the world of interpreting, since IS is not, (and is unlikely to become), a standardised or fully-fledged language. It is an improvised contact language that uses the common grammatical features of all signed languages and a small core vocabulary of signs (borrowed from various sign languages, but mainly from North America and Western Europe). IS is a restricted communication code which lacks the richness of expression that full languages develop, since it is only used in a limited number of situations, between people of varying cultural backgrounds and experience, who come together for one-off events. [4]

It is often difficult to transfer an equivalent level of technical detail from the source message into IS, because of vocabulary limitations, the inability to borrow from a common written language through fingerspelling, and broad diversity in the background knowledge of a mixed language audience. So how does it work? There are some consistent linguistic characteristics of IS interpretation, and strategies that skilled interpreters use to manage the information flow and make the TL message comprehensible to as many participants as possible including the following (McKee and Napier 2002):

- Extensive use of location and direction for verb agreement, pronoun reference, time reference;

- Non-manual grammar – for example, to mark topics, negation, questions, conditionals in sentences, and to add adverbial information;

- Use of classifiers in place of more 'frozen' or conventional vocabulary;

- Choosing more iconic signs and gestures, use of visual metaphor, and expanding word meaning by paraphrase;

- 'Showing' information through constructed action and dialogue (role-shifting, pantomime) wherever possible;

- A long lag-time to fully unpack large meaning chunks in the interpretation;

- Expressing concepts in more concrete or specific ways (by example rather than abstraction or generalisation);

- Selectively reducing, expanding, or occasionally substituting in order to convey a speaker's intent efficiently or in a contextually relevant manner;

- Signposting important information through articulation features such as pauses, holds and increased signing size or 'volume';

---

4   Few papers have been published on IS and IS interpreting, but some descriptions can be found in Moody (1987); Padden (1993); Supalla and Webb (1995); Rosenstock (2008).

- Using contextual knowledge (of the topic, and of 'jargon' signs coined at the particular event) to produce interpretation that is as relevant and clear to the audience as possible, with the least amount of ambiguity.

IS interpreters need to be extremely competent in their use of grammatical structures, preferably familiar with the vocabulary of more than one signed language, and to have broad experience communicating within the Deaf world. Interpreters working in the US and in the UK/Europe have more opportunity to develop IS skills, given the greater number of locally hosted international conferences and events. Needless to say, interpreters new to the profession are not expected to work at IS level. However, we can learn much from observing what IS interpreters do – their interpretations are extremely 'free', and their processing strategies are essentially those which all sign language interpreters need to use. As Moody (1994) notes, in IS interpreting there is 'no cheating' on the requirement to strip a source message from the words of its original form in order to work with its essential meaning. Optimising time lag is a key technique that IS interpreters use to determine SL meaning and create TL output in a visual-gestural package for a deaf audience – a relevant insight for all interpreters.

The various skills and techniques detailed in this chapter demonstrate that interpreters may develop specialist skills in certain areas, but it is worth noting that not all interpreters typically acquire all these skills. It is more common to find that interpreters work regularly in one of these areas or with a particular group of people, and thus develop the necessary skills and knowledge over a long period of time. For those who are keen to follow up on any of these specialist skills, further readings which discuss each area in more depth are listed in Appendix A.

The next chapter looks at the specific skills and knowledge required to interpret in Māori settings in New Zealand and in indigenous contexts.

Thought questions

1. Team interpreting:

(a) Imagine a client has rung to book you to interpret a three-hour meeting involving several deaf and hearing participants. How will you persuade them of the need for a team interpreter? List the key points you would raise.

(b) When an interpreter is 'off' (in passive role), what are some ways they can still be useful to their team interpreter?

2. Telephone interpreting:

(a) Thinking about the deaf client's background/expectations, why are interpreted phone calls potentially challenging?

(b) Thinking about the hearing client's background/expectations, why are interpreted phone calls potentially challenging?

(c) For the interpreter, a key skill in handling an interpreted phone call is managing turn-taking and timing. What are some strategies an interpreter may need to use to make the interaction as clear as possible for both parties?

3. Video remote interpreting:

(a) Brainstorm some things that a VRI interpreter would encounter that are different from a face-to-face interpreting situation. Which of these are positives and which are negatives?

4. Clients with minimal language competence:

(a) How might you recognize a deaf person with MLC? What would be some 'warning signals' that might alert you to their different communication needs?

(b) When communicating with an MLC client, what particular kinds of language and concepts might you anticipate difficulty with? Can you suggest some practical strategies for clarifying these areas as much as possible?

(c) If you sense that communication between you, an MLC client and a hearing client is not really working, what are three different ways you could respond to this situation?

5. Clients who are deafblind:

(a) What category of deafblind clients are interpreters most likely to encounter, and what are their typical characteristics in terms of *vision* and *language use*?

(b) In relation to DB interpreting, comment on the importance of:
    -   signing space
    -   lighting
    -   personal hygiene
    -   teaming

(c) With a DB client, what additional assistance might the interpreter need to provide beyond interpreting?

6. Relay interpreting:

(a) Can you identify three types of clients or situations where a deaf interpreter may be used to facilitate communication?

(b) Imagine you have called upon a deaf person to function as a relay interpreter in a mental health setting. The deaf person you are going to work

with has appropriate communication skills and a general understanding of the situation, but does not have any training in the specific
task of interpreting. What are some things you would want to discuss
with them before starting work together in the assignment? (Consider
points about role and functioning.)

7.   Oral interpreting:

(a)   Although oral interpreting (transliterating) is an English to English task,
what are some linguistic adjustments to the message that the interpreter
might need to make?

(b)   Ask some classmates or colleagues to try orally transmitting a short
passage to you (you could use headphones while they listen to a tape or
radio, or they could use headphones for the input). Identify (and discuss with them) the strategies that make comprehension easier or more
difficult for you – considering mouth, face, hands, or other features or
conditions.

8.   International Sign:

(a)   When communicating with a deaf foreigner, what are some sign language structures and/or visual communication strategies that you think
would be:
  –   *most useful* or easily understood across languages?
  –   *least useful* or understood across languages?

(b)   What makes IS interpreting a good demonstration of very free interpreting?

CHAPTER 9

INTERPRETING IN MĀORI AND INDIGENOUS AUSTRALIAN CONTEXTS

This chapter provides background information that is relevant to working with indigenous deaf people in New Zealand and Australia. The chapter is divided into sections pertinent to Māori and to Indigenous Australians.

Māori contexts

We define 'Māori contexts' for interpreting as including the following situations:

- A situation where most of the participants are Māori (for example, a family group conference), and/or where the focus (*take* or *kaupapa*) is Māori concerns – for example, a meeting (*hui*) or workshop (*wānanga*) about Māori or Māori deaf issues;

- Marae-based events (for example, *tangi*/funeral, *hui*) and ceremonies within these which are conducted in Māori (for example, *pōwhiri*/ welcome);

- Marae-based events specifically focused around deaf Māori where Māori, English and NZSL are used;

- Performance of rituals of *pōwhiri* and *karakia* (prayer/blessing) as part of public events such as conferences, graduations, building openings, VIP visits.

The deaf people in many of these situations will be Māori, but in some cases (especially public events and teaching situations) will also be non-Māori NZSL-users. The small number of interpreters who are Māori means that non-Māori interpreters are likely to work in some, or all, of the situations above.

As a starting point, non-Māori interpreters in Māori settings need to be aware that they are part of a tricultural exchange between hearing Māori and deaf (Māori or non-Māori) consumers, and themselves as a hearing, non-Māori person. As the cultural styles of each of these participants flavour how they behave and understand each other's meaning, a non-Māori interpreter should be aware of how their own cultural identity might impact such interactions, and how their communication behaviour could be adapted to reduce that impact. The details of the situations listed above are diverse, and so this section aims to introduce some basic cultural concepts relevant to working in settings involving Māori participants, language and protocols.

Cultural foundations of interpersonal relations

Even in Māori settings where communication is mainly in English, it helps if interpreters understand some of the cultural values underlying interpersonal behaviour. In Māori society, patterns of interaction are shaped by some fundamental concepts, which include:

Mana

Mana is power, esteem, dignity, social standing, authority – which can be gained through descent, seniority, and recognised achievement. Mana is maintained or diminished by the individual's own actions, as well as the behaviour and attitude of others toward them. *Whakamā* is a related concept which describes an individual's sense of lacking mana or self-esteem in a situation. A Māori person who feels whakamā (shamed, intimidated, unconfident) will not assert themselves.

Tapu

Tapu means to be under religious or ceremonial restriction or protection. Tapu is applied to categories of people (for example, men as a group, people of chiefly rank, and women when menstruating, pregnant, or childbearing), and to places or objects whose use is permanently or temporarily restricted by certain rules (for example, the *marae ātea* – open ground in front of a meeting house, an *urupā* – burial ground, landmarks such as a sacred mountain or river, the human head and associated things such as hats, combs). The counterpart of tapu is *noa*, which indicates an ordinary, common, or unrestricted status. New visitors to a marae are considered tapu (restricted, or potentially risky) until they have been welcomed and fed by the hosts (food is *noa*) – rituals which alter their status to noa, or 'ordinary', in the positive sense of being unrestricted.

Manākitanga

Manākitanga is the care, support, inclusion of others, which is a practical expression of *aroha* (compassion, empathy) that is expected behaviour in Māori contexts.

Kōtahitanga

Kōtahitanga refers to unity, collectiveness – placing the interests and the mana of the group above the individual.

These concepts influence social roles and expected behaviour. For example, an interpreter working with a Māori whānau (family) may notice that the father who accompanies his deaf son to a meeting speaks for the son, who remains passive; whereas the interpreter may assume that is due to the son's subordinate position as a deaf person, it may be equally due to cultural norms about parental mana (authority through seniority) and the protection and support (*tautoko*) of younger, more vulnerable ones. Another example is that if interpreting in a Māori home or a meeting, accepting a cup of tea or refreshment offered will make the hosts feel comfortable that their *manākitanga* (hospitality) has been recognised by the interpreter, and a connection established.

The Marae setting

The marae is the traditional venue for Māori ceremonies, community celebrations and meetings. These events may be attended by Māori, Pākeha, deaf and hearing who require interpretation between Māori, English and NZSL. Interpreters who are unfamiliar with the marae context might feel apprehensive about entering, let alone interpreting there. There is much symbolic meaning attached to the physical structures and use of space on a marae, and to the activities and communication that take place there.[1] But like any unfamiliar setting, (such as court, or church), basic protocols for behaviour and the meaning of events can be learned by interpreters; personal comfort will be gained through experiences of going onto the marae as a participant. Few people who have stayed on a marae leave without appreciating the warm sense of welcome and conviviality between hosts and guests. Tauroa and Tauroa (1986: 37) recommend many visits to gain a full understanding of how a marae works, because 'the marae represents people – it takes time to get to know people and to appreciate their feelings and beliefs.'

Language skills

Ideally, an interpreter working on a marae has a fluent command of Te Reo Māori and cultural knowledge (*tikanga Māori*), in order to translate directly from spoken Māori into NZSL, and vice versa. However, such skilled trilingual interpreters are, as yet, few in number. When Māori-speaking sign language interpreters are not available for marae events, relay interpreting is sometimes practised, where a Māori/English bilingual interprets Māori into English for an NZSL interpreter. Yet even for a skilled trilingual interpreter or a good relay team, equivalent translation of formal speeches (*whaikōrero*) and songs (*waiata*) into NZSL is sometimes impossible, because much language used in traditional oratory is steeped in archaic cultural references that have no equivalent form of expression in NZSL. The meaning of frozen

---

1   The following website provides a good introduction to marae layout and protocols, <www.maori.org.nz/tikanga/?d=page&pid=sp31&parent=26>. For a deeper discussion, see Salmond (2004).

language in chants, proverbs, poetry and songs cannot easily be retrieved, let alone translated meaningfully on the spot to an audience without deep background cultural knowledge. A tiny but familiar example is the phrase 'Tihei mauri ora', which is conventionally used to open a *whaikōrero*. This phrase can be translated literally as, 'I issue the sneeze of life' (Tauroa and Tauroa 1986: 114), but this reveals little about the deeper layers of cultural meaning embedded in the metaphor nor its discourse function. Where full translation is not possible in the situation, the interpreter can offer a paraphrase or description of the kind of language being used and its function or purpose, indicating why they cannot interpret fully.

Pōwhiri

The pōwhiri (welcome ceremony) is the most important protocol for NZSL interpreters to be familiar with, as this occurs across many settings. The ceremony itself follows a set process, and much of the language used in a pōwhiri has a formulaic structure even though content details vary (see Tauroa and Tauroa as a guide). For example, formal speeches generally acknowledge the deities, ancestors, the deceased, the living, and identify tribal and personal relationships before greeting the other party and raising specific topics of the day. Each speech is followed by a supporting *waiata*, many of which are commonly used and can be readily learned.[2] Although ceremonies of welcome (*pōwhiri*), farewell (*poroporoaki*), prayers (*karakia*), and songs are invariably in Māori, English (peppered with Māori vocabulary) is also used in less formal communication on the marae. Learning even basic Māori vocabulary and concepts makes the marae setting more comprehensible for interpreters; this includes, at a minimum, correct pronunciation, basic personal greetings and introduction (*mihimihi*), terms and concepts about the marae, and knowledge of *iwi* (tribal names and regions).

Placement in a pōwhiri

The division of roles between age groups and genders in a marae setting reflect aspects of *mana* and *tapu*. During a *pōwhiri* senior women will call (*karanga*) visitors onto a marae, but formal speeches on the *marae ātea* are, in most regions, performed by men. During speechmaking, younger men, and women generally take a background supporting position (for example, through *waiata* or *haka* in support of a speaker); in Māori terms, this division protects women and younger generations from becoming a target of conflict during potential disagreement with strangers (Tauroa and Tauroa 1986). Women contribute to the mana of the host people through other significant responsibilities within the marae, and express their views in other contexts – such as discussions inside the *wharenui* (meeting house).

2　Popular waiata are listed and translated in Tauroa and Tauroa (1986: 69-72).

Such conventions around the roles of women and men influence where an interpreter can be placed in a *pōwhiri*. A female interpreter should not stand directly next to a male speaker on the marae, but behind him, at an acceptable distance. Conversely, a male interpreter interpreting for a woman performing the *karanga*, should also stay in the background. A female interpreter may be directed to stay near the women, even if this is visually problematic for deaf participants trying to watch a male speaker, as trilingual interpreter Stephanie Awheto (2004) recounts:

> On one marae, the hosts put me next to a flagpole, because it had a carving of a wahine (woman) on it. They said 'You'll be safe standing there', even though the kaumatua (male elder) speaking was a good ten feet away from me. It was the safest place culturally for me to be. The other option was the second row behind all the men – so I went with the flagpole.

Spatial and social boundaries on the marae

Although the open space on a marae may appear to offer plenty of scope for interpreter placement, in fact spatial and activity boundaries are demarcated between host (tangata whenua: people belonging to the land) and visitor (manuhiri) groups; this has implications for interpreters who are newcomers to a marae they will work at. Newcomers, regardless of role or rank, do not cross an invisible line in the open space of the marae ātea until welcoming speeches have been exchanged, concluding with physical contact between hosts and guests in the form of *hariru* (handshake, hongi, kiss), and sharing the host's food. Even if only a drink and a biscuit, eating signals acceptance of hospitality (*manākitanga*) which upholds the hosts' *mana,* and also alters visitors' status from stranger and potential threat (*tapu*), to group member (*noa*). Sharing food in this context is therefore more than a polite gesture; it is expected behaviour that has cultural symbolism and a social function. After eating (*kai*), visitors are considered to be 'at one' with the tangata whenua, and gain freedom of movement on the marae premises.

Depending on how strictly traditional protocol is followed, and on how planned the situation is, it may be considered appropriate for an interpreter to go through a welcome process prior to interpreting on the marae. The following experience illustrates a situation where an interpreter's effectiveness (in terms of spatial positioning) was practically constrained by the interpreter's visitor status:

> One time I was interpreting a *tangi* on a marae, and the deaf people wanted me to move forward a bit so they could see me better, but I couldn't because of that invisible line – if I'd moved, I would have been in trouble with the hosts! (Awheto 2004)

In order for the interpreter to stand opposite a visiting deaf party to interpret the host speakers, they might be welcomed onto the marae beforehand so that they will be considered safe to perform their task within tangata whenua territory. A preliminary pōwhiri can be done by joining a group going on to the marae ahead of the deaf party's group, or by having a kaumātua (leader) of their group liaise with the hosts to pōwhiri the interpreter in advance. However this is handled, interpreters need to be conscious that the marae is not a public space to be entered freely by an outsider.

Observing customary protocols

At a *tangi*, issues of *tapu* surrounding death are significant. The interpreter should follow the lead of Māori participants in observing basic customary practices such as washing hands or sprinkling with water when leaving a burial ground to remove the *tapu* before resuming contact with the living.

Deaf participants on a marae may be unfamiliar with traditional protocols, having had few previous opportunities to learn directly about Māori culture.[3] A trilingual interpreter's role might extend to cultural guidance about expected behaviours and processes on a marae, in the same way that a diplomatic interpreter would provide this support for a foreign dignitary.

The interpreter's role in a Māori context

Defining the interpreter's role in a Māori setting must take into account a Māori social framework, which values the collective more highly than the individual. The concepts of *kōtahitanga* (one-ness) and *whānaungatanga* (relatedness) strongly underlie Māori ways of relating to others within a group. These concepts emphasise the inter-relatedness of various aspects of social life, and downplay 'compartmentalization and over-strict differentiation of roles' (Metge, 1976: 72). In other words, participation and personal connection are highly valued, and boundaries between professional and social relationships are less distinct. Māori participants are thus likely to see the interpreter as participating in the activity in a supportive role, rather than an 'outside' or neutral role. Stephanie Awheto (2004) explains her approach to defining her role in a Māori context:

> When I go into a Māori situation, I'll always say 'I'm here to *tautoko*' (support) – but I wouldn't say '*awhi*' (help). People see me as a support person, not just for the deaf but for the whole *whānau*. So your role is presented slightly differently than in a Pākeha setting. You have to put it in a way that's understandable for them. The interpreter, whether they are Pākeha or Māori, can say, 'I'm here to support the process, and my part in supporting this process is to translate everything that's spoken in the room'.

Of course, Māori contexts are not the only ones where interpreters feel tension between consumers' expectation of a personalised, reciprocal relationship on

---

3   Smiler's (2004) thesis describes the barriers that Māori Deaf people have faced in acquiring knowledge of their Māori cultural heritage, and provides contemporary insight on the cultural awakening that is now in progress for many Māori Deaf.

the one hand, and the profession's emphasis on maintaining of personal distance and neutrality, on the other. Interpreters also face this dilemma in their interactions with the Deaf community. Māori interpreters and deaf consumers suggest that the interpreter's conduct and demeanour can be responsive to the cultural preferences and style of Māori participants – without necessarily breaching any fundamental ethics – in order to establish a workable rapport with participants and to fit into the situation unobtrusively.

Awheto suggests that negotiating one's role and manner of working should be done in a style that is less directive and more collaborative, again respecting Māori norms about mana and tapu in personal relationships:

> With kaumātua (elders), I would do a *mihi* (greeting and personal intro-duction) and return their acknowledgement. And I take on a passive role: I don't go in there telling them, 'This is how it's going to work, and this is what I do. It's more like asking them if it's okay – taking a subservient role, saying 'Mātua (male elder), is it okay for me to be standing here so I can do this?', rather than saying, 'I am going to be standing here, and this is how I'm going to do my role'. I have to maintain a culturally appropriate relationship. Being a woman too, I take the role of being quieter – I let them take the lead as to where I stand. If their suggestion isn't going to work, I'll drop a hint like 'Maybe that will be a bit difficult Mātua, because they won't be able to see me – it might be good if we could do it there, for example.' In a Pākeha setting, I'd go in, introduce myself, and say exactly where I need to be – or say 'Where will you be sitting? I'll sit next to you'. So with Māori generally, I'm less directive. I will say, 'This is how it would *best* work', and wait and see how they can still manage to follow *tikanga* (customs) and accommodate for the deaf and my needs as well. So we get there in the end but it takes a little bit longer. (Awheto 2004)

This account highlights the greater value that Māori may place on process over outcomes. In other words, maintaining relationships and respecting social protocols are equally or more important than getting things done in a certain timeframe, or keeping activities and roles within strict categories.[4]

Furthering cultural knowledge

This section has just touched on some key elements of Māori culture that may affect the interactions that interpreters will mediate in Māori settings. There are many avenues and opportunities for interpreters in New Zealand to deepen their understanding of Māori culture and language. Preparedness for interpreting in Māori settings and interacting with Māori consumers also entails having some broader understanding of:

- Historical relations between Māori and Pākeha in New Zealand society;

- Traditional and contemporary notions of Māori identity;

- Kinship structures and tribal regions;

---

4 McKee and Awheto (2010) present a case study that further discusses considera-tions behind an interpreter's decisions about constructing her role in a Māori event.

- An awareness of how contemporary bicultural relations are affected by the principles and historical events originating in the Treaty of Waitangi.

Interpreting for deaf Indigenous Australians

Indigenous Australians (Aboriginal and Torres Strait Island people) who are deaf have diverse and often culturally complex backgrounds that can result in interpreting needs that are different from deaf non-indigenous Australians. One barrier to providing appropriate and effective interpreting services for this group is that Indigenous Australians are very scarce in the Auslan interpreting profession. Also, it is likely that most Auslan interpreters have had little contact with Indigenous Australian communities and are relatively unfamiliar with the thought-worlds of either deaf or hearing members. As in New Zealand, the profile of deaf Indigenous Australians, and their interpreting experiences and needs, are not well documented. In this section, we therefore present only an outline of some relevant considerations for Auslan interpreters working with Indigenous deaf people.

The following information is based heavily upon two key sources: O'Reilly (2005) and Fayd'herbe and Teuma (2010), which focus on the specific situation of deaf Indigenous Australians in Far North Queensland (FNQ). The authors of those works caution that not all of their observations and recommendations can be generalised to the circumstances of Indigenous deaf people elsewhere in Australia. Nevertheless, the information provides valuable insights for working in this context. For more detailed discussion about the points below, we encourage readers to consult the original sources.

Linguistic diversity

The cultures and languages of hearing Indigenous peoples in Australia are very diverse. Deaf Indigenous people are therefore also diverse, and often have complex combinations of language characteristics, cultural experience, educational and family background.

Rates of hearing loss are disproportionately high in Indigenous populations in Australia – disadvantaged living conditions have led to a high incidence of otitis media (a middle ear infection that can cause deafness if left untreated). Childhood deafness greatly increases the risk of difficulties with language development, education, mental health and interpersonal relations in adult life. These factors may be compounded by experiences of domestic violence, neglect, discrimination or trauma that are unfortunately prevalent in Indigenous Australian communities who have been historically displaced.

Deaf Indigenous Australians (in FNQ) usually participate in the community and cultural life of their hearing kin, yet many are linguistically isolated by deafness. Socioeconomic, cultural and geographical barriers to accessing early intervention and formal education mean that many do not acquire a fully developed signed (or spoken) language during childhood, nor form a strong affiliation with a local Deaf community. In comparison to the wider Deaf community in Australia, it appears that a relatively high proportion of Indigenous deaf people have limited language competence and understanding of the mores of non-indigenous society. Indigenous deaf people who participate in a Deaf community may communicate in Auslan and/or in a mixture of Auslan and Indigenous signs learned in the hearing community in which they were raised. Many Indigenous Australian cultures have native systems of signs, and deaf people raised within these communities often incorporate these and improvised home signs into a personal language system that differs from Auslan.

Due to this linguistic and cultural diversity, communicating with, and through, an Auslan interpreter from outside the community may not be straightforward or viable. Often, it is necessary to work with an Indigenous deaf person as an intermediary interpreter. O'Reilly describes this role as follows:

> An indigenous Deaf relay interpreter is a person who is Deaf and is of Aboriginal and/or Torres Strait Islander descent. This interpreter is multilingual with the ability to decipher regional indigenous dialects and is further able to apply advanced cross-cultural interpretation. An indigenous Deaf relay interpreter works in tandem with an Auslan interpreter and has the capacity to adapt to the communicative level of the indigenous Deaf client. (O' Reilly 2005: 9)

Fayd'herbe and Teuma explain that an Indigenous deaf relay interpreter can bring a better match of language style and contextual knowledge to the communication, and also, importantly, can facilitate the necessary relationship of trust that is difficult to achieve with a non-indigenous person, particularly in an unfamiliar situation.

Points of cultural awareness for interpreters

Suzannah O'Reilly's (2005) booklet on the interpreting needs and characteristics of deaf Aboriginal and/or Torres Strait Island people in FNQ makes recommendations about essential areas of background knowledge that Auslan interpreters should acquire in preparing to work with this group. Other writers on interpreting for hearing Indigenous Australians (for example, Cooke (2002) and Eades (1996)) also emphasise the impact of these factors on interpreted communication. Key points are listed below:

- Historical awareness of pre-European Indigenous cultures in Australia, the experience of colonisation, including paternalistic approaches of government institutions towards Indigenous people, and the impact of these on the circumstances of contemporary Indigenous communities.

• Familiarity with cultural customs, including political structure, social roles (for example, based on gender and age), kin relationships and associated restrictions on interaction, the existence of a native sign system, and non-verbal communication. Demonstrating a willingness to learn about Indigenous customs and perspectives through participation in community events and personal contact is appreciated, and builds rapport.

• Acknowledgement of a collectivist orientation to decision-making and information sharing. This means accepting that family members may attend appointments and expect to provide information and make decisions on behalf of a deaf person.

• Awareness of culturally-preferred terms for describing the identity of an Indigenous person: terms such as half-caste, full-blood, or judgements that someone does not 'look' Aboriginal, may be offensive. Whereas deaf Indigenous people regularly use the fingerspelled acronyms 'ATSI' and 'TI' to refer to Aboriginal and Torres Strait Island people, using these acronyms in spoken English is not so acceptable to hearing community members.

• Recognition of Indigenous communication behaviours: Indigenous people generally favour less direct communication strategies. For example, a Deaf Indigenous person may feel confronted by insistent hand-waving to demand attention and constant eyegaze, or by the asking of direct questions before a rapport has been developed. O'Reilly suggests that indirect gaze and a brief nod during introductions conveys courtesy and respect.

• Eliciting personal background information or a description of events may work better by encouraging a narrative recount rather than by a series of direct questions.

Issues for deaf Indigenous people in legal settings

Indigenous Australians are twice as likely to be victims of threatened or actual violence, and are 11 times more likely to be imprisoned than the rest of the population (ABS 2005). It has also been reported that 45.3 per cent of Indigenous Australian prisoners over 15 years old have a disability or long term health condition (ABS 2006); the majority also have low levels of education. This combination of factors suggests that deaf Indigenous people within the criminal justice system are at high risk of unfavourable outcomes.

We also know that deaf individuals who have significant linguistic and educational gaps, and cultural backgrounds that differ from the dominant culture of society, are particularly vulnerable in a forensic justice system that relies heavily on language-based evidence and processes of enquiry. Fayd'herbe and Teuma (2010) observe that many deaf Indigenous

Australian criminal suspects fall into this category, as a result of language deprivation in childhood which leads to cognitive deficits in abstract thinking and understanding of references outside the sphere of personal experience. (See the section in Chapter 8, 'Deaf clients who have minimal language competence', for further discussion of this topic.) These characteristics tend to be the underlying cause of social behaviour that breaches the law, and in turn make it difficult for them to understand their legal rights and how the legal process works. Their limited language competence and general world knowledge reduce the chances of a fair trial. Fayd'herbe and Teuma note that the Auslan interpreter brought into legal situations with such individuals may well be the only person to recognise the extent of linguistic disadvantage, and therefore has an ethical obligation to make this information known. Furthermore, the interpreter may need to take the lead in recommending improvements to the communication process, such as the following:

- team with an Indigenous deaf relay interpreter to mediate all communication;

- request preparation time with the client and the deaf relay interpreter, to establish rapport and to learn how the client communicates generally, and specifically, what methods they use to refer to people, places, times and events relevant to the case;

- use props and other visual communication techniques in interviews (see Chapter 8);

- assist other professionals to formally assess linguistic and psychological competence to stand trial. If no other specialist is available to provide this support, this might include explaining linguistic and cultural aspects of deafness that affect testing procedures and responses.

In legal situations involving Indigenous deaf persons, it is important that the interpreter errs on the side of caution and suggests the above measures in order to reduce the known risks of linguistic disadvantage, and the potential for a mistrial (that is, the outcome of a trial is found to be invalid due to flaws in the process), which can lead to the extra trauma of further legal proceedings.[5]

In summary

This chapter has looked at some of the key issues relevant to interpreters working with Māori and Indigenous Australian people in both indigenous and 'mainstream' contexts. The essential challenge for non-indigenous interpreters working with deaf individuals from these communities is to extend their own appreciation of cultural differences and meanings through

---

5   Examples of such cases are described in Fayd'herbe and Teuma (2010).

exposure to the customs, communication styles, and language use. Beyond those aspects of culture that can be observed and experienced, it is also essential to develop an understanding of thought worlds of consumers: that is, the values, beliefs, historical and personal experiences, political perspectives of indigenous communities, and the diversity of how these may be acquired and expressed by their deaf members in particular. A valuable practical strategy is to work collaboratively with a deaf or hearing member of the indigenous community, who has the skills to mediate cultural and linguistic differences between the interpreter and the deaf person, and help to build a sense of cultural comfort and confidence in the communication situation.

The next and final chapter provides an overview of working conditions and market specific information in Australia and New Zealand.

Thought questions

New Zealand

1. When interpreting in a Māori community context, such as a school-based hui, or a family conference situation, how would you approach explaining your role and setting up logistics? Identify any important considerations regarding who you talk to, how you negotiate, and what cultural factors you should be aware of in Māori participants' perception of the interpreter.

2. What is the significance of food at traditional Māori events? How should an interpreter participate with regard to eating?

3. Identify some important restrictions or cultural protocols on a marae that would practically affect how an interpreter functions in a powhiri.

4. On a scale of 1 to 5 (1 = minimal, 5 = strong), how would you rate your:

   (a) familiarity with Māori vocabulary;

   (b) level of experience socialising in Māori contexts.

Australia

1. In talking with an Aboriginal or Torres Strait Islander deaf person for the first time, give two examples of communication behaviours to be aware of in your interaction.

2. Identify at least three factors that are likely to elevate the difficulties and risks for an Indigenous deaf suspect going through the justice system.

3. How would you explain to a police officer the reason for, and benefits of, calling in an Indigenous deaf relay interpreter to work with you during an interview with a deaf Indigenous suspect or witness? What

might their objections be, and how would you counter them? (You could try this dialogue as a role play.)

4. On a scale of 1 to 5 (1 = minimal, 5 = strong), how would you rate your:

    (a) familiarity with Aboriginal or Torres Strait Island cultures, particularly social and communication norms?

    (b) level of previous contact with Indigenous people, deaf or hearing?

CHAPTER 10

WORKING CONDITIONS AND PROFESSIONAL PRACTICES

This final chapter provides a snapshot of the sign language interpreting profession in each country in terms of legislation, qualifications, training, interpreter demographics and supply and demand. It also outlines the pros and cons of different employment arrangements, and introduces basic business practices, occupational health and safety issues and membership of professional associations.

Working in Australia

Legislation

Sign language interpreting was able to move out of its welfare role and into a separate profession because of the joint arrival of anti-discrimination laws and multicultural policies. Various individual State anti-discrimination Acts (introduced during the 1980s) and the Commonwealth *Disability Discrimination Act* 1992 give some protection (but no absolute rights) to deaf people. Although there is no specific right to have an interpreter, these laws do state that people with disabilities (including deaf people) have the right to 'reasonable accommodation' of their disability (unless this causes 'unjustifiable hardship' for the employer, educational institution, service provider etc). 'Reasonable accommodation' can include provision of an interpreter, but these decisions are made on a case-by-case basis.

Multicultural policies and legislation established the interpreting language services for spoken languages (for example, Telephone Interpreter Service-TIS, Healthcare and other State government interpreting agencies) and State and federal portfolios (for example, Ethnic Affairs, Multicultural Affairs). Auslan has been added to the list of community languages accepted and provided by most of these organisations.

Qualifications

Australian interpreting qualifications are regulated by one organisation – the National Accreditation Authority for Translators and Interpreters (NAATI). Auslan has been included in NAATI's testing schedule since 1982 – this makes Australia one of the few countries in the world that accredits spoken language and signed language interpreters through the same system.

NAATI accreditation can be gained by either sitting for (and passing) a practical examination or by successfully completing a NAATI-approved course (at TAFE or university). All interpreters are expected to have NAATI accreditation before accepting paid interpreting work. Currently, there are two levels of accreditation for Auslan interpreters: 'Paraprofessional' (previously level 2) and 'Professional Interpreter' (previously level 3):

Paraprofessional level

This is the entry level for interpreting. NAATI defines it as:

> [A] level of competence in interpreting for the purpose of general conversations, generally in the form of non-specialist dialogues ... interpreting in situations where specialised terminology or more sophisticated conceptual information is not required [and]...a depth of linguistic ability is not required.

In reality, paraprofessional interpreters often work in settings that require professional level skills. They provide the bulk of interpreting services in educational and various community and employment settings, such as medical appointments, job interviews, staff meetings, and training workshops.

Professional Interpreter level

This is the recommended minimum level for interpreters, defined by NAATI as:

> [T]he minimum level of competence for professional interpreting ... [and] may be regarded as the Australian professional standard. Interpreters are capable of interpreting across a wide range of subjects involving dialogues at specialist consultations...[and] interpreting in both language directions for a wide range of subject areas usually involving specialist consultations with other professionals...[as well as] interpreting in situations where some depth of linguistic ability in both languages is necessary.'

Accredited Professional Interpreters work in a wider range of settings, including university lectures, conferences, public events and court.

As of January 2007, any interpreter newly accredited by NAATI (at Paraprofessional or Professional Interpreter level) is required to participate in a revalidation process. Interpreters must log a minimum number of working hours, and collect a required number of professional development points across different categories (for example, language, interpreting skills, ethics, etc) in order to demonstrate maintenance of their skills, regular activity as an interpreter, and retain their accreditation. Paraprofessionals have nine years to obtain Professional Interpreter accreditation, otherwise they have to re-sit their Paraprofessional test. Interpreters accredited before 2007 are encouraged to opt in to the revalidation system on a voluntary basis.

Training

For interpreters wanting to become accredited at the Paraprofessional level, training courses are available at Technical and Further Education (TAFE) colleges in most States. Currently students undertake a one-year part time course, and on successful completion, attain a TAFE Diploma and NAATI Paraprofessional-level accreditation.

In order to gain Professional Interpreter level accreditation, students can enrol in a Postgraduate Diploma of Auslan/English Interpreting at Macquarie University in Sydney. In the past, the Advanced Diploma of Interpreting (Auslan) has also been offered by TAFE colleges in Melbourne and Perth.

Demographics

According to NAATI (2008) figures, there are 888 accredited Auslan/ English interpreters nationally, 768 at Paraprofessional level and 120 at Professional Interpreter level (Bontempo and Napier, 2009b). A survey of 125 Auslan/ English interpreters conducted in 1999 (Napier and Barker 2004) found that:

- 83 per cent of interpreters were female;

- There was a ratio of 7:1 female to male interpreters;

- The majority of interpreters were aged between 26 and 35;

- 77 per cent of survey respondents had a post-secondary qualification;

- 42 per cent of survey respondents had some sort of qualification related to interpreting;

- 85 per cent of survey respondents had some form of interpreter training (including attending professional development workshops);

- 40 per cent of interpreters do more than half their work in education.

A further survey of 110 Auslan interpreters (Bontempo and Napier 2007) confirmed a similar profile, but found an increase in the number of post-secondary qualifications held. This study provided the following profile of a typical Auslan interpreter: female; 30-49 years of age; working part time; doing community interpreting assignments; accredited at Paraprofessional level; with English as a first language; formal interpreter training; and post-secondary qualification of some type.

Figure 10.1: Demand and supply of Auslan interpreting services[1]

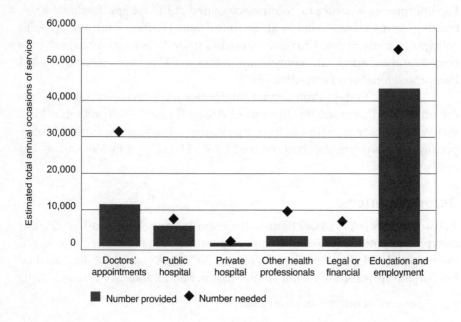

Figure 10.2: Interpreting assistance provided by family and friends

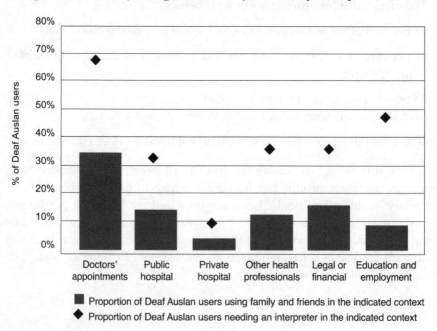

1   Orima Report, Commonwealth Department of Family and Community Services: *Report on Supply and Demand for Auslan Interpreters*, January 2004.

According to the Orima Report (2004), the main reasons for using family or friends to interpret were:

- Convenience;
- Shortage and unavailability of professional interpreters, particularly at short notice and in regional areas;
- Inability to pay for a professional interpreter;
- A preference for someone they know to interpret for them;
- Family members having a better understanding of their communication techniques; and
- Lack of awareness of the availability of professional interpreters.

In contrast, the main reasons given by deaf Auslan users for using professional interpreters rather than family members or friends were:

- Professional interpreters provided a better interpreting service;
- Family and friends were not always available or were unable to help;
- It enabled them to remain independent and not be a burden on family and friends; and
- They believed that deaf people have a right to use professional interpreters rather than family and friends.

Clearly there is a pressing need for more qualified Auslan/English interpreters.

Professional associations

There are two main interpreter associations in Australia: one for all spoken language interpreters and the other specifically for sign language interpreters.

Australian Sign Language Interpreters Association (ASLIA)

ASLIA is the national peak body representing sign language interpreters in Australia and has branches in most States. ASLIA National and its State associations rely on the voluntary input of board members to keep the association active. State associations take responsibility for collecting member fees, organising professional development, lobbying and developing policy on a State level. The national organisation hosts an annual ASLIA National Conference and Interpreter Trainers Workshop. It also-undertakes lobbying, policy development and input on a national level (for example, to federal government and NAATI). All practicing sign language interpreters are expected and encouraged to become members of ASLIA.

The Australian Institute for Translators and Interpreters (AUSIT)

AUSIT is the professional association for all spoken language interpreters and translators. They too have a Code of Ethics which is almost identical to the previous version of ASLIA's Code. Auslan/English interpreters can also become members of AUSIT – some State ASLIA branches have reciprocal membership arrangements with their local AUSIT branch, so that members can attend each other's professional development events and conferences.

Working in New Zealand

Legislation

Several laws in New Zealand directly or indirectly provide access to interpreted communication in different settings. As with Australian legislation, this right is mainly based upon health, disability and multicultural/ race discrimination perspectives, and is sometimes qualified:

- *New Zealand Sign Language Act* 2006 – recognises and promotes NZSL as an official language of NZ and guarantees the provision of competent NZSL interpreters in court.

- *Human Rights Act* 1993 – prohibits discrimination on the grounds of disability, in employment and the provision of goods and services.

- *New Zealand Bill of Rights Act* 1990 – includes a general right for all minorities to practise their culture and use their language. It also contains a specific right to free provision of an interpreter in court.

- *Children, Young Persons, and their Families Act* 1989 – requires that an interpreter be provided in government agency contact with young people and families, wherever practicable.

- The Code of Health and Disability Service Users' Rights (1996) – specifies that service users have the right to effective communication and 'where necessary and reasonably practicable', this includes the right to an interpreter.

- *The Mental Health (Compulsory Assessment and Treatment) Act* 1992 and the *Intellectual Disability (Compulsory Care and Rehabilitation) Act* 2003 require the provision of interpreter services (including NZSL), where it is 'practicable'.

In addition to legislated rights, several government agencies have policies which specifically recommend the use of interpreters. Guidelines for booking and working with NZSL/English interpreters are available to government agencies and others on the website of the Office for Disability Issues.

Qualifications

There is no independent system for accreditation of sign or spoken language interpreters within New Zealand, other than the Māori Language Commission which certifies Māori interpreters and translators. Many spoken language interpreters therefore apply for Australian NAATI accreditation. However, as NAATI's sign language accreditation is specific to Auslan, it is not available to NZSL/English interpreters. Although there is no national interpreter accreditation body, the Diploma of Sign Language Interpreting (DipSLI) is recognised as the minimum standard of qualification to work as an interpreter in New Zealand.

Training

Professional training for NZSL interpreters has been offered since 1992 through the Diploma in Sign Language Interpreting (DipSLI) program at Auckland University of Technology. This is a two-year full time undergraduate course, with an entry requirement of basic NZSL proficiency. Since the Diploma's introduction, it has become clear that an adequate level of bilingualism and interpreting competence takes a longer period of formal study; this course is likely to expand into a three-year Bachelor's degree in the near future. The exit standard for current DipSLI graduates is roughly equivalent to NAATI paraprofessonal level.

Te Reo Māori

Recently, the DipSLI program has recruited students who are speakers of Te Reo Māori, in order to address a demand for interpreters who can interpret between Māori, NZSL and English (in Māori settings and at public events where Māori is used as one of the languages of official proceedings). At this stage, the course does not specifically teach translation between Māori and NZSL, but aims to equip Māori interpreters with knowledge of sign language interpreting principles and techniques that they can apply to the use of Māori as a working language. The availability of trilingual interpreters is an important goal for Māori deaf people who want to participate in hearing Māori contexts and to access knowledge of their cultural heritage (Smiler 2004).

Demographics

There are approximately 60 qualified NZSL interpreters working full or part time; about two-thirds of these are based in Auckland, as the largest population centre, with the largest Deaf community. The ratio of interpreters to deaf people in Auckland was last estimated to be 1:23, in Wellington and

Waikato 1:50, while Canterbury, Palmerston North and Otago suffer from a shortage of interpreters at a ratio of 1:250.[2]

According to Deaf Aotearoa NZ (formerly known as Deaf Association of NZ), there are also about 20 known untrained interpreters who are regularly used due to under-supply of qualified interpreters, or sometimes the personal preference of deaf consumers.

Supply and demand

There is significant unmet need for interpreting in virtually all areas of life (Fitzgerald 2004), including health, mental health, education (all levels), legal situations, employment, government social services, public events, broadcasting, parent-teacher interviews, funerals, counselling, commercial and service transactions, sports and recreation, religious and community participation.

Unmet demand is related to factors such as funding limitations, inadequate supply of interpreters, and lack of awareness among service providers and consumers about the use of interpreters. These conditions are slowly but steadily improving as deaf consumers become more assertive about their rights, and interpreting is becoming a more established profession, supported by more widespread teaching of NZSL.

Professional associations

Sign Language Interpreters Association of New Zealand (SLIANZ)

The Sign Language Interpreters Association of New Zealand (SLIANZ) was incorporated in 1997 as the professional body which represents and advocates for sign language interpreters in New Zealand. SLIANZ does not have local branch structure, but local networks of interpreters are active in professional support and development in the main centres of Auckland, Wellington, and Christchurch. SLIANZ runs annual conferences and professional development workshops, promotes and informs about the use and training of interpreters, maintains a directory of qualified interpreters, promotes a code of ethics and practice and provides a complaints procedure, facilitates mentoring, and is a representative voice for interpreters in consultation with government and other relevant organisations.

SLIANZ maintains links with sign language interpreting organisations overseas, is a member of WASLI (World Association of Sign Language Interpreters), and is formally affiliated with the NZ Society of Translators and Interpreters (NZSTI Inc). The members of NZSTI are mainly spoken language interpreters and translators, but they share professional concerns and goals with sign language interpreters.

---

2   Source – Fitzgerald (2004), which compiled figures from data supplied by the Deaf Association of NZ and SLIANZ.

Occupational Health and Safety (OHS)

Most sign language interpreters work in isolation, without peer support or supervision, regardless of whether they are employed as staff interpreters, or are working on a freelance basis. Although employers are legally obliged to ensure a safe working environment, they are often unaware of the risks associated with interpreting work. As a result, it is essential for interpreters to be aware of their occupational health and safety rights and to be assertive and organised in advocating for their own needs.

Occupational Overuse Syndrome

The main health concern for sign language interpreters is Occupational Overuse Syndrome (OOS), previously known as Repetitive Strain Injury (RSI). OOS is an increasingly common work-related injury. Rather than one specific physical injury, OOS is a group of related physical conditions, any or all of which can be present. Common sites of injury include: wrist (carpal tunnel syndrome), arms (tendonitis), shoulder (bursitis), neck and back.

Causes

OOS problems arise for employees in many jobs that require repetitive movements, such as keyboard and cash register operators, and assembly line workers. The increased use of computers in our daily lives is also increasing the incidence of overuse injury. Key risk factors are:[3]

- Forceful, speedy repeated movements;
- Awkward hand positions and postures;
- Insufficient rest time between movements;
- Insufficient time for warm up and cool down of muscles;
- Insufficient recovery time between periods of intense work;
- Tight muscles in arms and upper body during work time.

Sign language interpreters are particularly at risk of acquiring OOS in classroom interpreting and public speaking situations. Madden states:

> In these physically and mentally demanding situations, the interpreter must produce clear signs, often in a large space in front of the body, and must keep pace with the presenter (no matter how fast he or she may be speaking). The process of interpreting in these types of 'machine-paced' situations is very demanding. (2005: 31)

---

3   From RID Standard Practice Paper: Cumulative Motion Injury, 1997 <www.rid. org/spp.html>.

Prevention

Increased litigation for workers compensation has raised awareness of OOS, and the motivation for employers to do something about it. Employer OHS policies and practices generally include general OOS injury prevention measures (for example, ergonomic furniture, adequate lighting). In relation to sign language interpreting, booking agencies and professional associations recommend:

- Allowing a regular rest break of five minutes for every hour of interpreting;

- Booking more than one interpreter for assignments longer than two hours;

- Limiting the number of hours worked in a single day;

- Limiting the number of days of interpreting work in a week.

Obviously prevention is better than cure; interpreters can develop work habits to minimise the risk of OOS occurring, including:[4]

- Using a less forceful or tense signing style;

- Fingerspelling with palms oriented naturally towards each other, rather than the palm turned outwards deaf clients;

- Doing stretching and warm up exercises for the body and hands, and cooling down after interpreting work;

- Doing strengthening exercises for arms and hands;

- Using micro-pauses to hang the arms down loosely, and stretching the wrists;

- Getting therapeutic treatments (for example, massage, acupuncture, physiotherapy);

- Counterbalancing interpreting stresses by regular exercise or activities that require large (and different) movements of the arms and upper body, increasing blood flow to affected muscles, which reduces pain.

Overuse injury develops in three stages, moving from temporary pain and discomfort in the affected area to persistent and sometimes permanent pain and damage. Interpreters affected by OOS symptoms need to seek medical attention and implement the above strategies as early as possible, to minimise the damage and maximise their recovery.

---

4   From RID Standard Practice Paper: Cumulative Motion Injury, 1997 <www.rid. org/spp.html>.

Other OHS hazards

In addition to OOS, sign language interpreters can also be at risk of emotional burnout because of stresses inherent in:

- Working alone without peer or employer support;

- Taking on too much educational interpreting work during term time, to compensate for the lack of work during school/university holidays;

- Interpreting in settings that are emotionally challenging (for example, mental health, court cases, or other distressing situations), without access to debriefing;

- Lack of feedback, personal development opportunities and a career path.

Unfortunately, at this stage of the development of the profession, there is still a lack of awareness about health and safety issues for sign language interpreters. Interpreters therefore need to be clear about the risks, and their rights, and to take care of themselves by educating employers and consumers about their needs.

Employment arrangements

Interpreters can work in different ways: as a self-employed freelance interpreter, as a staff interpreter in a Deafness-related organisation, as a staff interpreter in a mainstream organisation which employs deaf staff (less common) or in a combination of the above. Each of these employment arrangements has its own set of advantages and challenges in terms of working conditions and role expectations.

Freelance work

Many sign language interpreters in Australian and New Zealand work on a freelance basis. Freelancers are self-employed, taking on work through interpreting service agencies or directly from deaf consumers and contracting organisations, such as government agencies or educational institutions.
    Advantages of freelancing include:

- Variety in work settings and clients;

- Flexibility and control of work schedule and types of assignments;

- Some independence in setting terms and fees for work.

Interpreter's Toolkit:
Useful things for a freelancer to have on hand

- *Diary* – for carrying appointment details and adding new appointments.

- *Watch* – essential for arriving punctually, leaving promptly for the next appointment, and for time-keeping when team interpreting.

- *Mobile phone* – make sure it is switched off during assignments.

- *Map/Street directory* – for efficient navigation to job venues.

- *Timetables of public transport* – if working in a city environment.

- *Spare plain contrasting top* – for those times when you are called to interpret without notice.

- *Dictionary (English), pocket-sized* – handy for last minute preparation if you come across an unfamiliar word in a paper you are reading through just before an assignment. Useful sign language dictionaries unfortunately tend to be large or in electronic form – not so portable.

- *Pen and paper* – useful when team interpreting, to note down difficult terms, names, and figures while your partner is 'on'; also handy for noting challenging language or problems that arise, or feedback, to share later.

- *Small torch* – for the deaf client to shine on you in a darkened lecture theatre (for example, during a slide show or film), or handy in a 'blackout' situation where visual communication is completely cut off.

- *Business cards* – if consumers like your work, they may ask for contact details. (Be aware, however, that it may be a breach of contract and professional practice to give out a personal business card at a job where you have been booked through an interpreting agency.)

- *Water* – bring a bottle to have on hand during breaks (but if in a public setting, it looks more professional to use a glass).

- *Snacks* – for energy crises during or between unexpectedly long jobs. (Low blood sugar can affect concentration and energy.)

- *Painkillers* – for headaches etc.

- *Deodorant* – especially for all-day assignments or hot days.

- *Hairbrush/comb* – to maintain that impeccably groomed image.

- *Lip-balm or lipstick (optional)* – for preventing dry lips, or providing clearer lip definition when working in larger settings.

- *Tissues.*

Having more latitude to choose assignments according to your competence and interests is a potential advantage, although interpreters often find that this only happens when work is plentiful enough to be turned down. Concern with maintaining an income flow can sometimes override this advantage, and result in an interpreter accepting an assignment that is beyond their competence or is a conflict of interest.

Some drawbacks of freelancing are:

- Irregular income;

- No sick leave or paid holidays;

- Administration and preparation time may not be fully compensated;

- Needing a home office and covering mobile phone and internet costs;

- Responsibility for tax returns and possibly worker's compensation.

When freelance interpreters take on heavy work schedules because of the uncertainty of regular income, it can be difficult to maintain healthy and safe working conditions with regard to the number of hours worked continuously or levels of emotional stress. Networking with other interpreters, and having an independent supervisor or a mentor are good ways to offset the professional isolation and stress that can affect freelancers.

Securing work

In a community where demand for interpreters is greater than supply, many freelancers do not actively market themselves; most gain enough work through contacts with a network of clients and other interpreters, and through requests from interpreting agencies. Public awareness of the need for interpreting and its status as a professional service also affects freelancers' approach to seeking work, as this New Zealand interpreter comments:

> I think interpreting in this country is still seen by most people as a 'charity service', and it doesn't fit easily with the business model of 'marketing' oneself – there's a clash in ideology.

However, some do promote their services using strategies such as a personal website, a business card, a professional resume, and directly approaching potential consumers to inform them of their qualifications and availability.

Contracts

When an interpreter accepts an interpreting request, whether verbally or in writing, this is effectively a contract to perform work. It is important that terms of work are clarified and agreed at this point, so that the client knows what the interpreter will provide in terms of service, and what is expected in the way of payment and conditions. It is important to ensure all parties are clear about and agreed on: the length of the assignment, fees, whether travel and preparation time will be charged and opportunity for breaks or team interpreting.

Charging

Freelancers generally have a standard hourly rate that is determined by qualification, experience, and acceptable market rates. Many charge a minimum two hourly, or 'set up', fee per job, and charge by the half or full hour thereafter. Some choose to charge different fees to profit and non-profit organisations at their discretion, or charge a higher rate for especially demanding or specialised assignments, unusual conditions, or out of hours work. When significant preparation is required (for example, a meeting based on many documents or a conference), interpreters commonly negotiate a fee for preparation time into their contract.

Depending on local practice and personal preference, freelancers may either consider travel costs to be part of their basic hourly rate, or charge for travel expenses by mileage or by travel time. Some prefer to build travel into their usual hourly rate for jobs within a certain distance of home, but charge for travel time or mileage to assignments outside that area.

Cancellation and no-show policies

Once an interpreter has committed their time to a booked job, it is standard practice to charge for that time unless notice has been given by the client by an agreed deadline. Many interpreters charge the full fee if an assignment is cancelled within 24 hours (or sometimes longer periods depending on the length or regularity of the assignment). When a job turns out to be shorter than expected, interpreters generally charge for the full amount of time that was booked.

If an interpreter arrives as scheduled to an assignment but a client does not show up, general practice is that the job is still chargeable, since the interpreter cannot be re-booked to cover loss of income for that time. Interpreters should negotiate or inform the booking client or agency how long they will wait in a 'no-show' situation before leaving. For a one-hour appointment, 15 minutes might be reasonable, whereas for a full-day booking, the first hour may be a reasonable wait time to allow for a client's transport difficulties. It is wise to state deadlines for both cancellation and no-show situations in the initial negotiation of terms and conditions.

A standard set of written terms and conditions that covers fees, charges for travel and preparation, and cancellation policies can be given to consumers when confirming a booking (see Appendix E, for an example). Colleagues and booking agencies can give guidance on current rates and locally preferred business practices. Brief guidelines on how to communicate through an interpreter and a copy of interpreting ethics are also useful items in a 'customer information' package, so that you can create realistic expectations about your role and how you can provide service most effectively.[5]

---

5   Brochures produced by ASLIA and SLIANZ, or the RID Standard Practice Paper on Professional Sign Language Interpreting (available at <www.rid.org/spp.html>), or the guidelines for working with sign language interpreters (http://www.odi.govt. nz/resources/guides-and-toolkits/working-with-nzsl-interpreters/index.html) are examples of summaries appropriate for consumers.

Record keeping

A basic administrative requirement for freelance interpreters is having a system for recording bookings, assignment details, invoices, income, and expense details (such as travel, parking, accommodation). Assignment records for bookings should include: date and time, client, address details, situation, contact person for further information, and agreed fee (if non-standard). Some people use computer software to manage information storage and accounting tasks, while others are just as efficient using paper, pen, and file folders. The key thing is to establish a personal system and use it consistently. (See Appendix F for a sample invoice.)

Operating as a freelancer means running a small business, and it is essential to familiarise oneself with income tax obligations, and to know which operating expenses are tax deductible. This information can be gained from the Inland Revenue Department (New Zealand) or the Australian Tax Office (Australia).

Insurance

Insurance is something the freelancer needs to seriously consider, especially liability insurance, which offers financial protection against legal suits over interpreter error, and income protection insurance, which is a safety-net when a self-employed person is unable to work because of illness. In New Zealand and Australia, government compensation covers medical expenses and loss of income resulting from work-related injury; however, if a free-lancer falls acutely or chronically ill (that is, not through injury), income protection insurance supplements the basic government sickness benefit. Liability insurance is sometimes available through membership of a professional interpreter's association or an interpreting agency.

Salaried staff interpreter positions

Deaf organisation or interpreting agency staff interpreter

Some interpreting service agencies (for example, a Deaf Association or Society, or a medical interpreting service) offer salaried positions as a 'community interpreter'. The workload usually involves interpreting in a wide range of community settings for individual appointments, meetings, and public events, and sometimes other administrative or consumer education tasks as well. The benefits of an on-staff position can include:

- Stable employment with a regular income;

- No need to seek work and deal with the administration of self-employment;

- A variety of interpreting assignments and levels of challenge;

- Exposure to a cross-section of the Deaf community and life situations;

- Office space and facilities provided;

- Use of a work vehicle;

- Regular contact with colleagues who provide deaf-related or interpreting services;

- Professional supervision and support.

Extensive contact with a wide spectrum of Deaf community members and settings can be an excellent opportunity for new interpreters to develop their sign language flexibility and cultural familiarity. A more structured employment situation can also allow interpreters to focus their energy on their interpreting skills without the stress of finding work as a freelancer. Having the built-in professional support of colleagues and becoming a familiar face to the wider Deaf community can be an advantage in the early stages of an interpreting career.

Some interpreters find, however, that working in a non-profit organisation can have drawbacks in terms of pay scales, appropriate supervision and supported professional development. In voluntary-based service agencies, these systems may still be emerging.

Confidentiality of client information

In agency situations, the sharing of client information between staff can be an ethical concern; for example, a service coordinator might ask the interpreter how an interpreted job interview with one of their clients went, or the booking coordinator might expect the interpreter, rather than the client, to inform them of follow-on appointments needing an interpreter. These scenarios highlight potential conflict between maintaining confidentiality and effective teamwork within the agency.

Conversely, a deaf client arrested by the police in the weekend might expect the interpreter to fully inform their social worker at the office on Monday morning about their need for support at a forthcoming court appearance, whereas another client may be deeply concerned if the interpreter does *not* keep interpreted information strictly confidential.

Expectations and protocols about information sharing need to be clarified between agency staff and clients, otherwise confidentiality issues and role boundaries can create tensions for the interpreter in a staff team with differing roles.

Non-Deaf organisation staff interpreter

Governmental or education-related organisations who have deaf staff members may hire a staff interpreter for in-house interpreting. As well as stable employment, possible professional development and supervision, this situation offers the opportunity to gain in-depth contextual knowledge of the work environment, content, and terminology, which usually enhances interpreting performance.

Role boundaries for 'on staff' interpreters[6]

The main challenge for 'on staff' interpreters is managing role boundaries and relationships with deaf and hearing staff in the workplace. The interpreter in this situation has two identities and sets of responsibilities: the primary function and identity is as an interpreter between deaf and hearing personnel, while a secondary role is staff member of the workplace. Unlike a freelance interpreter who arrives, interprets, and leaves with minimal involvement, the staff interpreter remains in the workplace and must interact and maintain relationships with a range of colleagues.

Interpreters employed in this situation find it difficult to have 'neutral' relationships with either the deaf employee, or the hearing staff, since they are included in the social and political life of the workplace, for example, socialising in casual lunches, personal chats, and after-work events. However, reserving your opinions on work-related matters is essential to maintaining credibility in the interpreting role, as this school-based interpreter suggests:

> It's really important to remember that even when you're not interpreting, you need to be seen as a person who remains impartial at all times. Even in the staffroom at lunchtime – if staff are discussing the latest contract change, or that sort of thing, you need to watch what you say, because you could later be interpreting between management and staff, and you're meant to be impartial. If you've already been heard in the staffroom mouthing off your opinions about it, then it's really difficult to play that impartial role.

Another staff interpreter working in a social service organisation with a deaf staff member describes the kind of tension that sometimes arises where people within a workplace have varying understandings of the interpreter's function:

> One day, a hearing staff member was dealing with a dissatisfied client and their conversation got quite animated and audible to everyone sharing the office space. The deaf staff member was working at his desk, and when he noticed that something was going on, he asked me what they were saying. The hearing staff member involved in the conversation soon noticed me signing and said, 'You don't need to interpret this; it's a private conversation'. Later on, I approached the hearing staff member in private to explain that since the conversation was obvious and audible to everyone else in the room, it was part of the workplace environment, and that my role as an interpreter was to make this kind of information accessible to the deaf person. She insisted that I was inappropriate in relaying conversations that weren't specifically directed to the deaf person...I knew that ethically I did the right thing in this situation, and that I took appropriate steps afterwards to clarify my role and my reasons, but it's horrible to feel resented and distrusted when I'm just doing my job.

---

6   Hauser et al (2008) offers case studies and perspectives on issues and strategies for interpreters working with deaf professionals in various work contexts.

Working as an in-house interpreter requires a heightened sense of inter-personal awareness. Establishing regular dialogue between deaf and hearing staff and the interpreter can help everyone understand how they contribute to maintaining the interpreter's role boundaries and the deaf person's inclusion.

■ ■ ■ ■ ■ ■

One of the pleasures and privileges of working as a sign language interpreter is the incredible variety of settings and people that we interact with. However, our professional role is still relatively unknown to many of the people we work with in these settings, so our task includes a public relations component. The way we explain our role, and maintain appro-priate work practices, impacts on the immediate work situation, including our emotional and physical health, as well as on the profession generally.

We are in an era where deaf people's rights to interpreting services are gradually strengthening through a combination of public awareness and legislation. Currently in Australia and New Zealand, the supply of inter-preters does not meet the demand, even in the areas where the use of interpreters is legally required. The up side of this is situation is that work is readily available for qualified interpreters; the down side is that the market does not yet discriminate between qualified and unqualified interpreters across all settings.

Interpreters have considerable autonomy and choice in how they organise their employment – as freelancers, staff interpreters, a combination of these, or even choosing to supplement interpreting work with another type of work or study. This chapter has shown how each of these arrange-ments has a different balance of benefits and disadvantages in terms of income, administrative and professional support, role definition, and inde-pendence. Over and above interpreting skills and ethical knowledge, developing a professional approach in business practices is important to managing good client relationships and ultimately a successful career.

Thought questions

1. Imagine that you have been invited to talk for 30 minutes to a conference of managers across a range of government service agencies, about the use of sign language interpreters with deaf consumers. This is a valuable opportunity to inform managers' expectations about dealing with professional interpreters. List some points on what you would tell them about:

    –   the definition of a qualified, trained interpreter;
    –   how a professional interpreter will function on the job;
    –   what conditions interpreters might expect from hearing clients;
    –   how to obtain the services of an interpreter (in your area).

2. How might occupational health and safety concerns be slightly different for a full-time educational interpreter and a freelance community interpreter? What would you say are the key risks, and preventative strategies, for each to be aware of and put into practice?

3. Look at the example of interpreter 'Terms and Conditions' included in the Reference Materials section. Think about:
    –   Would this be a useful model for setting your own contractual terms? Why?
    –   Are there any aspects that you would want to alter or add?
    –   What are the benefits to freelancers and clients of having a document like this?

4. The situations of a freelance interpreter and staff interpreter positions create different combinations of opportunities and challenges around the interpreter's ability to maintain role boundaries. Identify positives and negatives in each employment situation, using the chart below.

	Freelance interpreter	Staff interpreter
Advantages to role clarity		
Threats to role clarity		

Appendix A – Recommended readings

Education

Seal, BC (1998), *Best practices in educational interpreting*, Allyn & Bacon, Needham Heights, MA.

Winston, E (ed), (2004), *Educational interpreting: How it can succeed*, Gallaudet University Press, Washington, DC.

VicCite report, *'Educational interpreting and note-taking in Australia'*, <http://online.nmit.vic.edu.au/viccite/publications.htm>.

Social service and government agencies

Gentile, A, Ozolins, U et al (1996), *Liaison interpreting: A handbook*, Melbourne University Press, Melbourne.

Roberts-Smith, L, Frey, R and Bessell-Browne, S (1990), *Working with interpreters in law, health and social work*, NAATI, Mount Hawthorn, WA.

Employment

Mindess, A (1999), Reading between the signs: Intercultural communication for sign language interpreters, Intercultural Press, Yarmouth, Maine.

Medical

Angelelli, C (2004), *Medical interpreting and cross-cultural communication*, Cambridge University Press, Cambridge.

Crezée, I (1998), *A Brief Guide to Healthcare Settings and Healthcare Terminology*, New Horizons Advisory Services, Auckland, NZ.

Metzger, M (1999), *Sign language interpreting: Deconstructing the myth of neutrality*, Gallaudet University Press, Washington DC.

Mental health

Austen, S and Crocker, S (eds)(2004), *Deafness in mind: Working psychologically with deaf people through the lifespan*, Whurr, London.

Cornes AJ and Napier J (2005) 'Challenges of mental health interpreting when working with deaf patients', *Australasian Psychiatry*, 13(4): 161-179.

Gutman, V (ed), (2002), *Ethics in mental health and deafness*, Gallaudet University Press, Washington, DC.

Hindley, P and Kitson, N (eds), (1998), *Mental health and deafness*, Whurr, London.

Legal

Berk-Seligson, S (1990), *The Bilingual Courtroom: Court Interpreters in the Judicial Process*, University of Chicago Press, Chicago.

Brennan, M and Brown, R (2004), *Equality before the law: Deaf people's access to justice* (2nd edn), Douglas McLean, Coleford, UK.

Colin, J and Morris, R (1996), *Interpreters and the Legal Process*, Waterside Press, Winchester.

Hale, SB (2004), *The Discourse of Court Interpreting: Discourse practices of the law, the witness and the interpreter*, John Benjamins, Amsterdam .

Laster, K and Taylor, V (1994), *Interpreters and the legal system*, Federation Press, Sydney.

Mikkelson, H (2000), *Introduction to court interpreting*, St Jerome Publishing, Manchester, UK.

Quynh-Du, Ton-That (1996) 'Legal Settings', in Gentile, A, Ozolins, U and Vasilakakos, M (eds) *Liaison interpreting: A handbook*, Melbourne University Press, Melbourne.

Russell, D (2002), *Interpreting in legal contexts: Consecutive and simultaneous interpretation*, Sign Media Inc, Burtonsville, MD.

Russell, D and Hale, S (eds) (2008), *Interpreting in legal settings*, Gallaudet University Press, Washington, DC.

Religious

Borrmann M (2004) 'Interpreting frozen text in the religious setting: The path toward dynamic equivalence', *Journal of Interpretation*: 75-94.

Frishberg, N (1990)(2nd edn), 'Interpreting in religious settings', in Frishberg, N (ed), *Interpreting: An introduction*, RID Publications, Silver Spring, MD.

Conference

Kopczynski, A (1980), *Conference interpreting: Some linguistic and communicative problems*, Adam Mickiewicz Press, Poznan, Poland.

Seleskovitch, D (1978), *Interpreting for international conferences*, Pen and Booth, Washington, DC.

Performance

Gebron, J (2000) (2nd edn), *Sign the speech: An introduction to theatrical interpreting*, Butte Publications, Hillsboro, OR.

Kilpatrick, B and Andrews, J (2009), 'Accessibility to Theater for Deaf and Deaf-Blind People: Legal, Language and Artistic Considerations'. *International Journal of Interpreter Education*, 1, 77-94.

Team working

Cokely, D and Hawkins, J (2003), 'Interpreting in Teams: A Pilot Study on Requesting and Offering Support', *Journal of Interpretation:* 49-94.

Mitchell, T (2002), 'Co-working and equal participation', *Deaf Worlds*, 18(2), 66-68.

Telephone interpreting

Dickinson, J (2002), 'Telephone interpreting – "Hello, is anyone there?"' *Deaf Worlds*, 18(2): 34-38.

Mindess, A (1999), *Reading between the signs: Intercultural communication for sign language interpreters*, Intercultural Press, Yarmouth, Maine.

Pollitt, K and Haddon, C (2005), 'Cold calling? Re-training interpreters in the art of telephone interpreting', in Roy C (ed), *Advances in teaching sign language interpreters*, Gallaudet University Press, Washington DC.

Wadensjö, C (1999), 'Telephone interpreting and the synchronization of talk in social interaction', *The Translator*, 5(2): 247-264.

Video (remote) interpreting

Braun, S. (2007). 'Interpreting in small-group bilingual videoconferences: Challenges and adaptation processes', *Interpreting*, 9(1), 21-46. Available: <http://www.benjamins.com/cgi-bin/t_articles.cgi?bookid=INTP%209%3A1&artid=693110960>

Spencer, R (2000), *Video Relay Interpreting Trial Report*, Australian Communication Exchange, Brisbane. Available: <www.aceinfo.net.au/Resources/Downloads/index.html#research>.

Deaf interpreting

Forestal, E (2005), 'The Emerging Professionals: Deaf Interpreters and Their Views and Experiences on Training', in Marschark, M, Peterson, R and Winston EA (eds), *Interpreting and Interpreter Education: Directions for Research and Practice*, Oxford University Press, New York.

Ressler, C (1999), 'A comparative analysis of a direct interpretation and an intermediary interpretation in American Sign Language', *Journal of Interpretation*, 71-104.

Clients with minimal language competence

Language Services Section (LSS) – New Jersey Administrative Office of the Courts (2004) *Guidelines for interpreting for deaf persons who do not communicate competently in American Sign Language*. Available: <http://www.judiciary.state.nj.us/interpreters/wrkgdeafjur.pdf>.

Clients who are deafblind

Mesch, J (2001), *Tactile Swedish sign language: Turn-taking and questions in signed conversations of deaf-blind people*, in Metger (ed), *Bilingualism and Identity in Deaf Communities*, Gallaudet University Press, Washington DC.

Smith, TB (2002), *Guidelines: Practical Tips for Working & Socializing with Deaf-Blind People*, Linstok Press, Burtonsville, MD.

Working with deaf professionals

Cook, AP (2004), 'Neutrality? No Thanks, Can a Biased Role Be an Ethical One?' *Journal of Interpretation:* 19-56.

Hauser, PC, Finch, K, and Hauser, A, (eds), (2008), *Deaf professionals and designated interpreters: A new paradigm*, Gallaudet University Press, Washington, DC.

Oral interpreting

Castle, DL (1984), 'Effective oral interpreters: An analysis', in Northcott, Winifred, H (ed) *Oral interpreting: Principles and practices*, University Park Press, Baltimore.

International Sign interpreting

McKee, R and Napier, J (2002), 'Interpreting into International Sign Pidgin: An analysis', *Journal of Sign Language and Linguistics*, 5(1), 27-54.

Moody, B (2002), 'International Sign: A practitioner's perspective', *Journal of Interpretation*. 1-48

Māori and Indigenous Australian settings

Metge, J and Laing, P (1984), *Talking Past Each Other: Problems of Cross-Cultural Communication*, Victoria University of Wellington Press, Wellington, NZ.

Moko-Mead (2003), *Tikanga Māori: Living by Māori Values*, Huia Publishers, Wellington.

Pere, RR (1991), *Te Wheke: A celebration of infinite wisdom*, AOAKO, Gisborne, NZ.

Salmond, A (2004), *Hui: A study of Māori ceremonial gatherings*, Reed Publishers, Auckland.

Tauroa, H and Tauroa, P (1986), *Te Marae: A guide to customs and protocols*, Reed Books, Auckland.

Appendix B – SLIANZ Code of Ethics

This Code of Ethics defines the principles of professional practice for all members of the Sign Language Interpreters Association of New Zealand (SLIANZ).

Impartiality

Interpreters shall never counsel, advise or interject personal opinions during the interpreting assignment. Interpreters shall not allow their personal interests and beliefs to influence the interpreting assignment. Interpreters shall remove themselves if the interpretation is influenced by a lack of impartiality.

Confidentiality

Interpreters shall treat as confidential any information gained through an assignment, including the fact of their having undertaken an assignment.

Competency

Interpreters shall only accept assignments in which they can reasonably expect to interpret competently having ascertained the level of skill required, the setting and the consumers involved. If an interpreter believes he/she is not able to interpret competently he/she will inform both parties and negotiate an acceptable solution.

Accuracy

Interpreters will, to the best of their ability interpret the meaning of the message in the manner in which it was intended without adding or omitting anything.

Professional Development

Interpreters shall continue to further their knowledge and skills by attending professional development or training activities, maintaining good working relations with colleagues, and keeping abreast of current literature and practice in the field.

Appendix C – ASLIA Code of Ethics and Guidelines for Professional Conduct

Preamble

The following document has been modelled on the Code of Ethics developed by the Association of Visual Language Interpreters of Canada (AVLIC). The work and consultation process undertaken by AVLIC with its members is acknowledged by ASLIA National.

Input received from members of ASLIA in the first round of consultation was included herein. A second draft of the proposed new Code of Ethics for ASLIA, was distributed for a further consultation round, including major stakeholders and once again with members of ASLIA with feedback requested by 15 July 2007. ASLIA National presented the final version of the new Code of Ethics which was ratified by the membership at our AGM in Sydney on 8 September 2007.

ASLIA expects all practitioners to maintain high standards of professional conduct in their identity and capacity as an interpreter. Members of ASLIA in particular, are required to abide by the Code of Ethics and follow the Guidelines for Professional Conduct as a condition of membership of the association.

This document articulates ethical principles, values, and standards of conduct to guide all practitioners in their pursuit of professional practice. It is intended to provide direction to interpreters for ethical and professional decision-making in their day-to-day work. The Code of Ethics and Guidelines for Professional Conduct is the mechanism by which the public is protected in the delivery of service. It should not be considered a prescriptive set of rules, but rather a set of principles and values which should be inherent in professional practice.

Values underlying the Code of Ethics and Guidelines for Professional Conduct

ASLIA values:

1. Professional accountability:

Accepting responsibility for professional decisions and actions.

2. Professional competence:

Committing to provide quality professional service throughout one's practice.

3. Non-discrimination:

Approaching professional service with respect and cultural sensitivity.

4. Integrity in professional relationships:

Dealing honestly and fairly with participants and colleagues.

5. Integrity in business practices:

Dealing honestly and ethically in all business practices.

Practitioners[1] are to understand that each of these core values and accompanying sections are to be considered when making ethical and professional decisions in their identity and capacity as an interpreter. These values are of equal weight and importance.

Code of Ethics and Guidelines for Professional Conduct

1. PROFESSIONAL ACCOUNTABILITY: Interpreters accept responsibility for all professional decisions made and actions taken.

1.1. Confidentiality

1.1.1. Practitioners will respect the privacy of all participants and hold in confidence all information obtained in the course of professional service, be that within an interpreting assignment or in the details about an assignment. Practitioners may be released from this

---

1 "Practitioners" for the purpose of this document, refers to both Deaf and hearing individuals who are engaged in interpreting assignments using Auslan. "Participants" refers to both Deaf and hearing participants in any interpreted assignment.

obligation only with the participants' authorisation or when ordered by law. Where necessary, a practitioner may exchange pertinent information with a colleague in order to provide consistent quality of service. This will be done in a manner that protects the information and the participants.

1.1.2. Practitioners need to be aware that other professional codes of conduct may impact upon their work. In such circumstances, practitioners will make appropriate professional decisions and conduct themselves in a manner befitting the setting and the profession.

1.2   Professional Conduct

1.2.1. Practitioners will hold the needs of participants' primary when making professional decisions.

1.2.2. Practitioners shall recognise that all work undertaken by them on an individual basis, whether pro bono or paid, will ultimately reflect the integrity of them and of the profession.

1.2.3. Practitioners shall conduct themselves in a professional manner at all times. They shall not badger or coerce individuals or agencies to use their professional services.

1.2.4. Practitioners shall take into account the limitations of their linguistic abilities, knowledge and the resources available to them prior to accepting work. They will remove themselves from a given setting when they realise an inability to provide professional service.

1.2.5. Practitioners must be aware of personal circumstances or conflicts of interest that might interfere with their effectiveness. They will refrain from conduct that can lead to substandard performance and/or harm[2] to anyone, including themselves and participants.

1.2.6 Practitioners who are ASLIA members are accountable to ASLIA National and to their State Association for their professional and ethical conduct. Further, practitioners are responsible to discuss and resolve, in a professional manner, issues arising from breaches of ethical or professional conduct on the part of individual colleagues after they are observed. In the case where these breaches are potentially harmful to others or chronic, and attempts to resolve the issue have not been successful, such conduct should be reported to ASLIA National, and/or their State Association, in a manner directed by the appropriate grievance procedure.

---

2   Harm refers to injurious behaviour that causes distress to the person. This can include but is not limited to actions which are sexual, physical, emotional or verbal in nature. It can also include performance of duties while under the influence of alcohol, drugs or mind-altering substances.

1.3 Scope of Practice

1.3.1 When functioning as part of a professional team (for example, but not limited to; education, legal, medical or mental health settings) it is understood that practitioners will limit their expertise to interpretation. In such settings, it may be appropriate for practitioners to comment on the overall effectiveness of communication, the interpreting process and to suggest appropriate resources and referrals. This should be done only within the context of the professional team.

1.3.2. Practitioners will refrain from using their professional role to perform other functions that lie beyond the scope of an interpreting assignment and the parameters of their professional duties. They will not counsel, advise, or interject personal opinions.

1.3.3. Practitioners will refrain from manipulating work situations for personal benefit or gain. When working as independent contractors, practitioners may promote their professional services within the scope of their practice. When working under the auspices of an agency or other employer, it is not ethical for the practitioners to promote their professional services independent of the agency or employer.

1.4. Integrity of Service

1.4.1 Practitioners will demonstrate sound professional judgment and accept responsibility for their decisions. Practitioners will make every attempt to avoid situations that constitute a real or perceived conflict of interest. Practitioners will ensure there is full disclosure to all parties should their ancillary interest be seen as a real or perceived conflict of interest.

2. PROFESSIONAL COMPETENCE: Interpreters provide the highest possible quality of service through all aspects of their professional practice.

2.1. Qualifications to Practice

2.1.1. Practitioners will be accredited by NAATI at Paraprofessional or Professional Interpreter level. Deaf Relay Interpreters will have completed appropriate training or testing. Practitioners will possess the knowledge and skills to support accurate and appropriate interpretation. It is recognized that practitioners work in a range of settings and with a variety of participants with diverse communication needs. This demands that practitioners be adept at meeting the linguistic needs of participants, the cultural dynamics of each situation, and the spirit and content of the discourse.

2.2. Faithfulness of Interpretation

2.2.1. Every interpretation shall be faithful to and render faithfully the message of the source text. A faithful interpretation should not be confused with a literal interpretation. The fidelity of an interpretation includes an adaptation to make the form, the tone, and the deeper meaning of the source text felt in the target language and culture.

2.3. Accountability for Professional Competence

3.3.1 Practitioners will accept full responsibility for the quality of their own work and will refrain from making inaccurate statements regarding their competence, education, experience or certification.

2.3.2. Practitioners are responsible for properly preparing themselves for the work contracted.

2.3.3. Practitioners will accept contracts for work only after determining they have the appropriate qualifications and can remain neutral throughout the assignment.

2.4. Ongoing Professional Development

2.4.1. Practitioners will incorporate current theoretical and applied knowledge into their professional practice. They will enhance that knowledge through continuing education throughout their professional careers and will strive to upgrade NAATI accreditation, as well participating in revalidation of accreditation procedures.

2.4.2. Practitioners will aim to be self-directed learners, pursuing educational opportunities which are relevant to their professional practice. This could include, but is not limited to, peer review, collegial consultation, mentoring, and obtaining regular feedback regarding specific areas of skill development.

3. NON-DISCRIMINATION: Interpreters approach professional services with respect and cultural sensitivity[3] towards all participants.

3.1 Non-discrimination

3.1.1. Practitioners will respect the individuality, the right to self-determination, and the autonomy of the people with whom they work. They will not discriminate based on ethnicity, gender, age,

---

3   Cultural sensitivity refers to being aware of and responding to the uniqueness of each individual and of each context within which we work.

disability, sexual orientation, religion, personal beliefs and practices, social status or any other factor.

3.2 Communication Preferences

3.2.1. Practitioners will respect and use specific forms of communication preferred by deaf and hard of hearing participants, as well as any hearing participants, to whom they provide service. Refer also to 1.2.4.

3.3. Deaf Relay Interpreters

3.3.1. The services of a Deaf Relay Interpreter may be required when working with individuals who use regional sign dialects, non-standard signs, foreign sign languages, and those with emerging language use. They may also be used with individuals who have disabling conditions that impact on communication. Practitioners will recognise the need for a Deaf Relay Interpreter and will advocate for their inclusion as a part of the professional interpreting team where applicable.

4. INTEGRITY IN PROFESSIONAL RELATIONSHIPS: Interpreters deal honestly and fairly with participants and colleagues while establishing and maintaining professional boundaries.

4.1. Professional Relationships

4.1.1. Practitioners shall understand the difference between professional and social interactions. They will establish and maintain appropriate boundaries between themselves and participants. Practitioners will assume responsibility to ensure relationships with all parties involved are reasonable, fair and professional.

4.2. Impartiality

4.2.1. Practitioners shall remain neutral, impartial, and objective. They will refrain from altering a message for political, religious, moral, or philosophical reasons, or any other biased or subjective consideration.

4.2.2. Should a practitioner not be able to put aside personal biases or reactions which threaten impartiality, the practitioner will examine options available to them. These may include not accepting the work, or withdrawing their services from the assignment or contract.

4.3. Respect for Colleagues

4.3.1. Practitioners will act toward colleagues in a spirit of mutual cooperation, treating and portraying them to others with respect, courtesy, fairness and good faith. Practitioners have a professional obligation to assist and encourage new interpreting practitioners in the profession.

4.3.2. Practitioners shall not abuse the good faith of other practitioners, breach trust, or use unfair tactics in dealings with colleagues or others.

4.4. Support for Professional Associations

4.4.1. Practitioners are expected to support ASLIA National, its State Associations, and other organisations representing the profession and the Deaf community.

5. INTEGRITY IN BUSINESS RELATIONSHIPS: Interpreters establish and maintain professional boundaries with participants and colleagues in a manner that is honest and fair.

5.1. Business Practices

5.1.1 Practitioners will refrain from any unfair competition with their colleagues, including, but not limited to:
a. engaging in comparative advertising
b. wilfully undercutting; or
c. artificially inflating fees during times when market demand exceeds supply.

5.1.2. Practitioners will conduct themselves in all phases of the interpreting situation in a manner befitting the profession, including negotiating work and contracts, obtaining suitable preparation material, choice of attire, presentation and professional demeanour.

5.1.3. Practitioners will honour professional commitments made when accepting work, and will follow through on their obligations. Practitioners may not unilaterally terminate work or a contract unless they have fair and reasonable grounds to do so. Termination for the purposes of gaining better paid work is not fair or reasonable.

5.1.4. Practitioners shall take reasonable care of material and/or property given to them by a participant or employer (for example, speech notes or a textbook) and may not lend such or use it for purposes other than those for which it was entrusted to them.

5.2. Accurate Representation of Credentials

5.2.1. Practitioners shall not by any means engage in, nor allow, the use of statements regarding their credentials that are false, misleading, incomplete, or likely to mislead participants or members of the public.

5.2.2. Practitioners will refrain from making inaccurate statements regarding their competence, education, experience or certification. This may include, but is not limited to, interpreter directories, business cards and forms, promotional materials, resumes or publications they have authored.

5.3. Reimbursement for Services

5.3.1. Practitioners will bill only for services provided. Practitioners will negotiate fees, including cancellation policies, preferably in writing or contract form, before service is provided. Practitioners will be sensitive to professional and community norms when establishing fees for services.

5.3.2. Practitioners may also provide pro bono service in situations where the profession of interpreting and the livelihood of other practitioners will not be threatened (refer to the ASLIA National pro bono interpreting policy).

References consulted

Association of Translators and Interpreters of Alberta Code of Ethics (draft, 1999) unpublished.

Corey, Corey & Callanan. (1993) *Issues and ethics in the helping profession.* Pacific Grove, CA: Brooks/Cole Publishing Company.

Humphrey, Janice (1999) *Decisions, decisions.* Amarillo, TX: H & H Publishers.

Code of Ethics for Psychiatric Nurses Association of Canada (February, 1998).

Camosum College Guidelines for Instructors, Victoria, BC (1997).

Code of Ethics: American Mental Health Counselors Association (1997).

Code of Ethics: Society of Translators and Interpreters of British Columbia (Fall, 1998).

Code of Ethics for the National Association of Social Workers, (revised 1990).

Appendix D – Deafblind Alphabet Chart

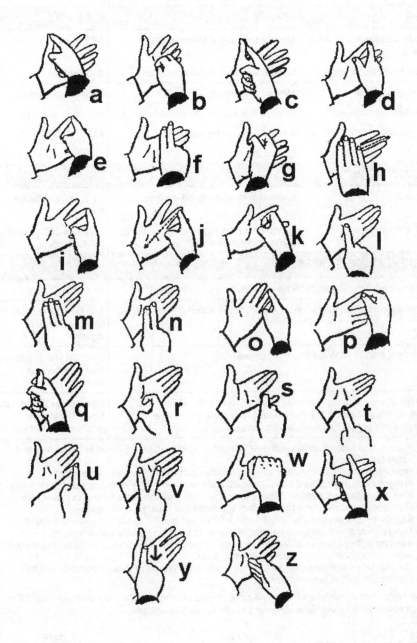

Appendix E – Sample Terms and Conditions

		EFFECTIVE AS OF *(date)*

(Name) / Sign language interpreter

FEES

Standard callout fee *(2 hrs or shorter)*	*Monday to Friday, 8.00am–6.00pm*	$80
Hourly fee *(2 hrs or longer)*	*Monday to Friday, 8.00am–6.00pm*	$40 per hour
Evening surcharge	*Monday to Friday, 7.00pm–6.00am*	booked time + 15%
Weekend surcharge	*Saturdays, Sundays and public holidays*	booked time + 25%
Travel costs	*Within 20 kms of Hataitai office*	$15
	Beyond 20kms	to be advised

PAYMENT TERMS

Due date	*Negotiable in advance, otherwise:*	21 days from invoice date
Late payment fee	*In addition to the invoice amount owing and if payment overdue:*	$10.00 + 25% of total invoice amount

CANCELLATIONS | LATENESS

Client cancellation more than 36 hours in advance of assignment:	no charge
Client cancellation with between 24 and 36 hours notice will be charged:	$40 OR 50% of booked time *(whichever is higher)*
Client cancellation within 24 hours will be charged:	standard fee OR booked time *(whichever is higher)*
In cases of client lateness the interpreter will remain for 30 minutes. Target clients who do contact the interpreter to make alternative arrangements or fail to show up will be charged:	standard fee OR booked time + travel costs *(whichever is higher)*

o A team interpreter is usually required for assignments that are 1.5 hours or longer and/or are highly technical.

o Preparation materials (meeting agendas, a list of participants' names, power point presentations, background information, etc.) are required, where possible, at least 3 working days before the assignment. If these cannot be provided, the client must accept that without sufficient preparation time the accuracy of interpreting could be compromised.

o Regular breaks are required: preferably for 5 minutes per 30 minutes of solo interpreting. Team interpreting breaks are negotiable in view of client's schedule and/or agenda.

o Interpreting beyond booked assignment time at the client's request (eg, clients are running well overtime) is entirely at the interpreter's discretion.

o The interpreter will not be responsible for any loss as a result of misinterpretation and/or miscommunication between parties.

These Terms and Conditions will cover all assignments accepted by the interpreter. At least 14 days written notice will be given for any changes to the Terms & Conditions.

NAME	SIGNED	DATE
POSITION	ORGANISATION	

Appendix F – Sample invoice

CHRIS TAYLOR

Auslan / English Interpreter
NAATI Paraprofessional Interpreter, ASLIA member

ABN: 12 345 678 123

Job Description:	Interpreting for recruitment interview
Venue:	Level 2, LMN Building, George Street, City
Client/s:	XYZ Corporation & Kim Smith
Contact person:	Lee Jones (ph: 1221 3443)
Date/s & Time/s:	11.15am – 12.15pm, Tuesday 11th October 2010
Pay rate:	$40 per hour*

Total fee: $80

Comments:

* N.B. All bookings are charged at a minimum of 2 hours.
This is not a tax invoice, ie, no GST has been charged.

Payment is requested within 28 days.

If you have any questions about this invoice, please contact me on:
(ph) 0123 456 789
Thank you

<u>Chris Taylor</u>   **Invoice number:** 09-10/14
11/10/10

NB   Please send payment to: *postal address*
        or deposit into account: *bank details*

REFERENCES

Angelelli, C (2003), 'The visible co-participant: The interpreter's role in doctor-patient encounters' in Metzger, M, Collins, S, Dively, V and, Shaw, R (eds), *From topic boundaries to omission: New research on interpretation*, Gallaudet University Press, Washington, DC.

Angelelli, C (2004), *Medical interpreting and cross-cultural communication*, Cambridge University Press, Cambridge.

Austen, S and S, Crocker (eds), (2004), *Deafness in mind: Working psychologically with deaf people through the lifespan*, Whurr, London.

Australian Bureau of Statistics (2005), *Australian Social Trends: Crime and Justice: Aboriginal and Torres Strait Islander People: Contact with the Law*, <www.abs.gov.au/ausstats/ABS@.nsf/2f762f95845417aeca25706c00834efa/a3c671495d062f72ca25703b0080ccd1!OpenDocument> accessed 5 September 2009).

Australian Bureau of Statistics, (2006), *Law and Justice Statistics – Aboriginal and Torres Strait Islander People – A Snapshot* <www.abs.gov.au/ausstats/abs@.nsf/mf/4722.0.55.003> accessed 17 February 2009.

AVLIC (1992), 'Interpreters in the educational setting: A resource document', Association of Visual Language Interpreters of Canada, Ontario, Canada.

Awheto, S (2004) Personal communication: interview with Rachel McKee, 9 October 2004, Hamilton, NZ

Baetens Beardsmore, H (1986), *Bilingualism: Basic principles*, Multilingual Matters, Clevedon.

Baker, M (1992), *In other words: A coursebook on translation*, Routledge, London.

Barnes, L, Harrington, F, Williams, L, Atherton, M (eds), (2007), *Deaf students in higher education: Current research & practice*, Douglas McLean, Coleford.

Bauman, DH-L (ed) (2007), *Open your eyes: Deaf studies talking*, University of Minnesota Press, London.

Bélanger, D (2004), 'Interactional patterns in dialogue interpreting', *Journal of Interpretation*: 1-18.

Bell, A (1984), 'Language styles as audience design', *Language in Society* 13: 145-204.

Bergson, M and D, Sperlinger (2003), '"I still don't know what I should have done": Reflections on personal/professional dilemmas in sign language interpreting', *Deaf Worlds* 19(3): 6-23.

Berk-Seligson, S (1990), *The Bilingual Courtroom: Court Interpreters in the Judicial Process*, University of Chicago Press, Chicago.

Beukes, A, and Pienaar, M (2009), 'Simultaneous interpreting: Implementing multilingual teaching in a South African tertiary classroom', in Inggs, J and Meintjes, L (eds), *Translation Studies in Africa: Central Issues in Interpreting and Literary and Media Translation*, Continuum, London.

Bidoli, CJK (2004), ' Intercultural Features of English-to-Italian Sign Language Conference Interpretation: A Preliminary Study for Multimodal Corpus Analysis', *Textus* 17: 127-142.

Bontempo, K and Napier, J (2007), 'Mind the gap! A skills analysis of sign language interpreters', *The Sign Language Translator & Interpreter* 1(2): 275-299.

Bontempo, K and Napier, J (2009a), 'Emotional stability as a predictor for interpreter competence: A consideration in determining aptitude for interpreting', Paper presented at the Symposium *Aptitude for Interpreting*, Lessius University College, Antwerp, Belgium, 28-29 May 2009.

Bontempo, K and Napier, J (2009b) "Getting it right from the start: Program admission testing of signed language interpreters", in Angelelli, C, and Jacobson, H (eds), *Testing and Assessment in Translation and Interpreting Studies*, John Benjamins, Amsterdam.

Borden, B (1996), *The art of interpreting American Sign Language*, Hayden-McNeil Publishing, Plymouth, Michigan.

Borrmann, M (2004), 'Interpreting frozen text in the religious setting: The path toward dynamic equivalence', *Journal of Interpretation*: 75-94.

Bot, H (2003), 'The myth of the uninvolved interpreter interpreting in mental health and the development of a three-person psychology', in Brunette, L, Bastin, G, Hemlin, I and Clarke, H (eds), *The Critical Link 3: Interpreters in the Community*, John Benjamins, Amsterdam.

Boudrealt, P (2005), 'Deaf interpreters', in Janzen, T (ed), *Topics in signed language interpreting*, John Benjamins, Amsterdam.

Bowen, M (1980), 'Bilingualism as a factor in the training of interpreters', Alatis, JE (ed), *Georgetown University Round table on Languages and Linguistics, 1980: Current Issues in Bilingual Education*, University Press, Washington, DC.

Bowman, J and Hyde, M (1993), 'Manual communication as support for deaf students in the regular classroom', *Australian Teacher of the Deaf* 33: 32-46.

Braun, S (2007), 'Interpreting in small-group bilingual videoconferences: Challenges and adaptation processes' *Interpreting* 9(1): 21-46.

Bremner, A and Housden, T (1996), 'Issues in educational settings for deaf students and interpreters'. Available: <http://www.deakin.edu/extern/rdlu/deafstud.html> accessed 1 February 2005.

Brennan, M and Brown, R (2004), *Equality before the law: Deaf people's access to justice*, Douglas McLean, Coleford, UK.

Brown, P and Fraser, C (1979), 'Speech as a marker of situation', in Scherer, K and Giles, H (eds), *Social markers in speech*, Cambridge University Press, Cambridge.

Campbell, L, Rohan, M, and Woodcock, K (2008), 'Academic and educational interpreting from the other side of the classroom: Working with deaf academics', in Hauser, P, Finch, K, and Hauser, A (eds), Deaf professionals and designated interpreters: A new paradigm, Galluadet University Press, Washington, DC.

Castle, DL (1984), 'Effective oral interpreters: An analysis', in Northcott, WH (ed), *Oral interpreting: Principles and practices*, University Park Press, Baltimore.

Chafe, W (1980), *The pear stories: Cognitive, cultural and linguistic aspects of narrative production*, Ablex, Norwood, NJ.

Coates, J and Sutton-Spence, R (2001), 'Turn-taking patterns in Deaf conversation', *Journal of Sociolinguistics* 5(4): 507-529.

Cokely, D (1983), 'Metanotative qualities: How accurately are they conveyed by interpreters?' *The Reflector* 5: 16-22.

Cokely, D (1992), 'Effects of lag time on interpreter errors', in Cokely, D (ed), *Sign Language Interpreters and Interpreting*, Linstok Press, Burtonsville, MD.

Cokely, D (1992), *Interpretation: A sociolinguistic model*, Burtonsville, MD, Linstok Press.

Cokely, D (2000) 'Exploring ethics: A case for revising the code of ethics', *Journal of Interpretation:* 25-60.

Cokely, D (2005), 'Shifting positionality: A critical examination of the turning point in the relationship of interpreters and the Deaf community', in Marschark, M, Peterson, R and Winston EA (eds), *Interpreting and interpreting education: Directions for research and practice*, Oxford University Press, New York.

Cokely, D and Hawkins, J (2003), 'Interpreting in teams: A pilot study on requesting and offering support', *Journal of Interpretation*: 49-94.

Colin, J and Morris, R (1996), *Interpreters and the Legal Process*, Waterside Press, Winchester.

Collins, J and Walker, J (2006), 'What is a Deaf interpreter?', in McKee, R (ed), *Proceedings of the Inaugural Conference of the World Association of Sign Language Interpreters*, Douglas McLean, Coleford.

Colonomos, B (1992), *The interpreting process,* unpublished teaching materials, The Bicultural Centre, Riverdale, MD. Summary available: <www.the interpretersfriend.com.pd.ws. pcsg_mdls/text.html>.

Compton, M and Shroyer, E (1997), 'Educational interpreter preparation and liberal education', *Journal of Interpretation* 7(1): 49-61.

Conlon, C and Napier, J (2004), 'Developing Auslan educational resources: A process of effective translation of children's books', *Deaf Worlds* 20(2): 141-161.

Cook, AP (2004), 'Neutrality? No Thanks, Can a Biased Role Be an Ethical One?' *Journal of Interpretation*: 57-74.

Cooke, M (2002), 'Indigenous Australian Interpreting Issues for Courts', Australian Institute of Judicial Administration Incorporated Publication Melbourne, <www.aija.org.au/ac01/Cooke.pdf> accessed 17 February 2009.

Corker, M (1997), 'Deaf people and interpreting – The struggle in language', *Deaf Worlds* 13(3): 13-20.

Cornes, A and Napier, J (2005), 'Challenges of mental health interpreting: Therapy has taught us that it's all our fault!' *Australasian Journal of Psychiatry*.

Coughlin, J (1985), 'Interpreter's training: Learning to control the bilingual switch mechanism', *Babel: International Journal of Translation* 30(1): 20 – 26.

Crezée, I (1998), *A Brief Guide to Healthcare Settings and Healthcare Terminology*, New Horizons Advisory Services, Auckland, NZ.

Davis, J (2003), 'Cross-linguistic strategies used by interpreters', *Journal of Interpretation*: 95-128.

Dean, R and Pollard, RQ (2001), 'The application of demand-control theory to sign language interpreting: Implications for stress and interpreter training', *Journal of Deaf Studies and Deaf Education* 6(1): 1-14.

Dean, R and Pollard, RQ (2005), 'Consumers and Service Effectiveness in Interpreting Work: A Practice Profession Perspective', in Marschark, M, Peterson R and Winston, EA (eds), *Interpreting and Interpreter Education: Directions for Research and Practice*, Oxford University Press, New York.

Dean, R and Pollard, RQ (2007), 'From theory to schema: Using Demand-Control in the practice and teaching interpreting', Unpublished manuscript, University of Rochester.

Dickinson, J (2002), 'Telephone interpreting – "Hello, is anyone there?"' *Deaf Worlds* 18(2): 34-38.

Dickinson, J and Turner, GH (2008), 'Sign language interpreters and role conflict in the workplace', in Valero-Garces, C and Martin, A (eds), *Crossing borders in community interpreting: Definition and dilemmas*, John Benjamins, Amsterdam.

Dion, J (2005), *The Changing Dynamics of the Interpreting Industry as influenced by Video Relay Service (VRS) and its Impact on the Deaf Community*, paper presented at the 3rd Supporting Deaf People Online Conference, 10-16 March. Available: <http://www.online-conference.net/sdp3/index.htm>.

Dugdale, PO (2000), *Being Deaf in New Zealand: A case study of the Wellington Deaf community*, unpublished doctoral dissertation, Victoria University of Wellington, NZ.

Eades, D (1996), 'Legal Recognition of Cultural Differences in Communication: The Case of Robyn Kina', *Language & Communication* 1 (3): 215–227.

Eighinger, L and Karlin, B (2003), 'Feminist-Relational approach: A social construct for event management', in Brunette, L, Bastin, G, Hemlin, I and Clarke, H (eds), *The critical link 3: Interpreters in the community*, John Benjamins, Philadelphia.

Elliott, RN and Powers, AR (1995), 'Preparing interpreters to serve in educational settings', *Journal of the Association of Canadian Educators of the Hearing Impaired* 21(2/3): 132-140.

Fayd'herbe, K and Teuma, R (2010), 'Interpreting for Indigenous Australian deaf clients in Far North Queensland, Australia within the legal context', in McKee, R and Davis, J (eds) *Signed Language Interpreting in Multilingual Contexts. Studies in Interpretation Series, Volume 6.* Washington DC: Gallaudet University Press.

Fenton, S (1998) 'Ethics in liaison interpreting', unpublished paper presented at the NZ Society of Translators & Interpreters Conference, July, Auckland, NZ.

Fischer, T (1993), 'Team interpreting: The team approach', *Journal of Interpretation* 6: 167-174.

Fitzgerald & Associates (2004), *New Zealand Sign Language Interpreter Issues: NZSL Interpreting in Court & Systems for Funding & Supply of Interpreter Services*, unpublished report of the Interpreter Issues Working Group to the Office of Disability Issues, December, Wellington, NZ.

Fleetwood, E (2000), 'Educational policy and signed language interpretation', in Metzger, M (ed), *Bilingualism and Identity in Deaf Communities*, Gallaudet University Press, Washington, DC.

Ford, L (1981), *The interpreter as a communication specialist*, presentation to the Third International Symposium on Interpretation of Sign Languages, Bristol.

Forestal, E (2005), 'The Emerging Professionals: Deaf Interpreters and Their Views and Experiences on Training', in Marschark, M, Peterson, R and Winston, EA (eds), *Interpreting and Interpreter Education: Directions for Research and Practice*, Oxford University Press, New York.

Frishberg, N (1990), *Interpreting: An introduction*, RID Publications, Silver Spring, MD.

Gebron, J (2000), *Sign the speech: An introduction to theatrical interpreting*, Butte Publications, Hillsbro, OR.

Gentile, A, Ozolins, U and Vasilikakos, M (1996), *Liaison interpreting: A handbook*, Melbourne University Press, Melbourne.

Gerver, D and Sinaiko, HW (eds), (1978), *Language interpretation and communication*, Plenum Press, London.

Gile, D (1995), *Basic concepts and models for interpreter and translator training*, John Benjamins, Philadelphia.

Goffman, E (1981), *Forms of talk*, Basil Blackwell, Oxford.

Goleman, D (1996), *Emotional Intelligence: Why it can matter more than IQ*, Bloomsbury, London.

Grosjean, F (1997), 'The bilingual individual', *Interpreting* 2(1/2): 163-188.

Gutman, V (ed), (2002), *Ethics in mental health and deafness*, Gallaudet University Press, Washington, DC.

Hale, SB (2004), *The Discourse of Court Interpreting: Discourse practices of the law, the witness and the interpreter*, John Benjamins, Amsterdam.

Harrington, F and Traynor, N (1999), 'Second-hand learning: Experiences of Deaf students in higher education', Pathways to Policy: Deaf Nation 2 conference, July, University of Central Lancashire, Preston, pp 219-238.

Harrington, F (2000), 'Sign language interpreters and access for Deaf students to university curricula: The ideal and the reality', in Roberts, R, Carr, SA, Abraham, D and Dufour A (eds), *The critical link 2: Interpreters in the community*, John Benjamins, Amsterdam.

Harrington, FJ and Turner, GH (eds), (2001), *Interpreting interpreting: Studies and reflections on sign language interpreting*, Douglas McLean, Coleford, UK.

Harrington, F (2005), 'Challenges of university interpreting', in Metzger, M and Fleetwood, E (eds), *Attitude, innuendo and regulators: Challenges of interpretation*, Gallaudet University Press, Washington, DC.

Harvey, M (1982), 'The influence and utilization of an interpreter for deaf persons in family therapy', *American Annals of the Deaf* 27(7): 821-827.

Harvey, MA (2003), 'Shielding yourself from the perils of empathy', *Journal of Deaf Studies and Deaf Education* 8(2): 207 -213.

Hatim, B and Mason, I (1990), *Discourse and the translator*, Longman, London.

Hauser, PC and Hauser, A (2008), 'The deaf professional-designated interpreter model', in Hauser, PC, Finch, K et al, (eds), (2008), *Deaf professionals and designated interpreters: A new paradigm*, Gallaudet University Press, Washington, DC.

Hayes, L (1992), 'Educational interpreters for deaf students: Their responsibilities, problems and concerns', *Journal of Interpretation* 5(1): 5-24.

Herbert, J (1978), 'How conference interpretation grew', in Gerver, HWSD, *Language interpretation and communication*, Plenum Press, New York.

Hindley, P and Kitson, N, (eds), (1998), *Mental health and deafness*, Whurr, London.

Hof, D (1994), 'The Interpreter as actor', in Erting, C, Johnson, R, Smith, D and Snider, B (eds), *The Deaf Way: Perspectives from the International Conference on Deaf Culture, July 1989*, Gallaudet University Press, Washington, DC.

Hoza, J (2003), 'Toward an interpreter sensibility: Three levels of ethical analysis and a comprehensive model of ethical decision-making for interpreters', *Journal of interpretation:* 1-48.

Humphrey, J and Alcorn, B (1996), *So you want to be an interpreter? An introduction to sign language interpreting*, H & H Publishers, Amarillo, Texas.

Hunter, K (1992), *The Remand of Ivan Curry*, documentary produced by Television New Zealand.

Hurwitz, A (1998), 'Current issues: Interpreters in the educational setting', Weisel, A (ed), *Insights into deaf education: Current theory and practice*, Academic Press of the School of Education, Tel Aviv University, Tel Aviv.

Hymes, D (1972), 'Models of the interaction of language and social life', in Gumperz, J and Hymes, D (eds), *Directions in sociolinguistics: The ethnography of communication*, Holt, Rinehart & Winston, New York.

Ingram, R (1974), 'A communication model of the interpreting process', *Journal of Rehabilitation of the Deaf* 7: 3-9.

Ingram, R (1985), 'Simultaneous interpretation of sign languages: Semiotic and psycholinguistic perspectives' *Multilingua* 4(2): 91-102.

Ingram, R (2000), 'Foreword: Why discourse matters', in Roy, C (ed), *Innovative practices for teaching sign language interpreters*, Gallaudet University Press, Washington, DC.

Jeffries, J (1992), *The Ivan Curry investigation*, Police Complaints Authority, Wellington, NZ.

Johnson, K (1991), 'Miscommunication in interpreted classroom interaction', *Sign Language Studies* 70: 1-34.

Johnston, T (2002), 'The representation of English using Auslan: Implications for Deaf bilingualism and English literacy', *Australian Journal of Education of the Deaf* 8: 23-37.

Jones, BE, Clark, G and Soltz, D (1997), 'Characteristics and practices of sign language interpreters in inclusive education programs', *Exceptional Children* 63(2): 257-268.

Joos, M (1967), *The five clocks*, Harbinger Books, New York.

Kanda, J (1988), *A comprehensive description of certified sign language interpreters including brain dominance*, unpublished doctoral dissertation, Brigham Young University, Provo, UT.

Karlin, B (2005), 'Should interpreters care?', paper presented at the 3rd Supporting Deaf People Online Conference, 10-16 March. Available: <www.online-conference.net/sdp3/index.htm>.

Kent, SO and Potter, A (2005), *The Interpreter and INTERRUPTING: Cultural and Group Dynamics*, paper presented at the 3rd Supporting Deaf People Online Conference, 10-16 March. Available: <www.online-conference.net/sdp3/index.htm>.

Kilpatrick, B and Andrews, J (2009), 'Accessibility to theatre for deaf and deaf-blind people: Legal, language and artistic Considerations', *International Journal of Interpreter Education*, 1(1), 77-94.

Kopczynski, A (1980), *Conference interpreting: Some linguistic and communicative problems*, Adam Mickiewicz Press, Poznan.

Kurz, I (1993), 'Conference interpretation: Expectations of different user groups', *The Interpreters' Newsletter* 5: 13-21.

La Bue, MA (1998), *Interpreted Education: A study of deaf students' access to the content and form of literacy instruction in a mainstreamed high school English class*, unpublished doctoral dissertation, University of Harvard, Cambridge, MA.

Lane, H, Hoffmeister, R, Bahan, B (1996), *A journey into the DEAF-WORLD*, USA, DawnSign Press, San Diego.

Language Services Section, Special Programs Unit (2004), 'Guidelines for interpreting for deaf persons who do not communicate competently in American Sign Language', New Jersey Administrative Office of the Courts. Available: <http://www.judiciary.state.nj.us/interpreters/policies.htm>.

Laster, K and Taylor, V (1994), *Interpreters and the legal system*, Federation Press, Sydney.

Lawrence, R (1987), 'Specialised preparation in educational interpreting', *Journal of Interpretation* 4: 87-90.

Lee, R (1997), 'Roles, Models and World Views', *Deaf Worlds* 13(3): 40-44.

Lee, J (2008), 'Telephone interpreting – seen from the interpreters' perspective', *Interpreting* 9(2): 231-252.

Leeson, L and Foley-Cave, S (2007), 'Deep and meaningful conversation: Challenging interpreter impartiality in the semantics and pragmatics classroom', in Metzger, M and Fleetwood, E (eds), *Translation, sociolinguistic, and consumer Issues in interpreting*, Gallaudet University Press, Washington, DC.

Leneham, M (2005), 'The sign language interpreter as translator: challenging traditional definitions of translation and interpreting', *Deaf Worlds*, 21 (1): 79-101.

Leneham, M (2007), Exploring 'power' and 'ethnocentrism' in sign language translation. *Babel: the journal of the Australian Federation of Modern Language Teachers Associations (AFMLTA)*, 41(3), 4-12.

Locker, R (1990), 'Lexical equivalence in transliterating for deaf students in the university classroom: Two perspectives', *Issues in Applied Linguistics* 1(2): 167-195.

Longacre, R (1983), *The grammar of discourse*, Plenum Press, New York.

Lörscher, W (1996), 'A psycholinguistic analysis of translation processes', *Meta* 41(1): 26-32.

Lucas, C (ed), (2003), *Language and the Law in Deaf Communities*, Sociolinguistcs in Deaf Communities, Gallaudet University Press, Washington, DC.

Lucas, C and Valli, C (1990), 'ASL, English and contact signing', Lucas, C (ed), *Sign language research: theoretical issues*, Gallaudet University Press, Washington, DC.

Macalister, J (2005) *A dictionary of Māori in New Zealand English*, Oxford University Press, Melbourne, Vic; Auckland, NZ.

Macintosh, J (1999), 'Interpreters are made not born', *Interpreting* 4(1): 67-80.

Madden, M (2005), 'The prevalence of chronic occupational physical injury in Australian Sign Language interpreters', in Metzger, M and Fleetwood, E (eds), *Attitude, innuendo and regulators: Challenges of interpretation*, Gallaudet University Press, Washington, DC.

Marschark, M, Sapere, P, Convertino, C, Seewagen, R and Maltzen, H (2004), 'Comprehension of sign language interpreting: Deciphering a complex task situation', *Sign Language Studies* 4(4): 345-368.

Mather, S and Winston, E (1998), 'Spatial mapping and involvement in ASL storytelling', in Lucas, C (ed), *Pinky extension and eye gaze: Language use in Deaf communities*, Gallaudet University Press, Washington, DC.

McCay, V and Miller, K (2001), 'Interpreting in mental health settings: Issues and concerns', *American Annals of the Deaf* 146(5): 429-434.

McCormack, H (2001) 'Between Two Worlds – Breaking the Sound Barrier' (interviewed and edited by Peter Beatson), *New Zealand Journal of Disability Studies*, 8: 3-35.

McIntire, M (1990), 'The work and education of sign language interpreters', in Prillwitz, S and Vollhaber, T (eds), *Sign language research and application*, Signum Press, Hamburg.

McIntire, M (1993), 'Getting out of line (and into space): A perspective on strategies for student interpreters', *Student competencies: Defining teaching and evaluating: Proceedings of the 9th convention of the Conference of Interpreter Trainers*, CIT, Sacramento, CA.

McIntire, M and Sanderson, G (1995), 'Bye-Bye! Bi-Bi! Questions of empowerment and role', *A confluence of diverse relationships: Proceedings of the 13th National Convention of the Registry of Interpreters for the Deaf*, RID Publications, Silver Spring, MD.

McKee, R (2008), 'Quality' in interpreting: A survey of practitioner perspectives', *The Sign Language Translator & Interpreter* 2(1): 1-14.

McKee, R L (2003), 'Interpreting as a tool for empowerment of the New Zealand Deaf community', in Fenton, S (ed), *For better or worse: Translation as a tool for change in the Pacific*, St Jerome, Manchester, UK.

McKee, R and Napier, J (2002), 'Interpreting into International Sign Pidgin: An analysis', *Journal of Sign Language and Linguistics* 5(1): 27-54.

McKee, R, Major, G, McKee, D (2008), 'Lexical Variation and Interpreting in New Zealand Sign Language', in Roy, C (ed) *Diversity and Community in the Worldwide Sign Language Interpreting Profession*. Proceedings of the World Association of Sign Language Interpreters conference, Segovia, July 2007. 89-106.

McKee, R and Awheto, S (2010), 'Constructing interpreter role(s) in a Māori trilingual context' in McKee, R and Davis J (eds) *Signed Language Interpreting in Multilingual Contexts. Studies in Interpretation Series, Volume 6*. Washington DC: Gallaudet University Press.

Mesch, J (2001), *Tactile sign language: Turn-taking and questions in signed conversations of deaf-blind people*, Gallaudet University Press, Washington, DC.

Metge, J and Laing, P (1984), *Talking Past Each Other: Problems of Cross-Cultural Communication*, Victoria University of Wellington Press, Wellington, NZ.

Metzger, M (1999), *Sign language interpreting: Deconstructing the myth of neutrality*, Gallaudet University Press, Washington, DC.

Metzger, M (1999), 'Replies and response cries: Interaction and dialogue interpreting, Review of Erving Goffman's Forms of Talk', *The Translator* 5(2): 327-332.

Metzger, M and Bahan, B (2001), 'Discourse analysis', in Lucas, C (ed), *The sociolinguistics of sign languages*, Cambridge University Press, Cambridge.

Mikkelson, H (1999), 'Relay interpreting: A solution for languages of limited diffusion?' *The Translator*: 5(2): 361-380.

Mikkelson, H (2000), *Introduction to court interpreting*, St Jerome Publishing, Manchester, UK.

Mindess, A (1999), *Reading between the signs: Intercultural communication for sign language interpreters*, Intercultural Press, Yarmouth, Maine.

Mitchell, T (2002), 'Co-working and equal participation', *Deaf Worlds* 18(2): 66-68.

Moko-Mead (2003), *Tikanga Māori: Living by Māori Values*, Huia Publishers, Wellington.

Montoya, LA, Egnatovitch, R, Eckhardt, E, Goldstein, M, Goldstein, R and Steinberg, A (2004), 'Translation challenges and strategies: The ASL translation of a computer-based psychiatric diagnostic interview', *Sign Language Studies* 4(4): 314-344.

Moody, B (1994), 'International Sign: Language, Pidgin or Charades?', Paper presented at Issues in Interpreting Conference, April, Durham University, UK.

Moody, B (2002), 'International Sign: A practitioner's perspective', *Journal of Interpretation*: 1- 48.

Moody, B (2007), 'Literal vs Liberal: What is a faithful interpretation?' *The Sign Language Translator and Interpreter*, 1 (2), 179-220.

Moody, B (2008), 'The role of International Sign interpreting in today's world', in Roy, C (ed), *Diversity and community in the worldwide sign language interpreting profession: Proceedings of the 2nd Conference of the World Association of Sign Language Interpreters*, Douglas McLean, Coleford.

Moody, W (1987), 'International Gestures', Van Cleve, JVV (ed), *Gallaudet Encyclopedia of Deaf People and Deafness Vol 3 S-Z Index*, McGraw-Hill Book Company Inc, New York.

Moser, B (1978), 'Simultaneous interpretation: A hypothetical model and its practical application', in Gerver, HWSD (ed), *Language interpretation and communication*, Plenum Press, New York.

Moser, P (1996), 'Expectations of users of conference interpretation', *Interpreting* 1(2): 145-178.

Moser-Mercer, B, Kunzli, A and Korac, M (1998), 'Prolonged turns in interpreting: Effects on quality, physiological and psychological stress (Pilot study)', *Interpreting* 3(1): 47-64.

Mouzourakis, P (2006), 'Remote interpreting: A technical perspective on recent experiments', *Interpreting* 8(1): 45–66.

Napier, J (1998), 'Free your mind – the rest will follow', *Deaf Worlds* 14(3): 15-22.

Napier, J (2001), 'Linguistic coping strategies of Sign language interpreters', *Linguistics*, Macquarie University, Sydney.

Napier, J (2002a), 'University interpreting: Linguistic issues for consideration', *Journal of Deaf Studies and Deaf Education* 7(4): 281-301.

Napier, J (2002b), *Sign language interpreting: Linguistic coping strategies*, Douglas McLean, Coleford, UK.

Napier, J (2003), 'Language contact phenomena: Comparing Auslan English interpreters and Deaf Australians', presentation to the Australasian Deaf Studies Research Symposium 2, Royal Institute of Deaf and Blind Children, September, Sydney.

Napier, J (2005), 'Consumer perceptions of sign language interpreting', in Mole, J (ed), *International Perspectives on Interpreting: Selected Proceedings from the Supporting Deaf People online conferences 2001 – 2005*. [E-Book]. Direct Learn Services Ltd, UK.

Napier, Jemina (2006) 'Comparing language contact phenomena between Auslan-English interpreters and Deaf Australians: A preliminary study', in Lucas, C (ed), *Multilingualism and Sign Languages. From the Great Plains to Australia. Sociolinguistics in Deaf Communities Series, 12*, Gallaudet University Press, Washington DC:

Napier, J (in press), 'It's not what they say but the way they say it: A sociolinguistic analysis of interpreter and consumer attitudes towards signed language interpreting in Australia', *International Journal of the Sociology of Language*.

Napier, J and Barker, R (2003), 'A demographic survey of Australian Sign Language interpreters', *Australian Journal of Education of the Deaf* 9: 19-32.

Napier, J and Barker, R (2004), 'Accessing university education: Perceptions, preferences and expectations for interpreting by deaf students', *Journal of Deaf Studies and Deaf Education* 9(2): 228-238.

Napier, J and Cornes, A (2004), 'The dynamic roles of interpreters and therapists', in Crocker, S and Austen, S, *Deafness in mind: Working psychologically with deaf people across the lifespan*, Whurr Publishers, London.

Napier, J and Rohan, M (2007), 'An invitation to dance: Deaf consumers' perceptions of signed language interpreters and interpreting', in Metzger, M and Fleetwood, E (eds), *Translation, sociolinguistic, and consumer issues in interpreting*, Gallaudet University Press, Washington, DC.

Nord, C (1997), *Translating as a purposeful activity: Functionalist approaches explained*, St Jerome Publishing, Manchester, UK.

O'Reilly, S (2005), *Indigenous Australian Sign Language and Culture: The Interpreting and access needs of Deaf people who are Aboriginal and/or Torres Strait Islander in Far North Queensland*. Cairns: Association of Sign Language Interpreters Australia (ASLIA) Winterschool.

Orima (2004), 'Supply and demand for Auslan interpreters across Australia', Department of Family and Community Services, Australian Commonwealth Government, Canberra.

Ozolins, U and Bridge, M (1999), *Sign language interpreting in Australia*, Language Australia, Melbourne.

Padden, C (1993) 'Restrictions', *Signpost* 6(4).

Padden, C and Humphries, T (1988), *Deaf in America: Voices from a culture*, Harvard University Press, Cambridge, Mass.

Padden, C and Humphries, T (2005), *Inside Deaf Culture*, Harvard University Press, Cambridge, Mass.

Patrie, C (1993), 'A confluence of diverse relationships: Interpreter education and educational interpreting', in *A confluence of diverse relationships: Proceedings of the 13th National Convention of the Registry of Interpreters for the Deaf*, RID Publications, Silver Spring, MD.

Pere, RR (1991), *Te Wheke: A celebration of infinite wisdom*, A0AKO, Gisborne, NZ.

Peterson, EH (1993), *The Message*, Navpress, Colorado Springs.

Phillip, MJ (1994), 'Professionalism: From which cultural perspective?' Paper presented at Issues in Interpreting Conference, April, Durham University, UK.

Pollitt, K (2000), 'On babies, bathwater and approaches to interpreting', *Deaf Worlds* 16(2): 60-64.

Pollitt, K and Haddon, C (2005), 'Cold calling? Re-training interpreters in the art of telephone interpreting', in Roy, C (ed), *Advances in teaching sign language interpreters*, Gallaudet University Press, Washington, DC.

Pöchhacker, F (2003), *Introducing interpreting studies*, Routledge, London.

Quynh-Du, Ton-That, (1996) 'Legal Settings', in Gentile, A, Ozolins, U and Vasilikakos, M (eds), *Liaison interpreting: A handbook* Melbourne, Melbourne University Press , Melbourne.

Ramsey, C (1997), *Deaf children in public schools: placement, context and consequences*, Washington DC: Gallaudet University Press.

Ramsey, C (2001), 'Beneath the surface: Theoretical frameworks shed light on educational interpreting', *Odyssey: Directions in Deaf Education* 2(2): 19-24.

Ressler, C (1999), 'A comparative analysis of a direct interpretation and an inter-mediary interpretation in American Sign Language', *Journal of Interpretation*: 71-104.

Riccardi, A (1998), 'Interpreting strategies and creativity', in Beylard-Ozeroff, A, Králová, J and Moser-Mercer, B (eds), *Translators' strategies and creativity*, John Benjamins, Philadelphia.

RID (Registry of Interpreters for the Deaf) (1995), *A Confluence of Diverse Relationships: Proceedings of the Thirteenth National Convention of the Registry of Interpreters for the Deaf*, RID Publications, Silver Spring, MD.

RID (1997), *Use of Certified Deaf Interpreters, Standard Practice Paper*. Available: <www.rid.org/spp.html>.

Roberts-Smith, L, Frey, R et al (1990), *Working with interpreters in law, health and social work*, NAATI, Mount Hawthorn, WA.

Robinson, D (1997), *Becoming a Translator: An Accelerated Course*, Routledge, London.

Rosenstock, R (2008), 'The role of iconicity in International Sign', *Sign Language Studies*, 8(2), 131-159.

Roy, C (1987), 'Evaluating performance: An interpreted lecture', *New dimensions in interpreter education: Curriculum and instruction, Proceedings of the 6th National Convention of the Conference of Interpreter Trainers*, RID Publications, Silver Spring, MD.

Roy, C (1989), 'Features of discourse in an American Sign Language Lecture', in Lucas, C (ed), *The sociolinguistics of the Deaf community*, Academic Press, New York.

Roy, C (2000), *Interpreting as a discourse process*, Oxford University Press, Oxford.

Russell, D (2002), *Interpreting in legal contexts: Consecutive and simultaneous interpretation*, Sign Media, Burtonsville, MD.

Russell, D (2008), 'Interpreter preparation conversations: Multiple perspectives', in Russell, D and Hale, S (eds), *Interpreting in legal settings*, Gallaudet University Press, Washington, DC.

Russell, D and Hale, S (eds) (2008), *Interpreting in legal settings*, Gallaudet University Press, Washington, DC.

Russo, T (2004), 'Iconicity and Productivity in Sign Language Discourse: An Analysis of Three LIS Discourse Registers', *Sign Language Studies* 4(2): 164-197.

Salmond, A (2004), *Hui: A study of Māori ceremonial gatherings*, Reed Publishers, Auckland.

Sameshima, S (1999), *Deaf students in mainstream Universities and Polytechs*, unpublished Masters thesis, Victoria University of Wellington, NZ.

Sanheim, L (2003), 'Turn exchange in an interpreted medical encounter', in Metzger, M, Collins, S, Dively, V and Shaw, R (eds), *From topic boundaries to omission: New research on interpretation*, Gallaudet University Press, Washington, DC.

Schank and Abelson (1977), *Scripts, plans, goals and understanding: An inquiry into human knowledge and structures*, Erlbaum, Hillsdale, NJ.

Scheibe, K and Hoza, J (1986), *Throw it out the window! (The code of ethics? We don't use that here): Guidelines for educational interpreters*, Interpreting: The art of cross cultural mediation, RID Publications, Silver Spring, MD.

Schein, JD and Delk, MR (1974), *The Deaf population of the United States*, National Association of the Deaf, Silver Spring.

Schick, B, Williams, K, and Bolster, L (1999), 'Skill levels of educational interpreters working in public schools', *Journal of Deaf Studies and Deaf Education* 4(2): 144-155.

Schick, B (2001), 'Interpreting for children: How it's different', *Odyssey: Directions in Deaf Education* 2(2): 8-11.

Schick, B and Williams, K (2001), 'Evaluating interpreters who work with children', *Odyssey: Directions in Deaf Education* 2(2): 12-14.

Seal, BC (1998), *Best practices in educational interpreting*, Allyn & Bacon, Needham Heights, MA.

Seal, BC (2004) 'Psychological testing of sign language interpreters', *Journal of Deaf Studies and Deaf Education* 9(1): 39-52.

Seleskovitch, D (1978), *Interpreting for international conferences*, Pen and Booth, Washington, DC.

Shaw, R (1992), 'Determining register in sign-to-English interpreting', in Cokely, D (ed), *Sign language interpreters and interpreting*, Linstok Press, Burtonsville, MD.

Shaw, R (1994), 'A conversation: Written feedback notes while team interpreting', *Mapping our course: A collaborative venture, Proceedings of the 10th National Convention of the Conference of Interpreter Trainers*, Charlotte, CIT, North Carolina.

Shaw, S, Grbic, N and Franklin, K (2004), 'Applying language skills to interpretation: Student perspectives from signed and spoken language programs', *Interpreting* 6(1): 69-100.

Siple, L (1993), 'Working with the sign language interpreter in your classroom', *College Teaching* 41(4): 139-142.

Siple, L (1995), 'The use of additions in sign language transliteration', State University of New York, NY.

Smiler, K (2004), *Māori Deaf: Perceptions of Cultural and Linguistic Identity of Māori Members pf the New Zealand Deaf Community*, unpublished Masters thesis, Victoria University of Wellington, NZ.

Smeijers, A and Pfau, R (2009), 'On the communication between general practitioners and their deaf patients', *The Sign Language Translator & Interpreter* 3(1): 1-14.

Smith, TB (1983), 'What goes around, comes around: reciprocity and interpreters', *The Reflector* 5: 5-6.

Smith, TB (2002), *Guidelines : Practical Tips for Working & Socializing with Deaf-Blind People*, Linstok Press, Burtonsville, MD.

Sofinski, BA, Yesbeck, NA, Gerhold, SC and Bach-Hansen, MC (2001), 'Features of voice-to-sign transliteration by educational interpreters', *Journal of Interpretation*: 47-68.

Solow, SN (1981), *Sign language interpreting: A basic resource book*, National Association of the Deaf, Silver Spring, MD.

Solow, SN (1988), 'Interpreting for Minimally Linguistically Competent Individuals', *The Court Manager* Spring 1988: 18 -21.

Solow, SN (1996), 'Interpreting in the legal setting involving minimally linguistically competent deaf individuals', *RID Views* (July).

Solow, SN (2000), *Sign language interpreting: A basic resource book*, Linstok, Burtonsville, MD.

Spencer, R (2000), 'Video Relay Interpreting Trial Report', Australian Communication Exchange, Brisbane.

Steiner, B (1998), 'Signs from the void: The comprehension and production of sign language on television', *Interpreting* 3(2): 99-146.

Stewart, D, Schein, J and Cartwright, B (1998), *Sign language interpreting: Exploring its art and science*, Allyn and Bacon, Boston.

Stewart, KL and Witter-Merrithew, A (2004), 'Teaching Ethical Standards and Practice within Pre-Service and In-Service Interpreter Education Programs', Supporting Deaf People Online Conference, February. Available: <www.directlearn.co.uk>.

Stratiy, A (2005), Best practices in interpreting: A Deaf community perspective, in Janzen, T (ed), *Topics in signed language interpreting*, John Benjamins, Amsterdam.

Stubbe, M and Holmes, J (2000), 'Talking Maori or Pakeha in English: Signalling Identity in Discourse', in Paul, A and Kuiper, K (eds), *New Zealand English*, Benjamins, Amsterdam/Victoria University Press, Wellington, NZ.

Suppalla, TW and Webb, R (1995), 'The grammar of international sign: A new look at pidgin languages', in Emmorey, K and Reilly, J (eds), *Language, Gesture & Space*, Erlbaum, Hillsdale, NJ.

Sutton-Spence, R and Woll, B (1998), *The linguistics of British Sign Language*, Cambridge University Press, Cambridge.

Sutton-Spence, R (2000), 'Aspects of BSL Poetry: A Social and Linguistic Analysis of the Poetry of Dorothy Miles', *Sign Language & Linguistics* 3(1): 79-100.

Swabey, L, and Mickelson, PG (2008), 'Role definition: A perspective on forty years of professionalism in sign language interpreting', in Valero-Garcés, C and Martin, A (eds), *Crossing Borders in Community Interpreting*, John Benjamins, Amsterdam.

Tannen, D (1984), *Conversational style: Analysing talk among friends*, Ablex, Norwood, NJ.

Tate, G and Turner, GH (2001), 'The code and the culture: Sign language interpreting – in search of the new breed's ethics', in Harrington, FJ and Turner, GH (eds), *Interpreting interpreting: Studies and reflections on sign language interpreting*, Douglas McLean, Coleford, UK.

Tate, G, Collins, J and Timms, P (2003), 'Assessments using BSL: Issues of translation for performance indicators in primary schools', *Deaf Worlds* 19(1): 6-35.

Tauroa, H and Tauroa, P (1986), *Te Marae: A guide to customs and protocols*, Reed Books, Auckland.

Taylor, M (1993), *Interpretation skills: English to ASL*, Interpreting Consolidated, Edmonton, Alberta.

Thoutenhooft, E (2005), 'The sign language interpreter in inclusive education: Power of authority and limits of objectivism', *The Translator* 11(2): 237-258.

Tray, S (2005), 'What are you suggesting? Interpreting innuendo between ASL and English', Metzger, M and, Fleetwood, E (eds), *Attitude, innuendo and regulators: Challenges in interpretation*, Gallaudet University Press, Washington, DC.

Turner, J, Klein, H and Kitson, N (1998), 'Interpreters in mental health settings', in Hindley, P and, Kitson, N (eds), *Mental health and deafness*, Whurr, London.

Turner, GH (2001a), 'Rights and responsibilities: the relationship between Deaf people and interpreters', Harrington, F and Turner, GH (eds), *Interpreting interpreting: Studies and reflections on sign language interpreting*, Douglas McLean, Coleford, UK.

Turner, GH (2001b), 'Interpreting Assignments: Should I or shouldn't I?', in Harrington, F and Turner, GH (eds), *Interpreting interpreting: Studies and reflections on sign language interpreting*, Douglas McLean, Coleford, UK.

Turner, GH (2005), 'Towards real interpreting', Marschark, M, Peterson, R and Winston, EA (eds), *Interpreting and Interpreter Education: Directions for Research and Practice*, Oxford University, New York.

Turner, GH (2007), 'Exploring inter-subdisciplinary alignment in interpreting studies: Sign language interpreting at conferences', in Pöchhacker, F, Jakobsen, AL, and Mees, IM (eds), *Interpreting studies and beyond: A tribute to Miriam Shlesinger*, Samfundslitteratur Press, Copenhagen.

Turner, GH (2007) 'Re-thinking the sociology of sign language interpreting and translation: Some challenges posed by deaf practitioners', in Wolf, M (ed), *Übersetzen – Translating – Traduire: Towards a Social Turn?*, LIT Verlag, Berlin.

Turner, GH and Pollitt, K (2002), 'Community Interpreting Meets Literary Translation: English-BSL Interpreting in the Theatre', *The Translator*, 8 (1): 25-48.

Van Herreweghe, M (2002), 'Turn-taking mechanisms and active participation in meetings with deaf and hearing participants in Flanders', in Lucas, C (ed), *Turn-taking, fingerspelling and contact in signed languages*, Gallaudet University Press, Washington, DC.

Vanderveken, D and Kubo, S (eds), (2001), *Essays in speech act theory*, John Benjamins, Philadelphia.

van Rooy, B (2005). 'The feasibility of simultaneous interpreting in university classrooms', *Southern African Linguistics and Applied Language Studies* 23(1): 81-90.

Verhoef, M, and Blaauw, J (2009), 'Towards comprehending spoken-language educational interpreting as rendered at a South African university', in Inggs, J and Meintjes, L (eds), *Translation Studies in Africa: Central Issues in Interpreting and Literary and Media Translation*, Continuum, London.

VicCite (2002), 'Educational Interpreting & Notetaking in Australia', Victorian Committee for Interpreting in Tertiary Education, Centre of Excellence for Students who are Deaf and Hard of Hearing, Northern Melbourne Institute of TAFE.

Wadensjö, C (1998), *Interpreting as interaction*, Longman, London.

Wadensjö, C (1999), 'Telephone interpreting and the synchronization of talk in social interaction', *The Translator* 5(2).

Wadensjö, C (2001), 'Interpreting in crisis: The interpreter's position in therapeutic encounters', in Mason, I (ed), *Triadic exchanges: Studies in dialogue interpreting*, St Jerome, Manchester, UK.

Wilcox, S and Wilcox, P (1985), 'Schema theory and language interpretation', *Journal of Interpretation* 2: 84-93.

Wilson, J (1996), 'The tobacco story: Narrative structure in an ASL story', in Lucas, C (ed), *Multicultural aspects of sociolinguistics in Deaf communities*, Gallaudet University Press, Washington, DC.

Winston, E (1989), 'Transliteration: What's the message?', in Lucas, C (ed), *The sociolinguistics of the Deaf community*, Gallaudet University Press, Washington, DC.

Winston, EA and Monikowski, C (2000), 'Discourse mapping-Developing textual coherence skills in interpreters', in Roy, C (ed), *Innovative practices for teaching sign language interpreters*, Gallaudet University Press, Washington, DC.

Winston, E (2001), 'Visual inaccessibility: The elephant (blocking the view) in interpreted education', *Odyssey: Directions in Deaf Education* 2(2): 5-7.

Winston, EA and Monikowski, C (2003), 'Marking topic boundaries in signed interpretation and transliteration', in Metzger, M, Collins, S, Dively, V and Shaw, R (eds), *From topic boundaries to omission: New research on interpretation*, Gallaudet University Press, Washington, DC.

Winston, E (ed), (2004), *Educational interpreting: How it can succeed*, Gallaudet University Press, Washington, DC.

Winston, E (2004), 'Interpretability and accessibility of mainstream classrooms', in Winston, E, *Educational interpreting: How it can succeed*, Gallaudet University Press, Washington, DC.

Winston, EA and, Monikowski, C (2005), 'Translation: The GPS of discourse mapping', in Roy, C (ed), *Advances in teaching sign language interpreters*, Gallaudet University Press, Washington, DC.

Wilcox, Sherman and Barb Shaffer (2005) 'Towards a Cognitive Model of Interpreting', in Janzen, T (ed) Topics in Signed Language Interpreting, Amsterdam: John Benjamins, 27-50.

Wilcox, Sherman and Barb Shaffer (2005) 'Towards a Cognitive Model of Interpreting', in Terry Janzen (ed) *Topics in Signed Language Interpreting*, Amsterdam: John Benjamins, 27-50.

Witter-Merithew, A and Johnson, L (2004), 'Market disorder within the field of sign language interpreting: Professionalisation implications', *Journal of Interpretation*: 19-55.

Witter-Merithew, A, and Mills Stewart, K (2006), *Ethical decision making: A guided exploration for interpreters*, Sign Media, Burtonsville, MD.

Witter-Merithew, A, Johnson, L and Taylor, M (2004), 'A national perspective on entry-to-practice competencies for ASL-English interpreters', in Maroney, E (ed), *CIT: Still shining after 25 years – Proceedings of the 15th National Convention of the Conference of Interpreter Trainers*, CIT, Western Oregon.

Zimmer, J (1989), 'Toward a description of register variation in American Sign Language', in Lucas, C (ed), *The sociolinguistics of the Deaf community*, Academic Press, New York.

INDEX